Contents

Dr Oladeji O. Ojo is Research Coordinator in the Development Research and Policy Department. Until his appointment in the Bank, he was Professor of Economics at the University of Ife (now Abafemi Awolowo University), Ile-Ife, Nigeria.

Dr Sheila Page is a Senior Research Fellow at the Overseas Development Institute, London.

Dr Christopher Stevens was a Senior Research Fellow at the Overseas Development Institute at the time he made his contribution. He is currently with the Institute of Development Studies at the University of Sussex, Brighton, UK.

Dr Temitope Oshikoya is a Senior Research Economist in the Development Research and Policy Department of the Bank.

Abbreviations

ACP	African, Caribbean and Pacific (countries)	IFAD	International Fund for Agricultural Development
AMF	African Monetary Fund	IFI	International Financial Institution
ASEAN	Association of South East Asian Nations	ILO	International Labour Office
BEAC	Banque des États d'Afrique Centrale	IMF	International Monetary Fund
		LDC	Less-Developed Country
CAP	Common Agricultural Policy	MFA	Multifibre Arrangement
CAR	Central African Republic	MFN	Most-Favoured Nation
CCP	Common Commercial Policy	MIC	Middle-Income Country
CFA	(Le Franc des) Colonies Française d'Afrique	NGO	Non-Governmental Organization
		NIC	Newly Industrializing Country
CMA	Common Monetary Area (Southern Africa)	NMP	Net Material Product
		NTB	Non-Tariff Barrier
CMEA	Council for Mutual Economic Assistance	ODA	Official Development Assistance
CN	Combined Nomenclature (a trade code of the EU)	OECD	Organization for Economic Cooperation and Development
DAC	Development Assistance Committee	OPEC	Organization of Petroleum Exporting Countries
DC	Developed Country	PTA	Preferential Trade Area (Eastern and Southern Africa)
EBRD	European Bank for Reconstruction and Development	SEM	Single European Market
		SITC	Standard International Trade Classification
ECOWAS	Economic Community of West African States	TRIPS	Trade-related intellectual property rights
ECU	European Currency Unit	UMOA	Union Monétaire Ouest Africain
EDF	European Development Fund	UNCTAD	United Nations Conference on Trade and Development
EIB	European Investment Bank		
EPZ	Export Processing Zone	UNDP	United Nations Development Programme
EU	European Union		
FDI	Foreign Direct Investment	UNFPA	United Nations Fund for Population Activities
FSU	Former Soviet Union		
GATS	General Agreement on Trade in Services	UNHCR	United Nations High Commission,(for Refugees)
GDP	Gross Domestic Product	UNICEF	United Nations Children's Fund
GSP	Generalized System of Preferences	UNRWA	United Nations Relief and Works Agency (for Palestinian Refugees)
IBRD	International Bank for Reconstruction and Development (World Bank)	VAT	Value Added Tax
		VER	Voluntary Export Restraint
		W FP	World Food Programme
IDA	International Development Association	WTO	World Trade Organization

List of Tables and Figures

Foreword

OMAR KABBAJ
President
African Development Bank

Since the middle ages, Africa has developed strong economic ties with Europe. In recent years, these ties have been strengthened by various agreements – the Lomé Conventions between Europe and a large number of African, Caribbean and Pacific (ACP) countries on the one hand, and some bilateral agreements between Europe and the North African countries on the other. By these arrangements, African exports enjoy relatively unrestricted entry into the EU market, while African countries were also treated preferentially in the allocation of EU aid. The consequence has been for Africa, substantial dependence on Europe for trade, capital flows and investment.

But all these may be changing as a result of some recent developments in Europe. One of these is the completion of the internal market of the European Union – Europe 1992 as it has come to be known. The other is the break-up of the former Soviet Union as a world power – a process which has opened up, politically and economically, the countries of the former Soviet bloc. These two events are likely to alter or revolutionize intra-European relations as well as Europe's relations with the rest of the world.

Of similar significance for African–European economic relations are two other developments. One is the successful completion of the Uruguay Round of trade negotiations and the other is the devaluation, in January 1994, of the CFA franc – the common currency of fourteen African countries. While the former has implications for trade with Europe (for example, the loss of preferences that could arise from global trade liberalization), the latter has implications for the future of monetary cooperation in Africa.

On the eve of Europe 1992, Africa derived much of its trade, capital flows and investment from Europe. This situation is likely to continue for some time to come. But as the analysis in the book illustrates, some recent developments are pointing in the direction of reduced interdependence between Africa and Europe in the years ahead. Hence, Africa needs to understand and take full account of the implications of these developments, otherwise it could face the prospect of a gradual loss of its major export market and of a major source of capital.

The purpose of this volume is to sensitize African policy makers on the issues involved so that individually and collectively, they could develop appropriate responses. The analysis in the book, however, remains, at best, broad generalizations. Some countries are likely to be affected more than others. Consequently, each country should see this contribution as providing tentative, albeit broad generalizations, with the task of evolving concrete national strategies being primarily that of national governments.

The publication of this book has been financed by a grant provided by the Swedish Board for Investment and Technical Support. I would like to thank the Government of Sweden for this assistance. This work is the outcome of Bank-sponsored research activity. The views expressed therein are therefore, strictly those of the authors. They do not necessarily reflect the views of the Bank's Board of Directors or its Management.

September 1995

This book was conceived as the proceedings of a workshop which the Development Research and Policy Department of the African Development Bank organized in 1992 on the consequences for Africa, of the completion of the internal market of Europe (Europe 1992) and the opening up, politically and economically, of the former Soviet bloc to trade and finance But two other events took place during the period leading to the finalization of the proceedings of the workshop which were to alter the initial conception and format of the book One was the successful completion of the most ambitious trade talks in world history – the Uruguay Round The other was the devaluation of the CFA franc in January 1994. When both events are combined with the original subject matter of the workshop, it becomes apparent that the issues at stake go beyond the consequences of Europe 1992 and of the events in the former Soviet bloc. Combined, all the issues impinge, directly or indirectly, on the very foundation of African–European economic relations.

Since the middle ages, Africa has developed strong economic ties with Western Europe The consequence for Africa, not surprisingly, has been heavy dependence on Western Europe for trade, capital flows and investment It is not the intention of this book to cry wolf where none exists, but it bears emphasizing at the outset, that there are forces in play which could reduce that dependence in the years ahead Those forces are rooted partly in some recent developments - Europe 1992, the opening up of the former Soviet bloc and the successful completion of the Uruguay Round discussed in this book The purpose of this book is to analyse critically those developments that could undermine future African–European economic relations in order to enhance Africa's understanding of the issues involved as a step towards developing appropriate defensive responses to them. While the book does not proffer a blueprint for continental response in this regard, it is hoped that it will assist in formulating appropriate policies, particularly at the national level.

In its present form, the book departs significantly from its original conception as the proceedings of a workshop in order to accommodate the events referred to earlier. Several people (including Drs Slimane, Yao and Shaaeldin) made useful comments on the papers presented at the workshop. While these comments are gratefully acknowledged, they are not included here because of the changed format of the book. Efforts have been made to incorporate the comments in the relevant chapters, however I am grateful to Chris Stevens and Sheila Page for readily agreeing to revise their contributions, which were rendered almost out of date by the delay in publication, and to Rosemary Anku for typing successive drafts of the book.

The research pro ject on which this book is based would not have been possible without the support and encouragement of Mr Delphin Rwegasira, Director of the Development Research and Policy Department Mr A London. the Deputy Director of the Department was similarly supportive. Although this project was conceived before he became the Department's supervising Vice President, Mr Ferhat Lounes has shown considerable interest in it since assuming responsibility for the Department. His frequent questions concerning the progress of the project served as further encouragement in its speedy finalization. Messrs S.A. Olarewaju and M. Wagacha read the entire manuscript and made useful suggestions. I am grateful to all these people for their support and encouragement; they are not to be held responsible, however, for the errors and omissions which the book might contain.

Oladeji O Ojo

Africa and Europe:
The Changing Economic Relationship
– An Introduction

●●●

OLADEJI O. OJO

Two major developments are currently under way in Europe. One is the completion of the internal market of the European Union (EU) countries which came into effect in 1992 (the so-called Europe 1992). This is an important part of the process of European economic integration which started in 1957 with the signing of the Treaty of Rome, and which is scheduled to end with the establishment of a monetary and economic union in 1997 or, at the latest, 1999. The other development (a more recent phenomenon), is the opening up, politically and economically, of the countries of the former Soviet bloc. Both developments are bound to have profound effects on Europe itself, on the world economy and on Africa, which has had a long historical relationship with Europe. Both developments offer considerable challenges and opportunities to Africa in the areas of trade and investment, including capital flows.

Beyond these two events, two additional developments are similarly important to Africa. One is the successful completion of the latest and most ambitious trade negotiation of the General Agreement on Tariffs and Trade (GATT), the Uruguay Round. This Round has tremendous implications for Africa in so far as it covers, for the first time, trade in agriculture, services and intellectual property rights. These are areas of vital importance to Africa. The Round is also important to Africa in another respect: as a generalized trade liberalization programme, it raises the spectre of loss of trade preferences which Africa (along with other countries of the Caribbean and Pacific countries) has been enjoying in European markets. The other development is the devaluation, in January 1994, of the CFA franc – the common currency of the thirteen former French colonies in Africa. While the devaluation of a currency – particularly that of a developing country – ordinarily would not provoke undue attention, the CFA devaluation calls into question the efficacy and the future of the monetary zone (the CFA franc zone) which issues the currency. In particular, it calls into question the future relationship between that zone and the French franc as Europe moves irrevocably towards monetary and economic union. The devaluation also raises questions about future strategies for African economic integration, and particularly about future monetary arrangements on the continent.

The present volume analyses the issues involved in these developments and how they are likely to influence the evolution of African–European economic relations in the years ahead. This introductory chapter provides a brief background to African–European economic relations. It also summarizes the key issues in each of the succeeding chapters. Chapters 2 and 3 address the consequences of Europe 1992 on Africa in greater detail (in the areas of trade, capital flows and foreign private investment). Chapter 4 reviews the future of monetary cooperation in Africa in the light of the recent devaluation of the CFA franc, while in Chapter 5 an attempt is made to analyse the likely consequences of the recent developments (economic and political changes) in Eastern and Central Europe on Africa. Chapter 6 discusses the implications of the Uruguay Round of trade negotiations for Africa. A concluding chapter sketches scenarios about the future of African–European economic relations.

Africa's Pre-1992 Relationship with Europe

The history of Africa's economic relationship with Europe dates back to the middle ages. Since then the relationship has gone through several phases, but trade and finance appear to have remained the more constant factors. In recent years, the flow of persons and services has become important in the relationship between Africa and Europe.

In discussing the relationship between Africa and Europe, it is important to make a distinction between sub-Saharan Africa and the North African countries. While in the latter (Algeria, Egypt, Morocco, and Tunisia) the relationship has been governed largely by bilateral association agreements, in sub-Saharan Africa cooperation agreements have been the rule. Between 1963 and 1975, the relationship between sub-Saharan Africa and Europe was governed by the Yaoundé Conventions (I and II). From 1975, the Lomé Convention (between the EU and African, Caribbean and Pacific countries) has become the legal basis of such cooperation. To date, four such conventions have been signed, the most recent in December 1989. Of the 69 African, Caribbean and Pacific (ACP) countries, 45 are African. By the provisions of the convention, the ACP countries are offered in principle, non-reciprocal trade preferences by their EU trading partners. Imports from ACP countries into the community are completely unrestricted, except for products covered by the EU's Common Agricultural Policy (CAP). As for manufactured goods, the Lomé Convention provides for duty- and quota-free access into the EU market of those ACP exports which satisfy the rules of origin. But there are safeguard clauses to prevent excessive imports capable of disrupting the EU market.

Partly because of the Lomé Convention and partly because of historical ties, Africa has become very dependent on Europe for the bulk of its trade. For example, on the eve of the Single European Market (SEM) about 52 per cent of Africa's exports, for the most part primary commodities, entered EU markets as against 41 per cent in 1975. The EU also accounted for 52 per cent of Africa's imports as against 50 per cent in 1975. This trade was dominated mainly by imports of manufactured goods.

The flow of aid has always been an important feature of African–EU economic relations. From European Currency Unit (ECU) 5.5 billion under Lomé II, the volume of aid has increased to ECU 12 billion under Lomé IV. The European Development Fund (EDF) is the main aid mechanism. The size of the EDF has increased progressively under each convention – under Lomé II, it was ECU 4.6 billion, whereas under Lomé IV it increased to ECU 10.8 billion. Although the total amount of aid under Lomé IV was 27 per cent highter than under Lomé III, aid under Lomé IV, in *per capita* terms, was less than under previous allocations. The bulk of assistance under the EDF is for the financing of projects mutually agreed to by the recipient country and the EU. EDF resources are characterized by a high, and recently increasing, grant element. While in the past Lomé Convention aid involved minimal conditionalities, in recent years its receipt could be tied increasingly to stringent conditionalities such as the implementation of structural adjustment programmes.

Some proportion of EDF resources is channelled through the European Investment Bank (EIB) to ACP countries in the form of risk capital and interest subsidies. Under Lomé II, EDF resources managed by the EIB amounted to ECU 815 million, made up of ECU 600 million for risk capital and ECU 215 million for interest subsidies. The Bank also provides loans from its own resources. Such loans have increased from ECU 885 million under Lomé II to ECU 1.2 billion under Lomé IV. Food aid is outside the EDF and, indeed the entire Lomé framework.

The Single European Market

The European economic integration process was set in motion in 1957 with the signing of the Treaty of Rome. Since then there have been many developments towards the achievement of that goal. These include the abolition of tariffs and quantitative restrictions on trade and the establishment of a common external tariff against third countries. But the Single European Act seeks to create a common market (the SEM) in 1922 by eliminating physical, technical and fiscal barriers to the flow of goods, services, persons and capital between member states. By this Act, member states were to eliminate all remaining barriers to the intra-Union flow of goods, services and factors by the end of the that year. There are other aspects of the process of European economic integration (economic and monetary integration, for example) which are proceeding in a parallel fashion but with a more distant deadline of 1997.

The attainment of a single market constitutes a major restructuring of the World economic landscape. It is a development which is bound to have far-reaching consequences not only for Europe itself but for the world economy in general. For Africa, which has had a long history of economic relationship with Europe, a single European market poses enormous challenges and opportunities in the areas of trade and finance, including capital flows.

IMPACT OF A SINGLE EUROPEAN MARKET ON AFRICA

Trade
In Chapter 2, Christopher Stevens investigates the opportunities and the challenges which the SEM could offer Africa in the area of trade. His argument is that such an analysis should proceed by examining the policy context in which Africa trades with Europe, one governed by the trade agreements which Africa has with the EU. The EU has several other agreements with different Less-Developed Countries (LDCs) and regional groupings. The outcome of these agreements is that the EU has constructed a pyramid of privileges in her trade relations with LDCs. At the apex of this pyramid are the signatories to the Lomé Convention (the ACP countries). In the middle are non-EU Mediterranean countries (Algeria, Egypt, Morocco and Tunisia) which have bilateral relations with the EU. The provisions of these agreements are less favourable than those with the ACP countries. At the base of the pyramid are the other LDCs, including those of South East Asia and Latin America.

Within this policy context, how will the SEM affect Africa? According to Stevens, there will be direct and indirect effects. The direct effects will come in the form of trade and investment creation within the EU as internal controls are dismantled and costs of production go down. The same direct effects will work in the opposite direction to produce negative effects on developing countries – trade diversion as production costs are lowered in the EU, and investment diversion as EU internal markets become more attractive.

The SEM will also produce indirect effects. While these will be positive for the countries of the EU, they will impact negatively on developing countries. For example, while the removal of internal barriers will imply less protectionism within the EU, the harmonization of community non-tariff barriers will probably induce more protectionism against third parties. Similarly, the harmonization of border controls will affect the flow of migrant workers, particularly from North Africa, adversely. The flow of workers' remittances to these countries will be affected adversely as a consequence.

These possible negative consequences of the SEM have prompted some observers to view it as a fortress. This threat of a fortress Europe is more imagined than real, however, because the EU has made its commitment to global trade liberalization known for some time now.

Under global trade liberalization, the system of preferences which Europe has built up for developing countries could be dismantled. Consequently, the real threat to Africa is the loss of preferences that could accompany global trade liberalization (such as obtains under the Uruguay Round) with increased access to Europe for non-ACP developing countries. Thus trade liberalization under GATT rather than SEM, could reduce Africa's share in Europe. There is also the possibility that SEM could make it easier for the more competitive African countries to penetrate EU national markets in which previously they have not been represented strongly, but it may also increase competition for some traditional products in the familiar national markets. Much will depend, of course, on Africa's ability to compete in the new Europe.

Capital Flows and Investment
The impact of the SEM on the flow of capital and private investment to Africa is analysed by Sheila Page in Chapter 3. After examining the well-known rationale for external capital in the development process of developing countries, she proceeds to analyse the trends in private investment and official capital flows to Africa. Europe, according to her, has been the major, but declining, source of official capital to Africa – 36 per cent in 1992 as against 40 per cent in 1989. Europe is also the major source of direct investment – about 70 per cent at the close of the 1990 decade. In relative terms, Africa has been receiving a large share of EU official and direct investment flows compared with other developing countries. For example, in 1991/2, sub-Saharan Africa received 47 per cent of EU official flows while the Middle East and North Africa received 20 per cent, compared to corresponding receipts of 24 per cent and 26 per cent respectively from all donors. Two conclusions can be drawn from this: anything that affects the total official flows of the EU is likely to affect its flow to Africa; and any change in its flows from the EU will have a major effect on Africa. It is in this sense that the SEM, as a major event in Europe, will have implications for capital flows and private investment to Africa.

In order to discern the direction of impact, however, it is appropriate to identify the determinants of the components of the various flows. Official flows – bilateral and multilateral – are motivated primarily by attempts to alter the macro-economic performance of an economy, either sectorally or in the aggregate. Consequently, willingness on the part of a country to adopt policy reforms would be a major determinant of this type of flow. Bilateral flows are further influenced by other factors – strategic and defence considerations, historical ties and, lately, the end of East–West rivalry. In recent times, these factors have assumed overwhelming importance in the allocation of bilateral flows. The proposals coming out of the negotiation of the Lomé V Convention illustrate this point. Europe is considering the allocation of increased resources to the Eastern European countries as a means of containing the crisis in that subregion, while it is also stepping up its assistance to the North African countries as a means of slowing down the flow of migration to Europe. Consequently, Africa, in particular sub-Saharan Africa, is gradually becoming Europe's third priority, behind Eastern Europe and North Africa, as strategic interests rather than budgetary considerations cause diversion of official development finance from Africa.

The flow of foreign investment on the other hand, is more sensitive to the prospect of adequate return on invested capital. This in turn is influenced by the macro-economic environment. Until lately, this environment has been lacking in Africa. While the adoption of market-oriented economic reforms on the continent is expected to change this, the prospects are not bright. By increasing growth and reducing costs within the EU, the SEM will increase the relative attractiveness of that market and therefore cause some investment diversion, particularly from the developing regions (such as Africa) where the cost of doing business is perceived to be relatively higher. This phenomenon is probably currently in operation – out of a total of $75 billion in direct investment that was made in developing countries in 1993, Africa received only $1.8 billion whereas China received $26 billion, Eastern Europe $5 billion and the rest ($42.2 billion) went to Asia and Latin America.[1] Thus, policy reforms notwithstanding, Africa continues to be an unattractive place for foreign direct investment.

Monetary cooperation
A principal component of the SEM is the programme for the establishment of economic and monetary union in Europe by 1997 or 1999 at the latest. This programme could affect significantly the 13 French-speaking African countries which belong to the CFA franc zone and share a common currency. The CFA franc has been fixed in value *vis-à-vis* the French franc since 1948 and is freely convertible to it. In January 1994 the currency was devalued by a massive 50 per cent.

Prior to and after the devaluation, the change in parity provoked commentaries from observers and policy makers alike. Ordinarily, the devaluation of a currency, in particular that of a developing country, would not provoke such commentaries. But the CFA franc devaluation is not just an ordinary devaluation: it touches on the efficacy of monetary cooperation between France (which guarantees the convertibility of the currency) and the African countries of the zone. It also presents a unique opportunity to Africa as it strives to achieve its goal of economic integration.

First, in addition to guaranteeing the free convertibility of the currency, France serves as the custodian of the common external reserves of the countries involved. Indeed, the convertibility of the currency is supported by the operations account, which functions as an overdraft facility in the French Treasury. In this role of creditor, France absorbs at the existing

[1] African Development Bank, *African Development Report*, 1995, p. 300.

exchange rate whatever supply of CFA francs exists on the foreign exchange markets. Since the January 1994 devaluation, questions have been raised as to whether or not France could continue to play this role, particularly as the EU (in which France is a major player), moves irrevocably towards monetary and economic union. Will France be willing to continue to guarantee the convertibility of the currency with all the costs that it entails? As CFA franc zone trade is progressively diversified into other EU markets, will an ECU peg be more desirable?

In keeping with the world-wide trend towards regionalism, Africa has set a 35-year timetable for the establishment of a monetary and political union, with monetary integration as a major component. In pursuance of that objective, some commentators have argued in favour of using the opportunity of the CFA franc devaluation to move forward with monetary integration on the Continent. What should be the most appropriate form of monetary integration for Africa? Should an African currency have an external anchor? If so, what type of anchor? These are the questions I discuss in Chapter 4.

Eastern Europe and Africa

When in 1985, Mikhail Gorbachev, then Soviet President, embarked on his policies of *glasnost* (openness) and *perestroika* (restructuring), few observers anticipated that a major revolution was in the making in Central and Eastern Europe. Between 1985 and 1991 the once monolithic CMEA (Council for Mutual Economic Assistance) collapsed and its member states embarked on major political and economic reforms. Politically, they have opted for Western-type democratic systems of government. Economically, they have replaced central planning with market-oriented economies. The opening up of these economies has effectively eliminated trade and other barriers between them and the rest of the world, thereby presenting immense opportunities and challenges to the world in general and to developing countries (including those of Africa) in particular. In Chapter 5, Ojo and Stevens analyse these developments and their likely impact on Africa.

According to them, the consequences of these events for developing countries will depend on the speed and extent of the changes in Central and Eastern Europe. A major economic restructuring in these countries is likely to lead first to rising prices and then to declines in living standards. There will be gainers, naturally, as well as losers. There could be resistance to reform if the austerity measures continue for long. And whether this could derail economic reform is a matter for speculation.

The reform and rehabilitation of the economies of Central and Eastern Europe will require immense financial resources. Most of these are likely to be foreign direct investment, commercial bank lending and some semi-concessional resources from the World Bank, the new European Bank for

Reconstruction and Development, the International Monetary Fund (IMF) and grant aid. To the extent that the resources are non-concessional, there may not be a diversion of resources from Africa. But if large-scale lending to these countries does occur, it could lead to an increase in world interest rates, and if this is not accompanied by an increase in the supply of funds it could affect all borrowers, developed and underdeveloped. For developing Africa, an increase in world interest rates would not augur well for its development prospects, including the external debt problem.

There could be changes in the political attitude of the West to developing countries as the West turns its attention to its neighbours. The cultural and ethnic affinity among Europeans could be a factor in this attitude. It may not, in the short run, imply a downgrading of interest in the affairs of developing countries, but in the long run there is a danger that such an interest could be crowded out. Already there are indications that strategic interests (for example, the containment of the crisis in Eastern Europe) are forcing a re-ordering of Europe's priority in aid allocation.

The Uruguay Round of Trade Negotiations

GATT was established on a provisional basis after the Second World War along with the Bretton Woods institutions, the World Bank and the International Monetary Fund (IMF). Although the idea of an International Trade Organization (ITO) on the same footing as the World Bank and the IMF did not materialize as planned, GATT was nonetheless established instead in 1946. GATT operates mainly as a forum for trade negotiation and as a court for the settlement of trade disputes.

Since its establishment, GATT has initiated seven rounds of trade negotiations. The most recent round – the Uruguay Round – was launched at a Ministerial meeting in Punta del Este, Uruguay, in September 1986, and was in part a culmination of the work begun in Geneva in November 1982. As the most ambitious of all trade talks, its objectives were to bring about further liberalization and expansion of world trade, strengthen the role of GATT and improve the multilateral trading system; increase the responsiveness of GATT to the evolving international economic environment; and encourage cooperation in strengthening the interrelationship between trade and other economic policies affecting growth and development.

The Uruguay Round Agreement was signed in April 1994 in the Moroccan city of Marrakech. Apart from a comprehensive liberalization of merchandise trade, it also covers trade in agriculture, intellectual property rights and services. It recommended the establishment of a comprehensive trade body – the World Trade Organization (WTO) – to replace GATT early in 1995.

Tariff reduction under the Uruguay Round is expected to yield significant gains for the world economy: about US$195 billion, of which $80 billion would accrue to developing countries. The benefits to developing countries are likely to be unevenly distributed, with Africa (in particular the sub-Saharan countries as net food importers), sustaining significant losses.

Oshikoya analyses these consequences for Africa in Chapter 6. Specifically, he argues that the implications of the Uruguay Round go beyond the potential income losses which Africa is likely to suffer. As a world-wide trade liberalization programme, the Uruguay Round is likely to reduce the value of preferences which Africa enjoys in its best market, Europe. By liberalizing trade, in particular trade in agriculture, the Uruguay Round will open up the European market to other developing countries which have not hitherto enjoyed unrestricted access to European markets. Not only will Africa suffer a loss of preferences, but it will also face stiff competition from more competitive developing regions of the world. Africa's market share in the EU, which has been declining for some time and for reasons unrelated to the SEM, is likely to decline further. This raises difficult problems for Africa: how to earn the necessary foreign exchange for financing development and for servicing its external debt.

2

The Single European Market:
Opportunities and Challenges in Trade

CHRISTOPHER STEVENS

The Single European Market (SEM) is of importance for Africa partly because of the policy changes specifically envisaged but, even more importantly, because it is part of a broader process. When combined with changes in the structure of the European economies, with generalized liberalization in the new World Trade Organization (WTO), and with the opening towards East Central Europe and the former Soviet Union (FSU), the net result may be a decline in Africa's relative position in its most important market.

A major problem facing those states likely to be affected by these events is that the speed and complexity of change make it hard to assess the nature and degree of any dangers. In the run-up to 1992 there was much talk about it leading to a 'Fortress Europe'. How likely is this to occur? If it does occur, is it a problem for Africa or only for the United States of America (USA), Japan and the Newly Industrializing Countries (NICs)? At a more technical level, will changes to European standards make it easier for Africa to penetrate all 15 European national markets or will it undermine existing flows by requiring goods to meet levels of sophistication that African producers cannot achieve?

This chapter provides a guide through the intricacies of the SEM and, where appropriate, related developments. The objective is to help African governments identify which changes might be beneficial and which adverse for their trade. As explained in the fourth section ('The Impact of the SEM on Trade'. p. 39), parts of the SEM occurred before 1992 and the process of building on the SEM towards closer political and monetary union will continue for the rest of this decade. Although the date of 31 December 1992 has passed, there is still much to play for.

The impact of the SEM changes on Africa will be filtered through the preferential trade agreements which almost all countries of the continent have with the EU. In the case of sub-Saharan African states, these trade provisions are incorporated into the Lomé Convention. The fourth Lomé Convention will continue until the end of this decade. Hence, its duration is broadly coterminous with the bulk of the changes occurring within Europe. Most of the North African states have bilateral trade and co-operation agreements with the EU. These are of more fluid duration but may reasonably be expected to last until the end of the century, at least.

The changes in Europe are many and complex; the countries of Africa are many and varied. Hence, a short chapter such as this cannot indicate precisely how each element of the SEM will affect each African state. Nor can it prescribe exactly what governments of Africa should do to protect their interests where this is necessary, and to advance them where this is possible. What it can do is to identify in broad terms the issues on which African governments need to concentrate their attention.

The next section ('The Existing Pattern and Volume of Trade', p. 13) describes the framework of trade policies that link Africa and the EU and the ways in which these are being affected not only by the SEM but also by other changes to the international economic environment. It then charts the progress of Africa's exports to the EU and imports from the EU in the context of the changing pattern of Europe's trade.

One conclusion is that there is a sharp contrast between Africa's position as most preferred (in terms of trade preference) yet least successful trading partner with the EU. This contrast has led some analysts to question whether trade preferences are effective. This debate is of importance because the combined effect of the SEM and the GATT Round will be to erode the value of trade preferences for Africa. The section also includes, therefore, an assessment of the utility of the trade preferences incorporated into the Lomé Convention and the North African association agreements.

The third section ('Distribution of Trade by Commodity and Country', p. 25) examines the commodity and country distribution of recent trade flows. Africa's exports to the EU are heavily concentrated on a very small number of largely unprocessed primary commodities. This over-concentration largely explains Africa's poor performance relative to other developing countries in exporting to the EU.

A conventional wisdom has developed that Africa is, somehow, incapable of exporting competitively. This conventional wisdom is wrong. An analysis of EU imports of traditional primary products indicates that during the 1980s the African, Caribbean and Pacific (ACP) countries as a whole performed as well as the less-developed countries' (LDC) average. Where Africa and other LDCs part company is that the latter have been more successful in diversifying out of traditional primary commodities, for which European demand is growing slowly, and into processed and manufactured products.

An analysis of non-traditional exports from Africa indicates that a significant number of countries from the continent have now begun to diversify out of this unsatisfactory product range. The success of Mauritius is well known, but Zimbabwe, Kenya, Botswana, Malawi and others in sub-Saharan Africa have also achieved some success, as have Tunisia and Morocco on a much larger scale. Although the absolute value of such non-traditional exports is still low in most cases, it is growing. In Kenya, for example, horticulture is now the country's third-largest merchandise export to the EU.

Although it is not possible to identify an unambiguous causal relationship, there is some reason to suppose that the preferential trade agreements of Africa have assisted this diversification. This suggests that further growth may be vulnerable to measures that aim at liberalization, such as the SEM and the GATT Round.

The fourth section ('The Impact of the SEM on Trade', p. 39) explains the various elements of the process that has become known as '1992'. It extends beyond an analysis of the simple removal of internal trade barriers to include broader visions, such as the Social Charter and monetary union, which may have an impact on Africa's competitiveness. Among the many actions being taken to remove internal constraints on trade, those that are most likely to affect Africa include the harmonization of excise taxes and technical standards, and the deregulation of air transport.

The external effects of '1992' may be divided into two categories, direct and indirect. The direct effects on both trade and investment will arise from changes to Europe's relative international competitiveness. Various estimates have been made of the size of these effects. One estimate for a group of African countries suggests that the overall impact will be positive.

The indirect effects arise from the measures that European governments may or may not take to protect their citizens and producers from the economic and social costs of the adjustment process. There are fears that Europe may become more protectionist in an attempt to transfer the burden of adjustment to third parties. It is in this context that the notion of a Fortress Europe has arisen. But Africa may have more to fear from a dismantling of current protectionist barriers. Its exports of bananas, sugar and clothing may become more difficult in future as the national markets into which these goods are sold are opened up to the winds of competition.

One area in which Africa may have just cause to fear a Fortress Europe is labour. The movement of human capital from one country to another in search of employment may be considered just as much a trade issue as the flow of goods. The free movement of labour within Europe is likely to lead to more uniform immigration policies. There is some reason to fear that the immigration policies of the more liberal states will be tightened rather than those of the least liberal being loosened. This would affect North Africa particularly severely as it is a major source of migrants into the EU.

The fifth section ('Prospects for Africa's Exports to Europe', p. 56) considers prospects for Africa's exports to Europe. These will be affected not only by the changes associated with the SEM but also by those that have been agreed within the GATT negotiations. They will also be affected by the success with which Africa diversifies from traditional to non-traditional products.

Africa's traditional exports are likely to be affected adversely by the GATT Round, albeit only to a moderate degree. They should not face major problems as a result of the SEM except in respect of commodities that cannot meet new technical standards and those commodities that might be affected if there is excise duty harmonization.

The impact of the GATT Round on non-traditional agricultural exports to Europe is unclear because the precise implications of the agreement on temperate agriculture will become apparent only over the next few years. Much depends upon the balance of liberalizing measures between different categories of temperate product.

Africa's manufactured non-traditional exports may be affected adversely by increased competition in Europe as a result of the SEM. Those countries that have already established a position in the market may be able to weather the storm but those just beginning are likely to find the environment more difficult than did the early starters.

The central theme of the final section ('Policy Recommendations and Conclusions', p. 59) is that each African state will be affected differently by the SEM, not to mention the other changes in Europe's external policies. It is vital, therefore, that each country identify precisely the areas in which it is most likely to be affected and seek the necessary expert advice to enable it to advance its interests. The major danger is that events will happen so fast that African interests will be left unprotected by default.

The Existing Pattern and Volume of Trade

The SEM will have a profound impact on trade between Africa and the EU, partly because it will alter the policy framework within which that trade takes place. All of the states of Africa apart from Libya have preferential trade agreements with the EU. The effective importance of these agreements may change as an indirect result of the SEM decisions.

THE POLICY FRAMEWORK

The present pattern of Europe's relations with the countries of the South has been woven from twelve bilateral sets of policies and a thirteenth, partly cross-cutting, Union-level set. The balance between the bilateral and Union levels is established by the distribution between them of those powers that are most relevant to LDCs. The SEM will alter this balance and, hence, the policy environment for Africa and the rest of the South.

The extent of Union-level relations is limited by the characteristic of the EU Commission that it does not possess the full array of attributes of a nation state. It cannot conduct a normal foreign or defence policy; even its responsibilities on debt are limited. Among this limited range of instruments there are three principal foundations for Union-level policies affecting the Third World. They are the common commercial policy (CCP), the common agricultural policy (CAP) and the partially common aid policy. All three may change as a consequence of the SEM.

Bilateral interests, such as those of France in Africa, have been indulged in the past, using both the instruments that have not yet been transferred to Union level and the national element of partially common policies, notably on trade and aid. Although the foundations of Europe's foreign trade regime are established at Union level, the CCP's purity has been reduced in practice as member states have adopted, to a greater or lesser extent, national policies that influence trade flows. Most important have been the growing number of non-tariff barriers (NTBs) to imports, such as bilateral voluntary export restraints (VERs) and national quotas within Union NTBs (see the fourth section, p. 39).

THE PYRAMID OF PRIVILEGE

The EU has a complex set of over 20 agreements with different LDCs and regional groupings which build upon these foundations to provide a combination of trade preferences, sometimes on CAP products, and of aid. This wide variety of treatment, however, is more apparent than real. In terms of practical provisions, the agreements boil down to three broad bands that form a hierarchy. With one exception, all those African states with which the EU has a preferential trade agreement are in the top two bands.[1]

- At the apex, in formal terms, are the 70 signatories of the Lomé Conventions (known collectively as the ACP countries), which include all the states of sub-Saharan Africa except South Africa together with states from the Caribbean and Pacific.

- In the middle are the non-EU Mediterranean states, almost all of which have a bilateral agreement with the EU. Algeria, Egypt, Morocco and Tunisia have such association agreements. The formal provisions of the agreements are in general less favourable than those of the ACP countries but, because of their location and higher economic base, these countries are often better placed to take advantage of such concessions as exist.

- At the base are all *other* LDCs, including those in South East Asia and

---

[1] The exception is South Africa. At the time of writing the final character of its trade agreement with the EU had not been decided.

Latin America, which, despite a rich variety of agreements, all receive broadly similar preferences.[2]

They form a hierarchy in the sense that the value of the provisions to those states at the top depends upon their being treated more favourably than those at the base. Hence, the Lomé preference on duty-free entry for coffee has been of value to Côte d'Ivoire only because its competitor, Brazil, has paid 4.5 per cent duty under the Generalized System of Preferences (GSP). Hence, the EU's GATT Round decision to cut tariffs on many tropical products will reduce the value of the preferences enjoyed by the ACP countries. The extreme case is provided by bananas exported by Cameroon, Côte d'Ivoire, Somalia and some other ACP countries, which until 1992 enjoyed an absolute preference in the UK, French and Italian markets over non-ACP supplies.

THE EFFECTS OF LIBERALIZATION

In consequence of the hierarchical nature of the EU's trade policy, changes to the treatment of some states affect the value of the preferences accorded to others. Improved preferences on clothing for Eastern Europe, for example, would devalue existing preferences to Mauritius, Morocco and Tunisia. Whereas generalized liberalization may well be a positive-sum game benefiting all states, a partial extension of preferences which effectively redistributes the economic rent arising from an artificial restriction of supply is more likely to be a zero-sum game in which gainers are counterpoised by losers.

The SEM is likely to be accompanied by such a shuffling of the hierarchy because a tension has developed between the orientation of Europe's economic interests and of its formal policies towards the South, especially those framed at Union level. A striking feature of the recent trade patterns described below is that they are the inverse of the pyramid of privilege: trade has grown fastest with some states at the base of the pyramid and slowest with those at the apex. In the case of the ACP countries, in particular, there has been a substantial decline in economic relations witnessed by a fall in the group's share of EU trade. Although it is only a part of the ACP group, sub-Saharan Africa experienced a similar decline. By contrast, trade relations with the Mediterranean, including North Africa, have remained strong, reflecting substantial European economic and political interests in the region.

This tension has been defused partially up to now because each EU member state has retained control over many of the most potent commercial policy instruments. Germany, for example, has been able to

---

[2] The principal distinction at the base is between the majority of LDCs and those that benefit from a superior tranche of the GSP intended originally for least developed states but extended in 1991 'temporarily', and in some cases partially, to some Latin American countries.

use export credits, investment promotion or debt rescheduling to promote its interests in South East Asia, regardless of the EU focus on the ACP group. Indeed, it may have preferred the Union to concentrate on the ACP countries so as not to queer its pitch in Asia. But as further powers are transferred from national to EU level, this capacity to run an independent shadow policy will wither; the emphasis of Union-level policy will acquire a direct importance for national interests.

As formal policy and effective practice have diverged, the framework of policies established after independence has become increasingly a hollow shell. Despite this, the old ways might have continued for some time under the weight of government inertia and the difficulty of devising new policies. Recent events, however, have begun to fracture the shell, a process which is likely to intensify in the medium term. It is within this framework that the effects of the SEM on EU–Africa trade have to be viewed.

The principal agent of change is trade liberalization, externally within the GATT Round and internally with the completion of the SEM. The value of trade preferences to the beneficiary is related inversely to the level of protectionism (at least if the matter is viewed only in a short-term, static perspective). If protection is high, the competitive advantage afforded by preferences may be substantial. By the same token, if protection is low, the opposite is true. With the successful completion of the GATT Round there is a reasonable chance that the 1990s will be a decade of liberalization. Hence, the whole edifice built up over the years by the EU is likely to subside gently as its foundations are weakened by liberalization.

THE VOLUME OF TRADE

Africa's trade relationship with the EU is asymmetrical. Europe is extremely important for Africa both as a market for its exports and as a source of its imports. For Europe, by contrast, Africa is a small and declining trading partner (see Table 2.1, p. 17). Hence, the SEM is of importance for Africa not only because of the shift in trade policy but also because these changes are occurring in its major trading partner.

Some 52 per cent of Africa's exports go to the EU. Perhaps more disturbing than this large figure is the fact that Africa's dependence on the EU has increased over the past 17 years; in 1975 the proportion was only 41 per cent. An even higher proportion of Africa's imports are sourced from the EU. Africa is more heavily dependent upon the EU than are other developing countries. In 1992 the EU absorbed only 25 per cent of all LDCs' exports and supplied 24 per cent of their imports.

The relative importance of EU–Africa trade is a function not only of each party's exports and imports but also of the volume of other regions' trade. There has been a substantial shift in the pattern of Europe's trade with the world over the past quarter century or so which has its origins in changes to the structure of production and in the creation of a common market. Africa has not shared fully in this new pattern.

TABLE 2.1
Africa's trade with the EU, 1975–92

	1975	1980	1985	1990	1992
Africa's exports:					
Value ($mn)	9,656	37,106	33,778	47,174	44,962
% of total	41	39	52	54	52
Africa's imports:					
Value ($mn)	13,331	41,995	30,342	41,906	42,452
% of total	50	51	53	56	52

Source: IMF, Direction of Trade Statistics, various Yearbooks.

The share of all third parties in total EU imports and exports has fallen since 1960 as the creation of the European Common Market has encouraged members to trade with each other (Figures 2.1 and 2.2). However, whilst non-EU developed countries (DCs) were more severely affected by this decline than were LDCs in the period 1960–75, since then the reverse has been true. The LDC share of EU imports has continued to fall (from 23 per cent in 1975 to only 12 per cent by 1992) whilst the DC share has stabilized at 24 per cent in 1992, compared with its 1975 level of 23 per cent. In the case of EU exports, the DC share has tended to hold up better than that of the LDCs throughout the period although, once again, the differentially poor LDC performance was more marked during the second part.

The sharpest fall in trade share has been experienced by sub-Saharan Africa and the other, small, members of the ACP group. Their share of external EU imports fell from 10 per cent in 1960 to 4 per cent by 1992 (Figure 2.3), and a similar picture applies to EU exports (Figure 2.4). The share of Latin America in both imports and exports also fell, whilst that of the Mediterranean held broadly stable. The only states to have experienced a steady rise in trade share are the East Asian NICs of Korea, Taiwan and Hong Kong, and the members of the Association of South East Asian Nations (ASEAN). Their respective shares of extra-EU imports rose from 1 per cent in 1970 to 5 per cent by 1992, and from 3 per cent to 5 per cent respectively. For exports, the rise was from 1 per cent to 5 per cent and from 3 per cent to 4 per cent respectively.

These changes in the positions of different regions in the EU's trade are related to the commodity composition of that trade (Figure 2.5). Over the period there has been a change in the relative importance of various sources for European growth, with non-traded services and intra-DC trade increasing in significance. The distortions caused by the CAP have simply accentuated a trend away from the traditional colonial trade pattern of

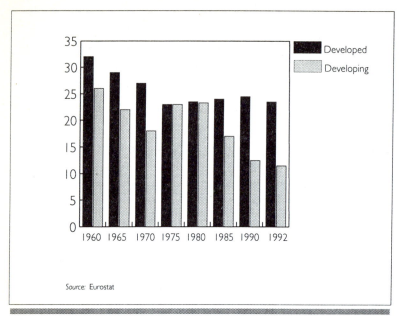

FIGURE 2.1 EU imports from developed and developing countries as a share of total imports (intra and extra), 1960–92

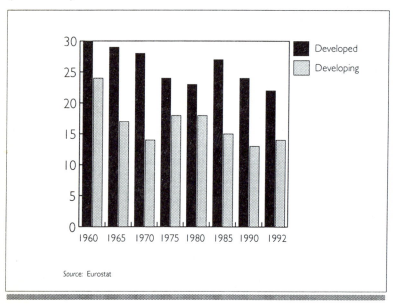

FIGURE 2.2 EU exports to developed and developing countries as a share of total exports (intra and extra), 1960–92

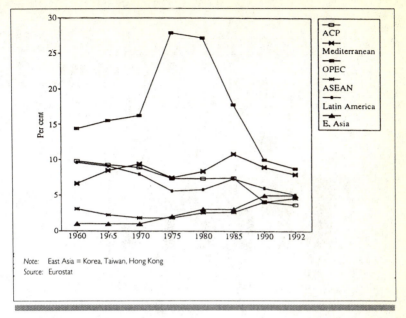

FIGURE 2.3 EU imports from developing countries by region as a share of extra-EU imports, 1960–92

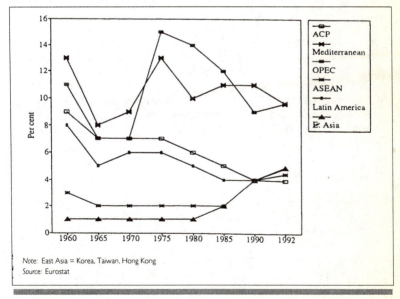

FIGURE 2.4 EU exports to developing countries by region as a share of extra-EU exports, 1960–92

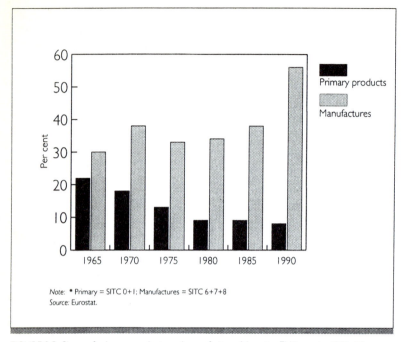

FIGURE 2.5 Share of primary products and manufactures* in extra-EU imports, 1965–90

importing raw materials from the South and exporting manufactures in return. In its place, a trade has developed with parts of the South that emphasizes a two-way flow of manufactures and services. The leaders of the new pattern of trade have been, on the European side, the states with relatively weak colonial ties (notably Germany) and, in the South, the countries of East and South East Asia. By contrast, Africa's exports have tended to be focused on the major ex-colonial states, France and the UK.

THE VALUE OF PREFERENTIAL TRADE AGREEMENTS

One potential effect on Africa of the SEM and other EU trade policy changes is that the region may lose its trade preferences: does this matter? The sharp contrast between the ACP group's position as most preferred yet least successful trading partner with the EU has led some analysts to question whether Lomé and, even, the Mediterranean association agreements are worth the candle and to assert that since their 'beneficiaries' have gained little from preferences, their potential losses from liberalization will be correspondingly modest (see for example Brown 1988, Davenport 1988).

In fact, the case against trade preferences has been overstated. The ACP countries' poor overall performance primarily reflects the fact that their exports are more heavily concentrated than are those of other LDCs on commodities for which world demand is growing slowly and which have suffered serious price falls since 1980. Because of this heavy concentration on traditional primaries, the ACP countries in practice benefit from rather few preferences, despite the apparent liberality of the Lomé texts. The Convention provides them with either zero or very limited preference over their major competitors for the vast majority of their exports.

As regards preferences, ACP exports to the EU fall into three broad groups. The largest group is of commodities that enter the Community market duty-free, but would do so even without the Lomé Convention, as do the exports of the ACP group's principal competitors. Hence, Lomé provides no preferences. The second group, accounting for a large part of the remainder, are products which enter duty-free under Lomé but do not do so under the GSP or most-favoured nation (MFN) provisions and do not compete directly with European production. Hence, the ACP states receive a tariff preference over other third party exporters to the EU. But the level of GSP or MFN tariffs, and hence the ACP margin of preference, is very low in many cases. Over half of sub-Saharan Africa's exports, by value, are normally accounted for by petroleum, gold, diamonds, copper and wood, all of which face zero MFN tariffs. Moreover, there are no major non-tariff restrictions on imports into the EU of most traditional ACP exports. Hence, the Lomé regime is unlikely to have significant dynamic effects on ACP exports of these commodities.

The third category is the smallest in terms of ACP export value but is potentially the most significant; many of the commodities covered by the North African agreements are also in this category. It consists of goods that are also produced within Europe and which benefit from substantial EU protection. Preferences on such goods are particularly valuable for three reasons. First, they may facilitate export diversification. Second, the preferred exporters, like European producers, are protected against competitive imports from other third party suppliers. And, not least, export earnings are increased by the artificially high prices in the European market brought about by the restriction of supply.

Most notable are products that fall within the CAP, plus clothing and textiles that are controlled by the Multifibre Arrangement (MFA). In the case of temperate agricultural products, Africa benefits from a number of openings to the European market, although these are usually restricted by quotas, calendars (that limit preferential access to certain periods of the year) or both. In the case of clothing, Africa is not subject to the MFA. The ACP states in sub-Saharan Africa are unconstrained by any quotas or duties, though there have been a number of instances of VER and anti-dumping actions, and the Lomé rules of origin are difficult to fulfil for woven clothing. The North African states are regulated by quotas, but

TABLE 2.2 Lomé IV preferences for fresh (or chilled) fruit and vegetables

Regime	Product(s)	Quota (tonnes)
Exemption from customs duties without marketing timetable	Radishes, leguminous vegetables, aubergines, celery other than celeriac, sweet peppers, courgettes, other vegetables, pistachios, pecans, other nuts, grapefruit, other citrus fruit, limes, melons, pawpaws, fruit of the species *Vaccinium myrtillus*, other fresh fruit	None
Reduction of the duty by 60%	Tomatoes (other than cherry tomatoes), from 15 November to 30 April	2,000 tonnes
Progressive abolition of customs duties	Cherry tomatoes, from 15 November to 30 April	2,000 tonnes
Progressive abolition of the customs duty	Onions, from 1 February to 15 May	800 tonnes
Progressive abolition of the customs duty	Garlic, from 1 February to 31 May	500 tonnes
Progressive abolition of the customs duty from 1 November to 31 December	Chinese cabbage	1,000 tonncs
Progressive abolition of the customs duty from 1 July to 31 October	Iceberg lettuce	1,000 tonnes
Progressive abolition of the customs duty from 1 January to 31 March	Carrots	800 tonnes
Progressive abolition of the customs duty	Horse-radish	
Progressive abolition of the customs duty	Salad beetroot	100 tonnes
Progressive abolition of the customs duty	Small winter cucumbers	100 tonnes
Progressive abolition of the customs duty from 1 October to 31 December	Artichokes	1,000 tonnes
• Progressive abolition of the customs duty from 15 August to 15 January • 40% reduction from 16 January to 31 January	Asparagus	
Progressive abolition of the customs duty	Other mushrooms	
Progressive abolition of the customs duty	Walnuts	700 tonnes

TABLE 2.2 cont. Lomé IV preferences for fresh (or chilled) fruit and vegetables

Regime	Product(s)	Quota (tonnes)
• Progressive abolition of customs duty from 1 November to 30 April	Figs (fresh)	200 tonnes
• Progressive abolition of the customs duty from 15 May to 30 September • Above this quantity and throughout the year an 80% reduction of the customs duty	Oranges	25,000 tonnes
• Progressive abolition of the customs duty from 15 May to 30 September • Above this quantity, and throughout the year, an 80% reduction of the customs duty	Mandarins and other similar citrus hybrids	4,000 tonnes
Progressive reduction of the customs duty by 50%	Apples	1,000 tonnes
Progressive reduction of the customs duty by 50%	Pears	1,000 tonnes
Progressive abolition of the customs duty from 1 September to 30 April	Apricots	2,000 tonnes
Progressive reduction of the customs duty from 1 November to 31 March	Cherries	2,000 tonnes
Progressive reduction of the customs duty from 1 December to 31 March	Peaches	2,000 tonnes
Progressive reduction of the customs duty from 15 December to 31 March	Plums	2,000 tonnes
Progressive abolition of the customs duty	Sloes	500 tonnes
Progressive abolition of the customs duty from 1 November to end February	Strawberries	1,500 tonnes
Progressive abolition of the customs duty	Mixtures exclusively of dried nuts (0801 and 0802)	
Reduction of the common customs tariff to: • 3% for fruit of the species • 5% for other fruits of the	Vaccinium macrocarpon and Vaccinium corymbosum Vaccinium species	

Source: Lomé IV, Annex XL.

these are set at levels that exceed by a substantial margin those that would probably apply if they were subject to the MFA.

The range of CAP products on which sub-Saharan African states benefit includes sugar, beef and horticultural products; the North African states also have preferences on the last of these. Although the mechanisms employed vary between these products, the fundamental nature of the benefit is the same in each. Because the CAP restricts supply to the EU market, prices prevailing in Europe are artificially high. The preferred exporters gain at least part of this economic rent for at least part of their exports. The reason for the 'at least part' *caveat* is that in some cases the EU treasury obtains part of the economic rent through the application of import tariffs, and because access to the EU market is normally limited to a fixed quota which may be less than total exports. If a country is able to sell only a part of its total exports to the EU, the effects of high European prices may have to be offset against lower returns in other markets. This would happen, for example, if the CAP resulted in world market prices being lower than they otherwise would be. Hence, the critical factors in determining whether, in the short term, the export revenue of LDC preference holders is higher or lower as a result of the CAP are: the proportion of exports that gain access to the EU market, the level of economic rent received by the exporter, and the price-depressing effects of the CAP in other markets.

Sugar
The EU–ACP Sugar Protocol is attached to the Lomé Conventions although it is not part of them. The principal reason for this distinction is that it is of 'unlimited duration', and therefore not subject to periodic renegotiation.

The Protocol provides nine African states (plus a further eight in the Caribbean and Pacific plus India), with a global quota of 1.3 million tonnes of sugar (white sugar equivalent) for which the EU guarantees to pay similar prices to those offered to European sugar beet producers. These prices are normally well above world levels. The Protocol, which represents a major breach in the CAP system of protection, was negotiated as part of Britain's accession to the Union. The imports are consumed almost exclusively in the UK market.

The share of sugar exports covered by the Protocol varies between the ACP beneficiaries. But in all, with the possible exception of Zimbabwe, the financial gain of high prices on the EU quota has almost certainly exceeded the financial loss due to the CAP-induced depression of world market prices.

Beef
Five African states (Botswana, Kenya, Madagascar, Swaziland and Zimbabwe) have a special regime for the export of beef to the EU. They benefit from a 90 per cent reduction in the variable import levy for a quota of beef.

The total quota under Lomé IV is 39,100 tonnes annually, but it is sub-divided into national quotas with discretionary provisions for a surplus on one state's quota to be transferred to another.

Horticulture
The CAP regime for horticultural products is complex. The basic rule is that the system for supporting European farmers is relatively lightly structured, without the mandatory intervention buying and variable import levies that have characterized the cereals and meat regimes. For the fresh products of most interest to LDCs the normal regime that applied to imports until the GATT Agreement was that the EU levied an *ad valorem* tariff and also established a 'reference price'. Countries exporting to the EU were obliged to sell their goods at a 'minimum import price' equal to the reference price plus the tariffs. Failure to comply resulted in a countervailing levy being imposed to bring the cost of imports up to the required level. Hence, it was possible to export fresh fruit and vegetables to the EU, but only if the landed price exceeded the level at which domestic produce was sold.

For Africa and some other third party suppliers (primarily states in the Mediterranean), concessions take the form of full or partial rebates of the *ad valorem* tariff. But there have been two provisos. The first has been that LDC preference holders must still respect minimum import prices. In other words, they have been unable to undercut domestic European produce but they have retained a larger share of the proceeds from any exports they do make, which has helped them to compete with other third party suppliers that have paid the full tariff.

The second proviso is that these concessions are limited for some products to a fixed quota or specific period of the year ('calendar') or both. Such quotas may be very small: the quota in Lomé IV for small winter cucumber is 100 tonnes for the whole of the ACP group (see Table 2.2). Moreover, it does not follow simply from the existence of a preference on paper that all (or any) African states can actually harvest a specified product within the calendar. There have been cases in the Mediterranean where the EU has granted a calendar-restricted preference for a product which, because of climate, the 'beneficiary' cannot produce at that time of the year!

Distribution of Trade by Commodity and Country

TRADITIONAL EXPORTS

To receive deep preferences, the ACP countries need to diversify their export products. The need for such diversification is particularly great since the central export problem for Africa and the other ACP states is one of over-reliance on slow growth product markets. Contrary to the

conventional wisdom, the ACP countries have not performed less satis-
factorily than other LDCs on their exports of tropical products even
though their preferences are modest. Rather, the problem is that their
exports are more heavily concentrated than are those of other LDCs on a
product range for which world demand is growing slowly. Africa has been
less successful than have other continents in diversifying into products
with a better market outlook.

An analysis of EU imports of the 13 tropical products of most
importance to the ACP countries suggests that they have performed as
well as the LDC average (Table 2.3). During the period 1978/9 to 1986/7 the
weighted average growth in the volume of EU imports for these thirteen
products from all LDCs was 4.0 per cent; for the ACP countries, the
increase was virtually the same, at 3.9 per cent. In the case of over half of
the commodities reviewed, EU imports grew faster (or declined more
slowly) from the ACP countries than from all LDCs. The problem for Africa
is that EU demand for these commodities has grown only slowly.

TABLE 2.3
Growth in import shares of crude tropical products,
1978/79 and 1986/87 (%)

	Average growth in share of EU imports		ACP tariff preference margin
	LDC 1978/9	ACP – 1986/7	
Bananas, fresh	1.6	3.4	20
Pineapples	9.0	8.8	9
Coffee beans	3.4	4.7	4.5
Tea	0.2	3.4	0
Cocoa beans	4.5	3.7	3
Tobacco	0.4	7.0	7.5
Palm nuts/kernels	−3.4	−2.9	0
Palm oil	4.9	6.3	5.5
Oilcake, meal	14.1	−3.1	0
Raw sugar	−0.0	1.2	L
Crude rubber	27.4	6.9	0
Sisal, etc	−1.0	−7.6	0
Wood, rough	−2.9	−2.1	0
Weighted averages*			
All products	4.0	3.9	–
Crude products	3.8	4.3	–

* Averages are weighted by 1986/7 total EU imports.
L Levy on non-ACP imports. The major ACP sugar producers have specific quantities of imports guaranteed at EU sugar prices.
Source: Davenport and Stevens, 1990.

African exports to the EU remain heavily concentrated on a very small number of traditional products. In 6 per cent of African states, one product group (at the 2-digit CN level) accounted for more than 90 per cent of the value of exports to the EU in 1990, and for 22 per cent of African states, two such products accounted for more than 90 per cent. Indeed, in 30 per cent of countries, one product accounted for more than 50 per cent, and in a further 32 per cent two products accounted for the same proportion of 1990 exports to the EU: in almost two-thirds of African states, therefore, one or two commodity groups accounted for over half of exports to Europe.

TABLE 2.4
Africa's main exports to the EU, 1992 (by value)

CN code	Description	Value (EU mn)	Cumulative share (%)
	Total trade	35,023	
27	Mineral fuels and oils	19,121	55
71	Precious/semi-precious stones/metals	1,485	59
62	Woven clothing	1,284	62
18	Cocoa and cocoa preparation	969	65
44	Wood and articles of wood	966	68
09	Coffee, tea, maté, spices	849	70
88	Aircraft and parts thereof	797	73
61	Knitted or crocheted clothing	563	74
17	Sugars and sugar confectionery	526	76
26	Ores, slag and ash	525	77
52	Cotton	521	79
74	Copper and articles thereof	506	80
03	Fish/crustaceans	490	82
76	Aluminium and articles thereof	404	83
08	Edible fruits and nuts	392	84
24	Tobacco and manufactured tobacco substitutes	347	85
15	Animal/vegetable fats/oils	253	86
85	Electrical machinery and parts thereof	235	86
28	Inorganic chemicals	228	87
16	Preparations of meat/fish/crustaceans	176	87
07	Edible vegetables	162	88
31	Fertilizers	158	88
41	Raw hides/skins	154	89
72	Iron and steel	151	89
40	Rubber and articles thereof	135	90

Source: Eurostat.

Most of these commodities are relatively unprocessed raw materials. In 1992, just 25 products accounted for 90 per cent of Africa's exports to the EU by value (Table 2.4). Out of the 16 most important, which accounted for over 80 per cent of the total, the only ones which were not relatively unprocessed primary commodities were woven clothing (4 per cent of the total), knitted clothing (2 per cent) and aluminium (1 per cent).[3]

There has been a slight improvement over the past two decades or so. In 1977 a larger share of total exports (94 per cent) was accounted for by only 18 products. Knitted garments were among them (although they accounted for only 1 per cent of the total) but woven garments were absent. Nonetheless, the overall picture remains one of a worrying dependence on primary products in exports to a market on which Africa is over-concentrated.

Not only is world demand for Africa's main exports relatively slow-growing, but the region also faces tough competition from other suppliers. In only one of the top 12 exports, in 1992, was Africa the dominant supplier to the EU market (Table 2.5). This was cocoa, where Africa supplied 83 per cent of EU imports from developing countries and 69 per cent of all imports from outside the Union. In only one other product (sugar) did Africa supply more than one-third of total extra-EU imports.

Africa is a significant supplier to the EU on some products, but these tend to rank rather low in the continent's total exports to the EU. In the case of cork and gums, for example, Africa supplies over one-third of EU imports from developing countries, and around one-fifth of all imports, but the products account for less than one-quarter of one per cent of total African exports to the EU. Table 2.6 lists the 12 product groups in which Africa supplied more than one-third of EU imports from developing countries in 1992. If the apparently anomalous line on aircraft is omitted (presumably being a re-export), most of the remainder are unprocessed raw materials. In all cases except fuels, they form only a very small share of total African exports. In many cases, also, although Africa supplies a large share of EU imports from developing countries, its share of total extra-EU imports is much lower.

NON-TRADITIONAL EXPORTS

Whilst such traditional export commodities still form the bulk of Africa's exports, the evidence of the 1980s is that a number of states have begun to break out of this unsatisfactory export product range, and while the EU's trade preferences have not had a major effect on trade patterns, there may have been some impact at the margins. They have not prevented the marginalization of sub-Saharan Africa in EU trade, but there are reasons to believe that this would have been more severe in the absence of the Convention.

[3] Excluding aircraft and parts, which probably represent re-exports.

TABLE 2.5
Africa's share of EU imports for principal exports

CN code	Description	EU imports from Africa: value (ECU mn)	as a % of extra-EU	as a % of all LDCs
	Total trade	35,023	7.18	24.04
27	Mineral fuels and oils	19,121	29.49	49.43
71	Precious/semi-precious stones/metals	1,485	9.87	34.15
62	Woven clothing	1,284	8.54	17.01
18	Cocoa and cocoa preparations	969	69.43	82.50
44	Wood and articles of wood	966	9.08	33.55
09	Coffee, tea, maté, spices	849	30.11	31.55
88	Aircraft and parts thereof	797	6.69	35.24
61	Knitted or crocheted clothing	563	6.03	10.72
17	Sugars and sugar confectionery	526	39.27	48.79
26	Ores, slag and ash	525	9.30	20.30
52	Cotton	521	15.18	33.11
74	Copper and articles thereof	506	9.99	27.58

Source: Eurostat.

TABLE 2.6
Products for which Africa is a major exporter to the EU

CN code	Description	EU imports from Africa: value (ECU mn)	as a % of extra-EU	as a % of all LDCs	as a % of total African exports to EU
	Total trade	35,023	7.18	24.04	
81	Other base metals	60	8.18	83.86	0.17
18	Cocoa and cocoa preparations	969	69.43	82.50	2.77
79	Zinc and articles thereof	22	5.99	75.36	0.06
27	Mineral fuels and oils	19,121	29.49	49.43	54.59
17	Sugars and sugar confectionery	526	39.27	48.79	1.50
76	Aluminium and articles thereof	404	8.12	47.26	1.15
75	Nickel and articles thereof	36	3.30	44.68	0.10
13	Lacs, gums, resins, etc.	59	25.43	41.77	0.17
88	Aircraft and parts thereof	797	6.69	35.24	2.28
45	Cork and articles thereof	5	17.89	35.21	0.02
71	Precious/semi-precious stones/metals	1,485	9.87	34.15	4.24
44	Wood and articles of wood	966	9.08	33.55	2.76

Source: Eurostat.

The number of states that have achieved significant diversification is still a minority within sub-Saharan Africa, but it is not an insignificant one. The success of Mauritius in developing its clothing exports is well known, but it is by no means alone. In Kenya, for example, horticultural exports have developed very rapidly over the last five years and are now the country's third-largest merchandise export to the EU. Some 28 African and other ACP states have emerged as significant exporters of non-traditional products and, although many have exported only a small number of items, one-third have exported six or more, and five have exported more than 15 (McQueen and Stevens, 1989). Moreover, diversification is not limited to the more advanced African states such as Kenya, Mauritius, Zimbabwe and Côte d'Ivoire. It has also included poorer countries at lower levels of economic development, such as Ghana, as well as Ethiopia and Sudan before civil disorder intervened. By 1987 such non-traditional exports accounted for about 8 per cent of total ACP non-fuel exports to the EU and were also prominent in exports to major non-EU markets, most notably the USA.

The principal product groups that featured in ACP non-traditional exports between the mid-1970s and mid-1980s are listed in Table 2.7. Of the groups in which the ACP countries achieved a significant increase in EU market share, those of most apparent potential for Africa are processed tropical products, horticulture, wood products and, especially, yarns/fabrics and clothing. Among the African states that have begun to

TABLE 2.7
ACP exports of non-traditional products, 1976–87

Product	Tariff	ACP exports to EU (ECU million)		% share of exporters' total exports to EU[†]	
		1976	1987	1976	1987
Canned tuna	24%	33.2	139.5	1.7	4.4
Leather & leather products	2.5-10%	37.5	73.6	2.8	2.7
Fresh flowers (1980–87)	17–24%	21.5	31.5		0.8
Vegetables	3–17%	36.2	48.6	2.8	2.4
Processed tropical agricultural products	17–24%	51.6	93.9	3.1	3.4
Wood products	4–10%	38.6	103.2	1.1	2.3
Yarns & fabrics	4–10%	28.8	94.0	1.0	2.1
Clothing	7.6–14%	28.8	237.7	1.2	5.7

† Total non-oil exports of the states exporting the product.
Source: McQueen and Stevens, 1989.

FIGURE 2.6
Selected sub-Saharan non-traditional exports to the EU (ECU million)

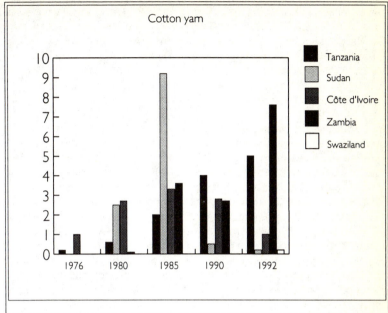

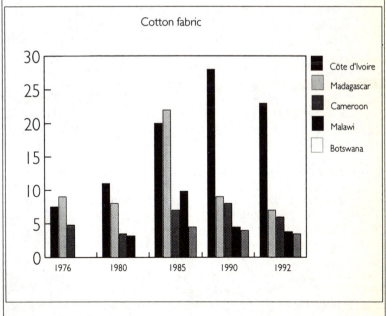

export textiles and clothing the most important are Mauritius and Zimbabwe, and of those exporting horticultural products Kenya is prominent. The experiences of these states (plus Ethiopia) are described in more detail below. But diversification is not limited to these states: Figure 2.6 illustrates the performance in various textile items of Botswana, Cameroon, Côte d'Ivoire, Madagascar, Malawi, Sudan, Swaziland, Tanzania and Zambia.

MAURITIUS

Mauritius has the most outstanding record among the ACP countries for stimulating non-traditional exports. Exports have been promoted through the Investment Incentive Schemes and, particularly, the Export Processing Zones (EPZ) Acts of 1970 and 1984.

Although initially successful, by the early 1980s these incentive schemes had produced what were considered generally to be disappointing results. After rapid growth from 644 employees in 1971 to 17,163 in 1976, EPZ employment increased only slowly to 24,952 in 1984 (under 8,000 jobs in eight years) while unemployment rose to 20 per cent in 1983 (Figure 2.7). One obvious explanation for this slowdown was the second oil shock in 1979, which induced world recession and ended the 8 per cent per annum growth rate that Mauritius had enjoyed since 1973. A further factor, however, appears to have been the results of the complex system of import protection and export subsidies which, through the price system, produced an incentive structure contrary to policy objectives.

Under a succession of IMF arrangements, backed by the World Bank, Mauritius from 1982 onwards introduced a package of liberalization measures. Exports began to surge once more. The spectacular growth in EPZ exports from 1984 onwards is shown clearly in Figure 2.8. Exports to all destinations increased in this year, but by far the greatest increase was in exports to the USA, which rose from Rs 184 million in 1983 to Rs 514 million in 1984. Exports to the USA continued to grow rapidly until 1986. But by 1988 growth had virtually ceased, with the imposition of import quotas by the US.

The EU has always been the most important market, accounting for over 80 per cent of exports in the 1970s. This only fell below 70 per cent in 1984-6 because of the growth in exports to the USA, but with quota restrictions now imposed on these exports the share of the EU is again increasing. Exports have been concentrated on France, which reached a maximum share of 44 per cent in 1975–7 and then fell sharply after VERs were introduced in 1977. These were suspended in 1981 and the export share has gradually increased (on a rapidly expanding total volume) since then. The United Kingdom was initially almost as important a market as France, but its share declined during the 1980s until it is now just below that of Germany.

Clothing has always been the mainstay of the EPZ and has been

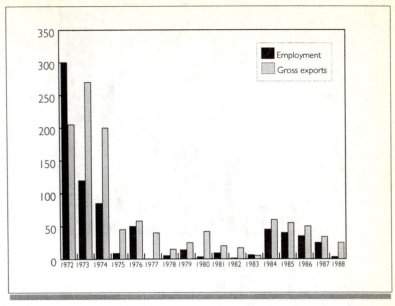

FIGURE 2.7 Mauritian EPZ growth: annual increases in employment and gross exports, 1972–88 (%)

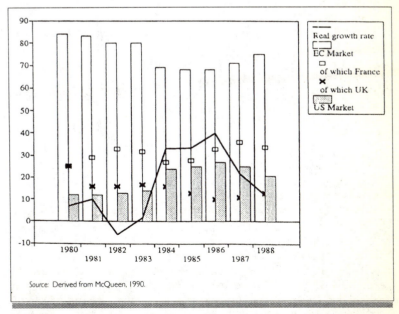

Source: Derived from McQueen, 1990.

FIGURE 2.8 Mauritian EPZ exports by real growth rate and destination, 1980–88 (%)

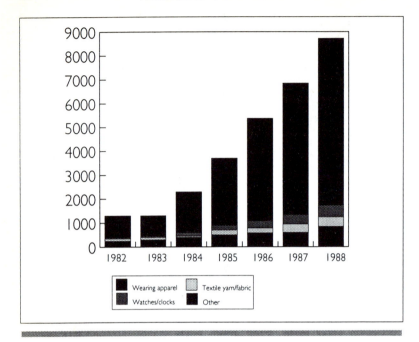

FIGURE 2.9 Mauritian EPZ exports by main commodities, 1982–88 (fob value: Rs million)

responsible for most of the rapid increase in exports (Figure 2.9). However, exports of watches and clocks and flowers (contained in 'other') have grown more rapidly, though of course from a much smaller base. There has also been diversification by product (at the 7-digit SITC level). In 1971, 21 products were exported by the EPZ; this had increased to 46 by 1976 and 70 in 1988.

ZIMBABWE

Zimbabwe's exports of non-traditional goods to the EU have expanded very rapidly since independence. From ECU 3.8 million in 1982, they had reached ECU 48.4 million by 1987, and this rate of expansion appears to have been sustained at least up until early 1990 (Riddell, 1990:18). There has been substantial expansion of exports of fresh flowers, canned meat, vegetables, fruit and juices, leather, cotton yarn and textiles, and clothing. The rapid rate of expansion is partly explained by the artificially low base-year levels caused by pre-Independence sanctions, but it also reflects a genuine effort to diversify into new markets (away from South Africa) and new products. The Lomé Convention preferences are perceived by Zimbabwean exporters to have been of value in facilitating this diversifica-

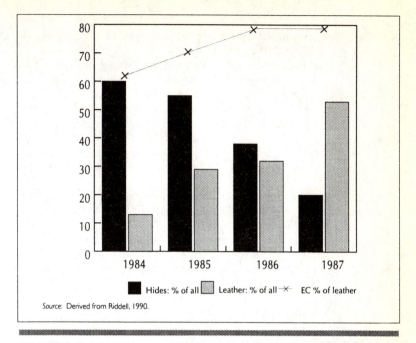

FIGURE 2.10 Zimbabwean exports of hides and leather to the EU, 1984-87 (Z$ million)

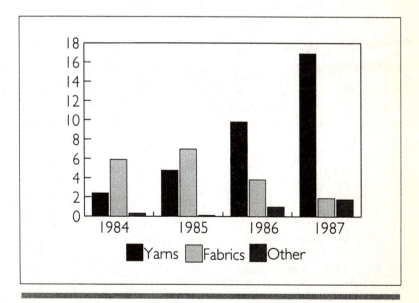

FIGURE 2.11 Zimbabwean exports of textiles to the EC, 1984–87 (Z$ million)

tion. Also important have been a number of government policies, including export promotion measures and the continuous, progressive depreciation of the Zimbabwe dollar.

Among the products that have featured in this diversification, leather, textiles and clothing are perhaps the ones of most interest to Africa. The EU is the major market for both hides and further processed leather. Since 1984, there has been a progressive shift of exports away from hides towards processed leather and an increase in the share of the EU in exports of the latter (see Figure 2.10). Attempts to export footwear have not been successful. This confirms a broader finding that Africa has had great difficulty penetrating the EU footwear market (McQueen and Stevens, 1989).

Zimbabwean exports of yarns to the EU have increased in terms of both value and share (Figure 2.11). The value increased from Z$2.3 million in 1984 to Z$16.5 million in 1987. Over the same period, the share of yarns exports destined for the EU increased from 16 per cent to 62 per cent. There was a similar trend for 'other textiles', although from a much lower base. However, in the case of fabrics the trend was in the opposite direction: exports to the EU fell both in terms of value and as a proportion of the total.

Among the factors contributing to the industry's ability to export to Europe has been the quality of domestic cotton supplied to the mills. Zimbabwe's niche in the European market is in the middle to lower range, but even so it has to pay serious attention to the quality of its inputs.

Some 10–15 per cent of clothing production is exported. After a fall immediately after independence, clothing exports have experienced a rapid and sustained expansion since 1983. The value of exports has risen, in current Zimbabwe dollars, by an average of over 60 per cent a year from 1984 to 1988, and it appears that this growth has extended into 1989. The two main categories of clothing exported to the EU are outer garments, both men's/boys' and women's/infants' (see Figure 2.12). The second most important market is South Africa (with 20 per cent of the total in 1988), followed by the USA (13 per cent) and the Southern African Development Community (SADC) (11 per cent).

The Zimbabwean exporters claim to prefer selling to Europe rather than to the USA because, once contact has been made and firm orders placed, it is their experience that follow-up orders are more likely to be made by European importers (Riddell, 1990:47). With US buyers, the likelihood of being dropped even after a big order has been secured remains quite high. One reason for this is that much of the US business is done indirectly through, for instance, East Asian companies that are not able to meet an entire order from their own factory. In Europe, Zimbabwean exporters fit into a niche between the big exporters from Asia and the fashion market European suppliers.

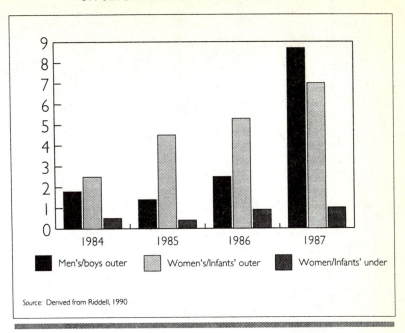

FIGURE 2.12 Zimbabwean exports of clothing to the EU, 1984–87 (Z$ million)

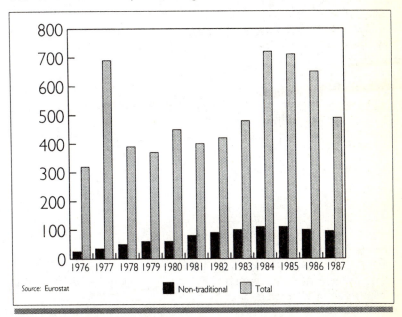

FIGURE 2.13 The growth of 'non-traditional' and total Kenyan exports to the EU, 1976–87 (Ecu million)

KENYA

The share of non-traditional commodities in Kenya's exports to the EU has increased substantially during the period since Lomé I was signed (Figure 2.13). Non-traditional Kenyan exports to the EU grew three times as fast as total exports between 1976 and 1987. In consequence their share (by value) of total exports rose from 10 per cent in 1976 to 23 per cent in 1987.

The term 'non-traditional' is used to refer to products that fall outside the group of largely unprocessed primary commodities that have been prominent exports for many years and are characterized by stagnant demand. This definition gives rise to certain anomalies. It includes both horticulture and canned pineapple, which some might argue have been a feature of trade sufficiently long for them now to be regarded as traditional exports. But they share with other actual and potential non-traditional products the characteristic that unit values are relatively high and markets buoyant. They are goods, therefore, into which diversification may be beneficial.

There has been a broadening of the range of non-traditional exports, thus defined. In 1976 the bulk were various kinds of processed fruit (mainly canned pineapple) and lightly processed hides and skins. A decade later a range of horticultural products and a small amount of clothing had joined the list. As a result of this rapid growth, horticulture is now Kenya's third-largest merchandise export to the EU, exceeded only by coffee, tea and, on the non-merchandise account, tourism.

Manufactures account for a relatively small but growing share of exports to the EU. In 1989, exports of SITC categories 6 and 8 accounted for 10 per cent by value of EU imports from Kenya, over twice the share in 1985. The relatively low share of manufactures may be gauged through a comparison with Kenya's total exports to the EU. In 1989, Kenya accounted for 3 per cent of total EU imports from the ACP countries and 0.4 per cent of imports from all LDCs, but for manufactures the shares were only 1.4 per cent of ACP countries and 0.15 per cent of all LDCs.

THE IMPACT OF PREFERENCES

How far can the growth of non-traditional exports be attributed to preferences? Given that North African non-traditional exports are of longer standing, and that their preference agreements are varied, the question can be posed most appropriately of the Lomé trade accords.

To answer the question, studies have been carried out in a select group of states which illustrate the differing importance of the various Lomé trade preferences in relation both to each other and to those offered by the ACP group's other trading partners (Stevens, 1990; Riddell, 1990; McQueen, 1990). They show also the interaction of demand-side constraints (such as the rules of origin) and those on the supply-side (notably unsupportive government policies) and the scope for aid to ease the bottlenecks that limit further diversification.

In none of the cases do the non-traditional exports 'solve' the problem of stagnant demand for traditional exports. The new markets into which they have diversified are highly competitive; diversification is a continuing exercise, not a once-for-all shift. But they confirm the findings of the statistical analysis, that sub-Saharan Africa and the other ACP states are not somehow incapable of diversification. Furthermore, they provide some evidence that the Lomé preferences have made a contribution.

It has not been possible to draw an unambiguous causal link between the Lomé Convention and the development of non-traditional exports. A host of factors is at work to explain both the success in exporting *these* new products and the failure to export *others* for which Lomé preferences are also substantial. Government policy in the exporting state is clearly a critical factor. In some cases, for example, the move into non-traditional exports has been very recent, partly because of the unsupportive nature of government policies in the earlier period. Nonetheless, there is some degree of circumstantial evidence to suggest that a link exists.

Whilst trade preferences are only one of many factors affecting exports, there exists circumstantial evidence to suggest that they have had a positive influence and, hence, that their loss through liberalization could slow down or even suffocate diversification into what are extremely competitive markets. Being part of the two most preferred regions, the African states will face the greatest adjustment to any such generalized liberalization.

The Impact of the SEM on Trade

WHAT IS THE SEM?

In one sense the SEM is a less dramatic enterprise than is sometimes portrayed. In a nutshell, all that the EU members have committed themselves to do is to take steps towards the creation of a customs union that they had promised to take thirty years before (for the original Six) when signing the Treaty of Rome. The reason why the customs union had remained uncompleted was that the remaining barriers were precisely those non-tariff ones that are politically the most difficult to remove.

The new impetus derived principally from two decisions. One was the approval of the Single European Act in 1987 which set the 1992 target. The other was the adoption, with the notable exception of matters affecting taxation and employment, of qualified majority voting within the European Council of Ministers in place of the previous unanimity requirement. This meant that the chances for the successful removal of barriers were improved since, on most issues, a single recalcitrant state can no longer block decisions.

Nonetheless, not all of the trickiest barriers were removed by 1 January 1993. An early casualty was that the EU Commission was forced to back down over *ex ante* harmonization of Value Added Tax (VAT) levels. Similarly, excise duties have not yet been harmonized. Even when a new Directive has been approved and gazetted, its provisions must still be incorporated into the national laws of the member states, which can be a lengthy process. And then, aggrieved parties may appeal to the legal system on some issues, embarking upon a process that could reach up to the European Court of Justice.

In the light of these considerations the SEM is best thought of as a process rather than being linked narrowly to the date of 1992. Some of the items on the agenda have already been brought into effect; other items may have to wait until towards the end of the century before all the legislation and judicial appeals have been completed. As the SEM has blossomed into wider concerns such as monetary and political union (see below), so the length of the process has grown.

The impact of the SEM may be profound simply because it brings into play a host of other issues on which an EU decision will be required to deal with the new circumstances. These consequential decisions may have effects on Africa that are just as potent as those arising from the SEM narrowly defined.

The CAP provides one example of these 'second round' effects. At present, despite its name, there is no *common* policy in the sense of uninhibited trade within the Union. In the period before 1992 a highly complex system of special (so-called 'green') exchange rates and border taxes grew up to enable some governments to secure higher prices for their farmers than did others. The removal of border controls as part of the SEM has rendered some of the existing controls inoperable in their present form. The EU's response to this new circumstance is likely to include the closer alignment of member state prices. This alignment could be upwards (which might tend to increase EU output) or downwards (with output declining); in either case, the effect on food importing and exporting states outside the EU could be substantial.

THE MAIN ELEMENTS OF THE SEM

There are two elements to the changes associated with the date of 1992. They are the dismantling of direct controls on trade and the removal of indirect barriers, and a set of grand visions. They differ in their timetables, chances of success, and implications for Africa.

Removing controls
The first element is the campaign against barriers at frontiers that halt the flow of people and of goods. This includes not only the removal of national quotas but also changes to the many national rules which, while not

ostensibly part of 'trade policy', effectively prevent goods being sold or persons moving freely from one member state to another. It includes the harmonization and/or mutual recognition of national policies that might otherwise inhibit the free flow of goods, such as technical standards. In many cases this will require not simply changes to rules but also a shift in attitudes.

Such changes may have complex effects on the pattern of demand for products of interest to Africa. A *harmonization of excise taxes*, for example, could increase demand for tropical beverages. Some member states tax heavily one or more of cocoa, coffee and tea; if these consumption taxes were reduced to the EU norm, demand would rise. One estimate of the effect of harmonizing consumer taxes on tropical beverages at 5 per cent is that world imports would rise by 1.9 per cent in volume and 3.8 per cent in value for coffee, by 1.4 per cent in volume and 1.8 per cent in value for cocoa, and by 0.2 per cent in volume and almost 1 per cent in value for tea. (Davenport and Page 1991: 62–3).

By contrast, the effect of harmonizing consumer taxes on tobacco would tend to lean in the opposite direction. It is likely that, because of concerns over public health, the relatively low consumer taxes in some southern EU states will be increased to the higher northern EU levels. It has been estimated that if tobacco tax rates for the whole Union were to be aligned on the average of the four states with the highest rates (Germany, Denmark, Ireland, and the UK) there would be a reduction in EU imports of some 4.1 per cent and a loss in LDC export revenue of around ECU147 million. (Davenport and Page 1991:63)

It is clear that there is no single 'African impact'. There will be a differential impact of such changes for Ghana (as a cocoa exporter), for Kenya (as a tea exporter), for Côte d'Ivoire (as an exporter of both cocoa and coffee) and for Malawi (as an exporter of both beverages and tobacco).

The SEM has implications for *air transport*. In the past, and to a substantial extent still, European air transport has been heavily regulated with most governments organizing a cartel in favour of their domestic carriers. The EU Commission is trying to introduce more competition into this regulated system. If it succeeds, third parties, such as those in Africa, will have the opportunity to liberalize air traffic with Europe, with differential effects on less competitive airlines which might suffer and on more competitive airlines and merchandise exporters which might gain from lower tariffs and larger markets. The North African states have long exported horticultural products to the EU and, as noted earlier, some countries South of the Sahara have begun to do the same. A critical factor in exporting many horticultural and floricultural products successfully is the availability of competitively priced air transport.

The *harmonization of technical standards* is an issue which has caused some concern in Africa. The EU is approaching standards in two ways, using the term 'standards' in a broad sense to include both product definitions and technical requirements. In the vast majority of cases no attempt is being made to define a single Union-wide standard. Rather, the principle to be adopted is that of 'mutual recognition'. This means that if a product meets the requirements of one member state, no other member state may ban intra-EU importation on the grounds that it fails to meet the national standard. For example, if an export from Senegal meets the requirements of France but not those of Germany, it should now be possible for such goods to be exported to Germany, albeit only indirectly via France.

Mutual recognition could have a substantial impact on some existing flows. For example, the application of this principle to chocolate means that British-style confectionery (which includes significant quantities of non-cocoa fats) may be sold for the first time in France and Belgium, where much higher proportions of cocoa are normally required in a product that is described as 'chocolate'. This could increase demand for palm oil but reduce demand for cocoa. Such effects would be of importance for African states which export palm oil, those which export cocoa and those which export both.

At the same time, Article 36 of the Treaty of Rome will continue to allow a member state to restrict imports even under the 'mutual recognition' principle if they fail to meet minimum health and safety or environmental standards. Although the continued validity of this Article will dilute the mutual recognition principle to a certain extent, the European Court of Justice has indicated that in defining such minimum requirements it will impose rigorous demands on those seeking to exclude imports. This should reduce the danger that Article 36 will be used as a protectionist device by those who claim that an import falls below some spurious standard.

In order to avoid frequent recourse to Article 36, the EU is attempting to codify uniform standards for products where there is a danger of adverse health, safety or environmental effects. The resulting harmonized standard is likely to be different from the standards currently employed in some national markets: more stringent in some cases and, possibly, less stringent in others. It may be difficult to disentangle standard harmonization from standard upgrading, especially in relation to products that are developing rapidly (such as high-tech goods) and those which are subject to volatile public concern over health, notably foods. The latter group is likely to be of most immediate concern to Africa. There has been concern amongst some LDCs, for example, about German objections to the use of pixin as a food colouring and about differing national regulations concerning EDTA as an additive to canned fish. Togo and Senegal will be affected adversely by the new regulations limiting residues of trace elements (including cadmium) in fertilizers.

Apart from cases where the new regulations relate to a physical characteristic of an African export that cannot be changed, the principal effect of both mutual recognition and uniform technical standards will be to increase competition. Prior to the '1992' programme there were some 218 EU barriers with which non-European exporters of manufactured foods had to contend. Of these, 64 were specific member state import restrictions, 68 were controls on labelling or packaging, 33 were bans on specific ingredients, 39 were rules on product description and 14 were instances of tax discrimination (Davenport and Page 1991: 60). Under the SEM this maze is being replaced by a single set of rules for all member states.

Since one of the effects of complex bureaucratic requirements is to favour more sophisticated exporters from more developed states over those from the poorest countries (because they can afford the human and financial cost of dovetailing their products to the varying rules), the overall impact of this simplification could be beneficial to Africa. But it is likely that some existing flows to niche markets in one or two European states may face a blast of tougher competition in the short term.

Whether such changes act as a barrier or an opportunity to African exports will vary according to the product and the exporter. Whilst there is no inherent reason why they should be a barrier, it is clearly vital that African exporters monitor closely the evolution of these standards in order to take advantage of any opportunities and guard themselves, through product improvement, against any barriers. Broad analyses, such as this chapter, may provide an introduction to the subject but the next, very necessary, step is to identify those standards that apply to each specific industry and to assess in relation to specific firms whether or not the changes will open new doors or present new barriers.

The grand visions
Alongside these changes to market regulation are a clutch of grand visions noted in the Single European Act. These include the 'social dimension' (which would establish minimum work and pay standards for all member states), economic and monetary union (which would provide the EU with a single currency and a central bank), a common foreign policy and, ultimately, full union.

Of most direct relevance to Africa are the social dimension and monetary union. If the Social Charter actually has teeth, as seems increasingly likely, it would tend to raise labour costs in the peripheral EU states. This might benefit African exporters by increasing their relative competitiveness, although if it results in stronger Southern European pressure for protection, the net result could be adverse.

Monetary union could affect the 13 African states that are members of the franc zone which are already experiencing problems with the system's operations. A source of stability in the past, which contributed to modest real Gross Domestic Product (GDP) growth until 1986, the franc zone has since entered a period in which its rigidities have hindered adjustment. A particular source of tension has been its restrictions on individual states realigning their currencies to accommodate higher levels of inflation. Such rigidities are likely to increase as Europe moves closer to monetary union.

As franc zone trade has diversified away from France towards other EU members and Japan, many of the fixed rate of exchange benefits with the French franc have been eroded. As realignments between the franc and other European currencies have become more infrequent so the CFA franc has become pegged, effectively, to the European Currency Unit (ECU). The principal worry for CFA franc countries will be that this may intensify their difficulties in maintaining a fixed exchange rate. Inflation in a European Monetary Union is likely to follow what have been historically low German rates dictated by the tight monetary policy of the Bundesbank rather than the somewhat higher rates tolerated in France until relatively recently. This will place further pressure on franc zone competitiveness. An explicit shift to an ECU-peg of a fixed but adjustable type would require financial support for an intervention fund to support the exchange rate under pressure if France abdicated full responsibility for this role.

The Direct Effects

The potential effects of this wide range of SEM measures on third parties fall into two categories: direct and indirect.

- Direct effects result from changes in the European economy induced by '1992'. The scale of the trade creation and trade diversion that will result is uncertain and the scope for government action to influence the impact on the South may be limited. Nonetheless, African states need to take a view of the possible direction and scale of such effects.

TABLE 2.8

Potential external effects of the SEM

Positive	Negative
Direct effects	
Trade creation	Trade diversion
(from faster EU growth)	(lower costs of EU production)
Investment creation	Investment diversion
(from faster EU growth)	(increased attractions of EU)
Indirect effects	
Less protectionism	More protectionism
(no national NTBs)	(more severe Community NTBs)
More liberal trade policy	Less liberal trade policy
(majority voting)	(to alleviate social costs)
More cost-effective aid	Lower total aid budget
(EU-wide procurement typing)	(less commercial incentive)
	(increased social fund demand)
Easier migration	More restrictive migration
(removal of national barriers)	(reinforcement of EU barriers)

• Indirect effects are the outcome of political decisions that become necessary because of the SEM and to influence the impact, domestically and internationally, of these economic changes. Governments have substantial scope either to maximize or to minimize adverse consequences for third parties.

The broad range of effects is set out in Table 2.8. This underlines the unfortunate 'two-handed' nature of this level of SEM analysis: the potentially adverse effects on the right side of the table are simply the inverse of the potentially positive effects on the left side! Whether, in the event, each element falls into the left or the right column depends on how it is implemented as well as the product and the African state in question.

The net direct trade impact on the outside world will be the result of two broad changes operating in opposing directions. To the extent that the SEM removes barriers between EU national markets and results in faster economic growth, third parties may benefit. The acceleration of growth should result, other things being equal, in increased EU imports, while the removal of internal barriers will make it easier for third party exporters to exploit the full potential of European demand.

Against this, the creation of more efficient production units within Europe will tend to increase the competitiveness of domestic supplies relative to imports. So the share of the EU market supplied by imports may decline and EU exports to third markets may become more competitive. Whether or not the absolute level of imports falls depends upon whether this trade-diverting effect is larger or smaller than the trade creation of faster EU economic growth. And the overall impact on third parties will also depend on their net trade position in respect of the goods in question: for states that are net importers (which will probably include many African states) the effect of more competitive European production will be a favourable movement in their terms of trade.

TABLE 2.9
Estimates of trade creation and diversion for individual developing countries (ECU million, based on 1987 data)

	Morocco	Tunisia	Côte d'Ivoire	Kenya	Zimbabwe
Trade creation					
Primary goods	24	26	41	9	9
Manufactures	99	96	12	5	14
Sub-total	123	123	53	14	24
Trade diversion (manufactures)	-106	-108	-16	-7	20
Net total	17	15	37	7	4
As % exports to EU	0.8	0.9	2.6	1.2	1.3

Source: Davenport and Page, 1991.

Although neither the direct nor the indirect effects can be forecast with accuracy, some estimates have been made of the trade-creating and trade-diverting effects of the SEM, both globally and in relation to specific countries and regions. For example, calculations made by Davenport and Page (Table 2.9) of the principal, identifiable direct and indirect effects on five African countries indicate positive net effects for all, ranging from the equivalent of a boost to Morocco's exports of 0.8 per cent to one of 2.6 per cent for Côte d'Ivoire (relative to 1987 exports to the EU).

Similar considerations apply to the effects on foreign direct investment (FDI). Economies of scale in information on investment opportunities abroad could increase the level of EU FDI. Joint efforts to promote FDI in some, such as the Maghreb, could lower the risks to investing firms through an EU investment guarantee instrument. On the other hand, the complete liberalization of intra-EU capital movements, together with incentives given for intra-Union firms to cooperate, could divert FDI in favour of the EU regions which currently have the most barriers (the Southern countries).

The Indirect Effects

Protectionism. The position is even more uncertain in respect of indirect effects such as those related to protectionism. There are likely to be squeals of pain from the less efficient European industries that survive in their present form only because of the current imperfections in the EU market. These will be translated into political pressures on governments to shift the burden of adjustment to non-European producers through increased protectionism. It is concern over such pressures that has led to the publicly aired fears that a Fortress Europe will appear.

There are two ways in which the level of protectionism might be affected by '1992'. One, especially imponderable, factor concerns the extent not only to which national governments will listen to protectionist demands from their industries but also the extent to which they will be successful in persuading their EU partners to accede to such demands. The adoption of majority voting will allow a protectionist majority to override a liberal minority, but it will also allow the opposite to occur; where, in the new Union, will the balance of opinion lie?

The other concerns the abolition of national non-tariff barriers (NTBs) to imports. As noted above, the EU has had two tiers of NTBs: Union-wide barriers, plus additional national restrictions imposed by some member states on some products from some countries. The national tier was made possible by Article 115 of the Treaty of Rome, which permitted states to restrict imports from their neighbours of goods originating outside the Community. This Article has become inoperative as part of the SEM exercise; the abolition of customs controls on internal borders has removed the power of member states to limit imports from their neighbours and, hence, their opportunity to police national quotas.

The extent to which national NTBs have developed is very unclear, with widely varying estimates of the number imposed. Among the problems encountered in compiling a list is that some NTBs were secret, some were unenforced and some, in the form of intra-industry voluntary export restraints (VERs), may not even be known to the authorities. One set of illustrative figures is provided in Table 2.10, which lists the requests for protection under Article 115 approved by the Commission in the period 1979 to 1987 according to the requesting country. The list is an incomplete one, since there is a variety of other ways through which states can impose national controls, but it probably provides a good indication of differences in the supplementary protection sought by the various member states.

TABLE 2.10
Article 115 case acceptances, by member state, 1979–87

	1979	1980	1981	1982	1983	1984	1985	1986	1987	Total
Benelux	44	25	17	19	22	14	4	0	1	146
Denmark	3	4	0	0	0	0	0	0	2	9
France	124	105	80	85	57	39	66	67	62	685
Germany	6	1	2	2	4	0	0	0	0	15
Greece			0	0	0	0	0	0	0	0
Ireland	33	57	32	26	48	59	57	45	52	409
Italy	17	23	23	29	37	34	30	20	23	236
Portugal								0	1	1
Spain								4	13	17
UK	33	7	12	13	20	19	9	5	3	131

Source: A. Sapir, 'Does 1992 come before or after 1990?', CEPR Discussion Paper No. 313 (London, 1989).

The table suggests that the countries making most use of national NTBs were France, Ireland and Italy. This view is reinforced by Table 2.11, which lists developing country manufactures subject to Article 115 in the recent past and also identifies the countries most frequently targeted: they are almost exclusively the states of East Asia.

Table 2.12 rearranges the data in Table 2.10 according to the type of product for which Article 115 restrictions have been requested. Overwhelmingly the most important product is textiles (including clothing), followed by other 'sensitive manufactures'. The predominance of clothing/textiles is because the most extensive set of national quotas is that negotiated under the framework of the MFA.

Given the need for Africa to diversify its exports the increased competition for clothing may be the greatest problem in the longer term, but in the immediate future the difficulties created for two traditional exports – bananas and sugar – are attracting more attention.

TABLE 2.11

Developing countries' manufactures subject to Article 115
in 1988 and 1989 (first seven months) (excluding textiles and clothing)

EU country	Product	Exporting countries
1 Import exclusion		
France	Footwear	Taiwan
	Slippers	China
	Umbrellas	Taiwan, Singapore, China
	Toys	China
	Car radios	Korea, China
	Televisions	Korea, Taiwan
Italy	Footwear	Korea, Taiwan
	Silk	China
Spain	Umbrellas	Taiwan
	Handtools	China, Taiwan, Hong Kong
	Sewing machines	Brazil, Korea, Taiwan
	Televisions	Korea
	Slide fasteners	Taiwan
	Video recorders	Korea
	Imitation jewellery	Korea
	Cars	Korea
2 Surveillance†		
Belgium	Brooms and brushes	China
Denmark	Bicycles	China
France	Footwear	Korea, Taiwan
	Umbrellas	China, Taiwan
	Radio aerials	China, Korea, Taiwan
	Televisions	Korea, Taiwan
Greece	Electric motors	Taiwan, Hong Kong
	Batteries	Taiwan, Hong Kong
	Electric transformers	Taiwan, Hong Kong
	Toys	Taiwan, Hong Kong
Ireland	Footwear	Taiwan
	Tableware	China
Italy	Silk	China
	Slide fasteners	Taiwan
United Kingdom	Leather gloves	China
	Footwear	China
	Tableware	China
	Colour televisions	China

† Excluding surveillance allowed to Spain and Portugal under transitional arrangements.

Source: Davenport and Page, 1991.

TABLE 2.12
Article 115 case acceptances, by member state, 1979–87

	1979	1980	1981	1982	1983	1984	1985	1986	1987	Total
Textiles	199	164	120	116	131	120	119	102	105	1,176
Other manufactures	59	53	43	52	49	37	45	36	49	423
Agricultural products	2	5	3	6	8	8	12	3	3	50

Source: A. Sapir, 1989, op. cit.

Bananas. At present about half of the EU's consumption of bananas is supplied by the ACP states and by the Union itself (the French overseas *départements* of Guadeloupe and Martinique, as well as Crete and the Canary Islands), while the other half consists of 'dollar' bananas, mostly from Latin America. The former half traditionally has entered the EU under special arrangements designed to preserve traditional markets. Thus, France provided a guaranteed market for bananas from its overseas *départements* and from Cameroon and Côte d'Ivoire. Italy and Britain provided similar guarantees for Somalia and for the English-speaking Caribbean and Suriname respectively. These guarantees were enforced through controls on intra-EU trade, legitimized by Article 115, to prevent dollar fruit being re-exported from, say, Germany to France. With the SEM, Article 115 has become inoperative.

Even without the SEM, the European market outlook for ACP exports is not good in the long term. ACP bananas do not compete only with the dollar variety; they also compete with other fruits. The evidence suggests that the high relative price of bananas on the protected markets has constrained the growth of consumption. Figures for the current level of *per capita* consumption, and recent growth rates, are highest in those markets where prices are lowest. The highest level of *per capita* consumption in the EU is found in Germany (at 12 kg) and lowest in the UK (at 6.5 kg) (Davenport and Page, 1991). Whereas the annual average rate of growth of banana imports by volume over the period 1983–88 was 12 per cent in Benelux and 10.8 per cent in Germany, it was only 0.3 per cent in France. By contrast, prices in national currency terms rose in France over the period (by 10 per cent) and in the UK (by 17 per cent) but fell in Benelux and Germany (by between 20 per cent and 26 per cent).

Such comparisons should not be taken too far. There are factors other than price that influence taste patterns and consumption levels for bananas. Hence, although banana prices are relatively high in France,

consumption (at 8 kg per head) is only slightly below the level in Benelux.
Nonetheless, European consumers are becoming increasingly sophisticated, the range of fruits available to them is widening rapidly, and the
structure of the retail trade is changing to facilitate the rapid distribution
of perishable fruits from all corners of the world. Such circumstances will
tend to exacerbate, rather than alleviate, the problems of high-cost
suppliers of traditional fruits.

Before 1993 the EU and ACP producers also enjoyed a 20 per cent tariff
preference over Latin American producers of bananas (except in Germany,
where most bananas enter duty-free for historical reasons), but this was
thought unlikely to be sufficient to allow most Caribbean exporters to

FIGURE 2.14

Annual gross mark-ups 1988 and 1989 for ACP and dollar bananas in the UK market

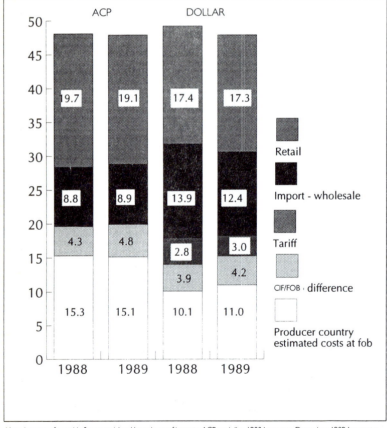

compete without the market guarantees. The African producers appear to have more room for manoeuvre being, in general, lower cost, but it is doubtful that they could compete head on with the Latin American exporters. Because the banana trade in the French and UK markets has been controlled for so long, it is difficult to identify how far prices of African exports could be cut and still remain viable. However, figures compiled by the UK Ministry of Agriculture for the British market in 1988 and 1989 suggest that the average CIF price of ACP fruit would have to be reduced by about 15 per cent if the tariff were to apply only to Latin American fruit (Figure 2.14).

Lomé IV repeats the commitments made in its predecessors to maintain preferential access for the traditional suppliers after '1992'. But, in order to give effect to these commitments, the EU has had to introduce special measures that would not otherwise have figured on the '1992' agenda.

The solution that the EU has adopted is to implement a two-tier import regime. As before, ACP bananas enter the Community duty free, but Latin American fruit are now subject to a two-tier tariff. The first two million tonnes of imports from Latin America pay a specific duty of ECU100 per tonne; for imports above this tariff quota, the duty increases to ECU850 per tonne. Is this high or low? To put the figures in perspective, they can be compared with the unit value of imports in order to obtain an *ad valorem* equivalent. The unit value of EU imports from Latin America was ECU412 per tonne in 1992, at which level the lower tariff for the first two million tonnes was equivalent to 24 per cent and the higher tariff was a penal 206 per cent.

The object of the two-tier tariff is to allow the Latin American countries to continue to supply their traditional share of the market while imposing a serious barrier to attempts to increase their market share at the expense of preferred suppliers. ACP suppliers no longer have an absolute advantage in the UK and French markets, but they have a substantial tariff advantage provided that the Latin American tariff quota has been set at a level that will leave space for them. The critical questions for African banana exporters, therefore, are how large the tariff quota will be and whether the new regime will survive. Neither question has yet been answered definitively.

The Latin American suppliers claimed that the tariff quota of two million tonnes was insufficient. It was certainly smaller than the volume of Latin America's banana exports to the EU in 1992 (which totalled 2.8 million tonnes). Hence, a continuation in 1993 and beyond of this level of exports would have resulted in a part of a shipment paying the punitive 206 per cent rate. The Commission's response was that two million tonnes represented the historic level of Latin American exports to the Community and that the increases in the years leading up to 1992 had been part of a deliberate strategy by the dollar exporters to increase their market share with a view to the completion of the SEM.

Eventually a compromise was hatched between the EU and some of the Latin American banana exporters, under which the tariff quota was increased to 2.1 million tonnes in 1994 and 2.2 million tonnes in 1995. In addition, the EU agreed to reduce the tariff on this volume of bananas from ECU100 to ECU75 per tonne (equivalent to an *ad valorem* tariff of 17.5 per cent at 1992 import unit values).

It is not certain, however, that this agreement will stick. The deal was done with four of the most important Latin American suppliers – Costa Rica, Colombia, Nicaragua and Venezuela – and includes specific quotas for each of the four countries based on their past share of the EU market. Other Latin American exporters – Ecuador, Guatemala, Honduras, Panama, Mexico and the Dominican Republic – rejected the agreement, and in September 1994 US banana exporters petitioned the US Clinton Administration to investigate the deal under its 301 procedure on the grounds that it adversely affected their interests. The outcomes of this, and of any GATT complaint by the hostile Latin American exporters, have yet to be determined.

Sugar. The problems for sugar do not arise from any change in EU law as such, and may occur well after 1992, but they loom on the horizon and should be taken into account by the African states that have an effective quota under the EU–ACP group Sugar Protocol. These are primarily Malawi, Mauritius, Swaziland and Zimbabwe.

Part of the problem arises from the dependence of the Sugar Protocol on the maintenance of a genuine demand for cane sugar in the EU market. At present, this demand is based primarily in the UK, where most ACP cane sugar is refined by a single company, Tate and Lyle. Given the surplus supply in the EU, the maintenance of a market for cane sugar is a delicate operation. In the past there have been periods of fierce competition on the UK market between Tate and Lyle and the main beet suppliers, British Sugar Corporation. There is nothing to prevent sugar from continental Europe being marketed in the UK and thus setting off a renewed bout of competition. But the combination of border formalities and cross-Channel trans-shipment costs has kept such trade to a low level.

With the completion of the SEM and, more particularly, the Channel Tunnel, it will be much simpler – and cheaper – to move sugar from, say, northern France and Belgium into south-east England. This could set off a battle for market shares that would have one of two likely consequences. Either the cane exporters would accept a cut in price in order to share the cost of waging the battle, or the cane refiners would go out of business. The low-cost ACP sugar exporters such as Malawi, Mauritius, Swaziland and Zimbabwe probably could live with a price cut, though it would be very unwelcome; the high-cost Caribbean and African producers probably could not. Hence, the effect of either option would be to drive some cane sugar exporters out of the market and reduce the export revenue of the remainder. Although the Sugar Protocol, which is of unlimited duration, would remain intact, its main *raison d'être* would have been removed.

Migration
The movement of labour may be considered as analogous to a trade issue. It is certainly an area likely to be affected by the SEM. The removal of internal barriers may be accompanied by changes to the external barrier. Such changes will be occurring at a time when the supporters of liberal migration policies are on the defensive.

The danger as perceived among many EU policy makers is that markedly unequal rates of population and economic growth on the northern and southern shores of the Mediterranean are creating pressures for migration flows into the EU that exceed politically tolerable levels. Commission officials talk of the Straits of Gibraltar as being 'Europe's Rio Grande'.

The Mediterranean periphery is already the main source of legally registered aliens (and probably of illegals as well). Of the 12.9 million aliens residing legally in the EU in 1987, 7.9 million originated outside the EU, and some 75 per cent of these came from the Mediterranean periphery (Tovias, 1991). Over 4 million of the non-EU aliens are in the economically active social groups. They still form a very small share of the total EU population of 324 million, but they are not evenly spread among member states.

The two principal hosts are Germany (with 41 per cent of the 1987 stock) and France (with 27 per cent). These two countries also have the highest proportions of non-EU foreign workers in relation to labour force: 3.6 per cent in the case of Germany, and 2.3 per cent for France (with Luxembourg, UK, Netherlands, Belgium and Denmark having shares of over 1 per cent but less than 2 per cent). Estimates of illegal migrants reach up to 1 million in France, 600,000 in Italy, and 90,000–170,000 in Spain; in May 1991 5,000 illegal Moroccan workers were expelled from Spain in a single week (Tovias, 1991).

The numbers wishing to migrate can only increase. Current demographic projections put the year 2000 population of Turkey at 65 million and that of the three Maghreb states at 72 million (an increase of 28 million over 1988). It is improbable that their economies will expand sufficiently rapidly to absorb all of this increase in the labour force. One International Labour Office (ILO) forecast is that there will be some 4 million people of working age unable to find suitable work in these four countries by the end of the decade (Tovias, 1991).

The fear of a Fortress Europe has been expressed primarily in relation to goods; perhaps it is more realistic to expect it to emerge in relation to people: tighter border controls and more stringent health checks on aliens. The free movement of labour with the SEM will require changes to member state policies. Although the right applies only to EU citizens, the removal of frontier controls will make it easier for aliens to move across borders, albeit illegally. All member states will have an interest in the policing of their neighbours' external borders. There will be pressure for more uniform immigration laws and enforcement. The classic example of the decisions that will have to be taken is provided by Kenya. At present, Kenyans have free access to six member states and require visas in the other six. Following the completion of the SEM the same provisions will probably soon apply to all. Which is more likely: that those states currently requiring visas will grant free access or that the others will in future impose visas?

Aid
Aid provides another example of the indirect effects of the SEM. There are no direct references to development aid in the plan to complete the market but, as in many other cases with '1992', there may be an indirect link. It is not likely that there will be any major changes in the near future but there could be subtle changes in the medium to long term resulting from both the SEM and other facets of European integration. There are four principal ways in which the SEM may affect both the absolute level of aid and its distribution.

The most straightforward effect on EU aid will occur if the logic of open procurement for internal government contracts is extended to aid. The EU Commission's programme of directives designed to create the SEM included measures that require each EU member state to accept tenders from companies based in other members when awarding contracts for public works. There are no plans at present to extend this open procurement policy to aid contracts but it is clearly within the 'spirit of 1992' that this should happen in due course. If in due course procurement is widened, it would tend to improve the value for money of the member states' bilateral aid by allowing recipients to source goods and services from the cheapest EU supplier.

A second, less desirable effect may follow from this. If the member states are no longer able to use their programmes to support domestic industries they may become less willing to provide aid. The quality of the aid cake may improve but its size may diminish. The impact of both the open procurement and the aid volume effects will vary between LDCs. Both will tend to be greater in respect of those states (donors and recipients) for which aid is currently tied.

There may be a third effect on the channels through which aid is provided. At present, only around 14 per cent of the aid provided by the twelve EU states is channelled through the EU institutions. The remainder is disbursed bilaterally, through the multilateral institutions or via non-governmental organizations. Open procurement may reduce the member states' interest in running their own bilateral programmes. It could lead, therefore, to a diversion of aid to the EU level and/or to one of the other delivery vehicles. Since companies from ACP states are permitted to tender for aid contracts under the Lomé Convention, a shift from bilateral to EU-level aid could increase intra-African trade.

The remaining potential effects concern the possible diversion of aid away from some existing beneficiaries. This may have both intra- and extra-EU facets. The creation of the SEM will cause serious adjustment problems for some parts of the Union. There will be pressure to increase budget spending in support of depressed parts of the Community. If there is also a tight budget constraint this increase in intra-EU aid may occur at the expense of extra-EU aid. As the favoured recipient of European aid at present, such a diversion might adversely affect Africa.

REGIONAL IMPACT

How far can this welter of conflicting possibilities be rationalized to provide guidance for states from Africa? On which of the issues should governments from these states concentrate their diplomatic efforts to ensure that the effects are in the 'potentially positive' rather than the 'potentially negative' column, and on which should technical assistance be directed?

Apart from the NICs, most Third World states will be affected less by the overall dynamics of the EU economy than by changes to the markets for specific products which bulk large in their exports. A first step, therefore, is to isolate those effects of the SEM most likely to have an impact on major groups. This is summarized in Table 2.13, which lists for various country groupings those elements of the SEM which could have the most serious adverse effects.

The North African states are vulnerable to the widest range of possible SEM negative effects. Because of their position in the upper echelons of the EU's pyramid of privilege, the internal liberalization aspects of the SEM could increase competition in their traditional markets. As their economies are similar to those of the southern EU states, the potential for

TABLE 2.13
Potential dangers of the SEM for different LDCs

Country group	Potential dangers
NICs, Middle-Income Countries (MICs)	Increased protectionism
North Africa	Trade diversion Investment diversion Restricted migration
SSA and other ACP	Trade diversion
Latin America	Investment diversion Increased protectionism

investment diversion is significant. And, as the principal source (together with other non-EU Mediterranean states) of migrants into the EU, they stand to be most affected by any toughening of immigration policies.

The potential trade diversion for sub-Saharan Africa derives from the effect of the SEM on intra-EU trade barriers. The non-traditional exports of most sub-Saharan African states are concentrated in a relatively small number of product categories, many of which are 'sensitive' and are at present subject to national as well as EU restraints. The effects of removing these national import barriers will vary between African states. In the case of textiles/clothing, for example, the national quotas of the MFA may constrain the exports of the most competitive suppliers; by the same token, they may provide a degree of protection to the less competitive suppliers, especially if they have trade preferences in the more protected EU member state markets. Hence, the removal of national quotas may threaten existing markets for the less competitive. The effects must also be seen in the context of the likely overall changes in the MFA, which is to be phased out following the completion of the GATT Round, but probably not until the next century for the most sensitive items.

The removal of border controls as part of the SEM, for example, will remove the power of member states to limit imports from their neighbours and, hence, their opportunity to police any national NTBs that may be in place. The countries that make most use of national NTBs are France, Ireland and Italy. Those with the fewest restrictions over and above EU-level quotas are Germany and Denmark. Hence, states that export primarily to France, Ireland and Italy have more reason to be worried about possible increased competition from the NICs and other third party exporters than do countries exporting primarily to Germany/ Denmark or having a broad geographical spread. France tends to be the largest market for the manufactures exports of both the ACP and the Mediterranean African states.

Prospects for Africa's Exports to Europe

The prospects for Africa's exports to Europe are intimately linked to the speed of diversification. The market outlook for almost all of Africa's traditional export commodities ranges from stagnant to bleak. If Africa remains as heavily dependent on this small group of products in the future as it has in the past the likelihood is that its share of Europe's imports will continue to fall.

The most important features of the SEM, therefore, are those that relate to diversification. Will the SEM make it easier or harder for Africa to shift its exports into commodities for which Europe is a more attractive market? A similar question may be asked of the GATT Round.[4] It is not

---

[4] See Chapter 6.

possible within the scope of this chapter to provide an exhaustive analysis of the GATT Round. However, it is both possible and desirable to identify those aspects of the GATT Agreement which would tend to reinforce (or offset) the effects of '1992'.

One of the principal conclusions to be derived from the preceding section is that the SEM may make it easier for the more competitive African states to penetrate European national markets in which they have not previously been strongly represented, but it may increase competition for some traditional products in the familiar national markets. Much depends, therefore, on the supply response of African states to this changed demand situation. The changes described in the preceding pages do not present Africa with an insuperable challenge. But it is clear that the force of the challenge will vary between products.

THE EFFECT OF THE SEM ON PROSPECTS

The SEM is likely to have a differential impact on broad commodity groups of interest to Africa. In general terms it is helpful to distinguish between its effects on traditional exports, non-traditional agricultural products and non-traditional manufactures.

The impact of the SEM on traditional primary exports is likely to be limited to a small number of identifiable cases. These include bananas and sugar, where the removal of intra-EU trade barriers will increase competition for African exporters, beverages and tobacco, which could be affected by harmonization of excise duties, and some foodstuffs and food-related products that would be adversely affected by new, more stringent health standards. For the bulk of Africa's traditional primary exports, however, '1992' is unlikely to provoke major changes one way or the other.

Non-traditional exports fall into two broad groups: CAP products and sensitive manufactures. The SEM will not have major effects on Africa's exports of CAP products under the Lomé and North African preferences. But it will have an effect on the competitive environment for exports of sensitive manufactures. The removal of barriers to intra-EU trade will tend to increase competition in the most protected national markets. The product group of most concern to Africa is clothing. The larger African clothing exporters are now well established in a number of EU national markets which include both more- and less-protected ones. Whilst they may find the profitability of exports declines with the completion of the SEM, it is reasonable to expect that they will be able to adapt to the new conditions. For those countries just embarking on diversification into clothing, however, the changes may be more difficult. Establishing a toehold in a new product market is always a difficult process. If the SEM proceeds as planned, new entrants will not have as substantial a boost from trade preferences as did their predecessors.

THE EFFECT OF THE GATT AGREEMENT ON PROSPECTS

The SEM will result in increased competition, however, only if the removal of internal barriers is not accompanied by a reinforcement of the external barrier. Hence, the effects of '1992' cannot be viewed in isolation from the changes negotiated under the GATT Agreement.

While African diversification into CAP products is unlikely to be affected significantly by '1992', it will be influenced by the GATT Agreement. The conventional wisdom has tended to be that a reduction of subsidies to farmers in the Organization for Economic Cooperation and Development (OECD) states would lead to a fall in production and a consequent increase in world prices. This price effect of liberalization will depend largely on the behaviour of farmers in responding to the new levels of subsidies which, in turn, will be influenced heavily by the differential impact of such subsidy cuts. It is unlikely that there will be uniform, across-the-board cuts in all subsidies on all commodities; the GATT Agreement reductions apply, in the main, to broad product groups. For example, if the CAP were to be reformed to reduce fiscal subsidies in the form of intervention buying or export restitutions but not to remove consumer subsidies effected through import restrictions, there would be a tendency for livestock products to be the most adversely affected, for sugar and horticulture to be lightly affected (and therefore relatively more attractive) and for cereals to be moderately adversely affected. If, in addition, the effect of reform is to drive small, inefficient farmers out of the sector and for large, efficient farmers to maintain their incomes through increased production, the overall effect could be for the output of some commodities to rise.

The importance of such differential effects on Africa is clear. Cereal imports into Africa have risen significantly in recent years but horticultural exports to the high priced European market have also risen. Clearly, the terms of trade between cereal imports and horticulture exports will be influenced by the differential effects of CAP reform on these two sub-sectors, as well as by changes to the world markets for Africa's traditional agricultural exports.

These traditional agricultural exports are likely to be adversely affected by the GATT Agreement. As explained above, a reduction in MFN tariffs on Africa's major traditional tropical product exports will reduce the Lomé margin of preference. An attempt has been made to estimate the effect of the erosion of preferences resulting from the GATT Agreement on sub-Saharan Africa. A review of all the most important sub-Saharan African exports to the EU (Stevens and Kennan, 1994) suggests that the erosion of preference *as a result of the GATT Round* will be modest: of the order of 4 per cent of total exports, of which over one-half is accounted for by a single product, coffee. The reason for the emphasis in the previous sentence is that the situation could change substantially if the GATT Round is followed by a reduction in the EU's tariffs under the GSP. Until the rates applying under the proposed new European Union GSP are known, the extent of the erosion cannot be calculated.

Policy Recommendations and Conclusions

THE RELATIVE IMPORTANCE OF THE SEM FOR AFRICA

Perhaps the most important point to emphasize in this concluding section is that this chapter, and the recommendations that flow from it, cover only a part of the picture. They deal almost exclusively, because of the subject matter, with trade relations between Africa and Europe. These relations are important and the actions recommended to secure Africa's position in its largest global market following the changes associated with the SEM should be given the most serious consideration.

But although Europe is part of the solution, it is also part of the problem. Africa has two central problems with its exports. One is that its exports are heavily concentrated on a small number of commodities, world demand for which is growing slowly. The other is that its international commerce is concentrated on one region of the world where trade has grown relatively slowly. If one of the challenges facing Africa is to diversify out of traditional commodities, another is to effect a similar shift away from traditional markets. The success of Malaysia in finding a profitable market for its refined palm oil, despite stagnant demand in the OECD, by developing new markets in the Middle East and South Asia is a classic example of the room for manoeuvre that may exist if exporters are able to look beyond the well-worn paths of traditional commerce.

The following conclusions and recommendations emphasize the need to make the most of the European market, but they should not be interpreted as detracting from the need also to promote intra-African trade and to exploit new markets outside the region. In one area these two concerns overlap. It is argued above that the erosion of the EU's traditional trade policy instruments through liberalization, together with the shift of commerce-related powers from the national to the Union level, will provoke a reshuffling of Europe's pyramid of privilege.

At present Europe's trade preferences divide the African continent into three groups: those states that are signatories of the Lomé Convention; those that have bilateral association agreements; and those that have nothing. If there are to be changes in Europe's trade policy Africa should seek to ensure that, at best, they provide more support than the present regime to intra-African commerce and, at worst, that they do not divide the continent even more than at present. One of the attractive features of the Lomé Convention, for example, is that it encourages trade between signatories in order to fulfil the EU's rules of origin. Thus far, this provision has remained largely a dead letter because there is insufficient complementarity between most of the sub-Saharan African states. The extension of the provision to North Africa and to South Africa could provide a significant boost to intra-African trade.

FORTRESS EUROPE OR INCREASED COMPETITION?

The principal conclusions on the impact of the SEM on Africa's trade with the EU are summarized above. Rather than repeat the points of detail, it may be more helpful to provide here a very broad summary of the nature of the impact.

Much has been heard of the danger that the SEM will give rise to a Fortress Europe, but for Africa such fears miss the mark. It is, indeed, possible that Europe will attempt to transfer the burden of adjustment to third parties by reinforcing external protection. It would be prudent for African states, like all others, to keep such possibilities constantly in mind. But it seems unlikely that this will be the principal avenue for any adverse effects of the SEM on Africa. Moreover, a dominating concern with Fortress Europe risks diverting African attention from the avenue that is most likely to be disruptive to current trade patterns. The principal danger for Africa is the complete opposite of Fortress Europe; it is that the SEM, like the GATT Agreement, is an exercise in liberalization.

There are two reasons why Africa has more to fear from the liberalizing than the protectionist tendencies of the SEM. The first is that it does not, in the main, export the goods and services most at risk from a Fortress Europe. These are goods and services in which the level of protection is currently relatively low but where new barriers may be put in place as a consequence of the Single Market. On the other hand, Africa has a strong interest in goods with the opposite characteristics: those in which the level of protection is currently high and in which some liberalization is likely as a consequence of the removal of national trade barriers.

The second reason is that all the African states except South Africa and Libya are situated in the upper echelons of the EU's pyramid of privilege. Trade preferences have been useful for some African countries, even though they have not been a sufficiently powerful policy instrument to offset the forces tending to marginalize the continent in Europe's trade. The potential value of a trade preference is related inversely to the level of protection. If protection is high then a trade preference may provide a substantial competitive advantage over non-preferred suppliers. It is little surprise that the commodities into which Africa has diversified are precisely those in which EU levels of protection are currently high: CAP products for which preferences exist and textiles/clothing. The combination of internal liberalization under the SEM, external liberalization within the GATT and the extension of trade preferences to East Central Europe and the FSU are coinciding to provide a substantial jolt to the commercial environment within which African exporters have been able to operate for the last fifteen or more years.

The example of bananas is given prominence in this chapter because it illustrates the point that liberalization rather than protection poses the most potent threat to Africa. The case of bananas is not as great a problem for Africa as it is for the Caribbean islands. Nonetheless, African interests are at stake and similar problems may be faced in the future by African sugar exporters. Quite clearly, these problems arise not because of a Fortress Europe but because the ramparts of the French, British and Italian national fortresses are being stormed.

THE NEXT STEPS

The overall impact of the enlarged SEM will be to make it easier for competitive suppliers that are able to increase the volume of their exports to sell to all 15 EU national markets; less competitive suppliers, dependent upon traditional links to the more protected national markets, by contrast, will face tougher competition, particularly if they are unable to adapt their product to new standards. Into which category do African exporters fall? The answer is, of course, that African exporters do not all fall into the same group. The impact of the SEM will vary not only between each African state but also between different groups of producers within each state.

Broad analyses such as those contained in this chapter have an important role to perform in focusing attention on those aspects of the complex process of '1992' that are more, and those that are less, likely to be important. But they serve only as an introduction to the vital task facing each country of Africa. This is to identify precisely which of the 279 Directives that form the core of '1992' narrowly defined are important for their exporters and to monitor the indirect effects of the SEM as they evolve to influence those likely to affect their interests. The recommendations that flow from this conclusion are the following.

RECOMMENDATIONS FOR AFRICAN GOVERNMENT ACTION

Some of the African governments are monitoring closely the evolution of events in Europe to identify the consequences for their exporters. This monitoring must be continued and, in some cases, extended. Politico-economic analysis must be supplemented in many cases by legal scrutiny. In the case of the SEM, in particular, changes to European policy will be effected through alterations to the law. Assessing the implications for third parties involves, therefore, legal scrutiny of the draft and final texts of European Directives and the resulting national legislation as they become available. For those African countries able to do so, it makes a great deal of sense to retain the services of a firm of trade-oriented lawyers in Europe. For those African states without adequate financial means for this there is clear scope for technical assistance from the international community (see below).

In addition, events in several different fora need to be analysed together. For those African states with substantial diplomatic representation in Brussels, Geneva, Washington and the commercial centres of the principal European countries, the task is merely one of coordinating and integrating the advice being received in the national capital. For some African states, however, it is not possible to have adequate representation in all these centres. Here again, there is a clear role for the international community to perform (see below).

In their efforts to react to the changes in Europe, African governments must not lose sight of the fact that in most states of the region the task of producing for export and identifying markets lies with the private sector. It is of vital importance that information on market changes obtained by government representatives is passed on to those firms and private sector associations that have need of it. This is not a straightforward task. In many countries of the world communication between the public and private sectors is not as timely or problem-specific as it could be. The SEM is likely to produce such a rapid flood of changes that any inadequacies in existing communication channels should be remedied as a matter of priority.

TASKS FOR THE INTERNATIONAL COMMUNITY

The challenges facing the states of Africa are substantial; since not all will have the resources to respond as extensively as they might wish, there is a clear role for the international community to assist through technical help. Among the areas in which assistance may be most needed are the following:

* assistance to identify changes in standards and norms that will affect existing or potential new exports;

* analysis of any EU decisions on the harmonization of excise taxes to identify the differential impact on commodities of importance to the African region;

* analysis of the implications of the GATT Agreement for Africa;

* analysis of the implications of the EU's new GSP for Africa;

* analysis of the new agreements with the East Central European and FSU states;

* identification of alternative markets for African exports that may be adversely affected by the SEM and identification of new market opportunities for all African states.

In all cases, the international community's assistance should focus on those African states least able to undertake such activities from their own resources and, within all states of the region, small- and medium-sized enterprises that lack the information or resources to identify the challenges or to take advantage of opportunities.

References

Brown, Drusilla K. (1988), 'Trade preferences for developing countries: a survey of results', *The Journal of Development Studies*, 24, 3. London: Frank Cass.

Davenport, Michael (1988), 'European community trade barriers to tropical agricultural products', ODI *Working Paper No. 27*. London: Overseas Development Institute.

Davenport, Michael and Page, Sheila (1991), 'Europe: 1992 and the developing world', *ODI Development Policy Studies*. London: Overseas Development Institute.

Davenport, Michael and Stevens, Christopher (1990), 'The outlook for tropical products', in Stevens, Christopher and Faber, Doeke (eds) *The GATT Uruguay Round and Europe 1992: Implications for ACP–EU Co-operation*. Maastricht: Centre for European Development Co-operation Management.

McQueen, Matthew (1990), 'ACP export diversification: the case of Mauritius', ODI *Working Paper No. 41*. London: Overseas Development Institute.

McQueen, Matthew and Stevens, Christopher (1989), 'Trade preferences and Lomé IV: non-traditional ACP exports to the EU', *Development Policy Review*, 7, 3. London: Sage; September.

Riddell, Roger C. (1990), 'ACP export diversification: the case of Zimbabwe', ODI *Working Paper No. 38*. London: Overseas Development Institute.

Stevens, Christopher (1990), 'ACP export diversification: Jamaica, Kenya and Ethiopia', ODI *Working Paper No. 40*. London: Overseas Development Institute.

Stevens, Christopher and Kennan, Jane (1994), 'How will the EU's response to the GATT Round affect developing countries?', IDS *Working Paper 11*. Brighton: Institute of Development Studies.

Tovias, Alfredo (1991), 'The Single Market and labour mobility', paper presented at United Nations Symposium on 'The Implications of the Single Market Act for non-Member Countries', Geneva, 27–31 May.

3

The Single European Market:
Opportunities and Challenges in
Capital Flows and Private Investment

SHEILA PAGE

The formation of the Single European Market (SEM), or Europe 1992, affects both official and private flows of capital from Europe to the rest of the world. African countries particularly must be concerned by these effects for at least four reasons. First, they are at a stage of development when countries are very dependent on capital flows in aggregate, and when the type, or allocation, of flows could have major effects on the future pattern of their economies. Second, the members of the EU are responsible for a high share of the funds which they receive. The third reason arises from their close trade relationships with the EU, which have been discussed in Chapter 2. The countries which may expect particularly strong effects on their trade from the SEM are also likely to see changes in flows of investment related to traded commodities. A final reason is that other changes in world economic and political conditions may also threaten their access to European capital, notably the easing of international tensions and the emergence of eastern Europe as a competitor for funds.

This chapter will look primarily at the first and second reasons for African concern cited above The next section ('The Role of Foreign Capital in Economic Development', p. 65) will look at both its quantitative role, as a source of additional savings or short-term support, and at its potential for effecting technological change by facilitating the acquisition of knowledge. The third section ('Trends in Private Investment and Official Capital Flows from Western Europe to Africa', p. 68) will give a detailed survey of the various current sources and types of capital, and its allocation in Africa. For direct investment, it will also look at the composition by industry.

It will then be possible, in the fourth section ('Current Intentions and Determinants of Official and Investment Flows', p. 98), to examine how different factors affect flows of capital. The fifth section ('Impact of 1992 on Official Capital Flows and Investment', p. 101) will use the analysis and data provided in previous sections to look at the changes which result from the Single European Market, and indicate which are likely to be most important. The conclusion (p. 107) will place these in the context of what Africa can realistically expect from foreign capital at this stage of its development, given general expectations for capital flows and how they are determined, and suggest the most important areas for policy.

The Role of Foreign Capital in Economic Development

The two, linked roles which have been assigned traditionally to foreign capital in development are to provide additional savings in countries which are, almost by definition, capital-scarce, and to provide external resources in countries which need to import more than they export in order to grow more rapidly than their trading partners. This is necessary in order to catch up with those already more developed. The need for capital may be intensified if the income elasticity of exports is less than that of imports. There are, however, a variety of other potential effects of foreign capital in general or of certain forms which have been identified.[1]

In the lowest-income countries, extra savings are needed to accelerate the development of the infrastructure of development. This motive, combined with the desire to increase the rate of development relative to industrial countries, suggests a need even in more advanced countries for capital at concessional or zero cost. This must be from official flows. Such flows are unlikely to create an identifiable and capturable return to the provider.

For countries where there is sufficient infrastructure for the additional costs of doing business in an underdeveloped system not to outweigh the extra benefits to be expected from providing capital as a scarce resource, there is clearly a possibility of attracting inflows which require a return, whether in the form of loans at commercial interest rates or equity investment, but which will still contribute to more rapid growth in income, and thus to catching up. The level of development at which the extra costs, and extra risks, of investing in a developing economy become less than the extra return will depend on various factors in both the investing and the receiving country.

Some types of investment are traditionally largely self-contained, with little dependence on the economy or the infrastructure of the host country (mining is the traditional example) and may be attractive to foreign investment regardless of local conditions. As a corollary, however, they may have relatively little impact on the economy unless steps are taken to secure some of the 'rents' of the investment in addition to direct effects. The cost of capital in the investing country and world demand obviously

[1] For a fuller discussion see Page, 1990, Chapter 14; Collas-Monsod, 1991, summary table 5; Encarnation and Wells, in Moran *et al.*, 1986.

influence new flows at the margin. These parameters and the risks of changes or fluctuations in them also affect the costs which a host country must assess in deciding whether the investment will produce a net increase in income and wealth.

There are additional uses for short-term capital, most obviously the 'smoothing' function of short-term borrowing for a country which faces fluctuations in its import or export values without an adequate cushion of foreign exchange reserves. This is particularly important for developing countries because all three factors influencing the need for such capital apply strongly to them: the prices of their exports are likely to have a high variation; their poverty makes them particularly vulnerable to income fluctuations; most lack large foreign reserves. For all these macro-economic roles of foreign capital, the economic conditions and policies, that could change because of the SEM can influence the supply of or demand for inflows.

The various additional possible contributions of foreign capital, over and above these macro-economic and developmental roles, normally accrue from the use to which the capital is put or from the form in which it is made available. The one which has attracted most attention in recent years is the improvement of the level of technology in the recipient country. This must go beyond simply providing the income to buy technology (which would merely be a special case of the foreign exchange benefit). But in many cases technology requires either a particular set of experts or a type of industrial organization, which can be provided in the context of either official flows, through technical assistance, or private flows, through a foreign investor. Or the technology may belong to a commercial organization which chooses to supply it only in association with foreign investment. This is an additional, and non-capital, contribution to growth and often to development, in the sense of structural change. This function can be an argument for putting resources into acquiring foreign capital as part of a development strategy, if the capital sought is in fact available.

Knowledge of markets and marketing in industrial countries can be considered a particular form of technical expertise. It is a way in which foreign capital, if it is associated with foreign investors or appropriate official expertise, can improve the performance of a developing country's exports, both existing and new. The contribution may go beyond simply providing expertise to providing the market (sales to related companies) or to removing barriers to exports (lobbying against protection). These are contributions additional to foreign capital's role in reducing exchange constraints.

Both the technology and the market-access effects depend critically on the form in which capital is provided, and therefore are sensitive to changes in it. It also appears to be the case that they depend on the nationality of the provider. Some differences are obvious: countries which are more advanced in technology or which have larger markets may have more to offer. Countries differ in the role of technical assistance in their official capital flows. Others may be less obvious. It appears (Page, 1987) that Japanese investors are particularly likely to bring high technology, but to restrict its spread; that US firms are particularly concerned with marketing, and that Europeans are likely to behave more like local firms. Therefore the potential benefits from these additional effects may depend on the national composition of foreign investment or of public funding.

Whether foreign capital flows contribute directly to exports for more general reasons, is uncertain. This could happen because foreign private investors are more likely to have high export ratios or because support for public sector spending may go preferentially to infrastructure which is related to the external sector. Both arguments are used, with increasing flows of foreign capital seen as being part of a general process of the 'opening' of an economy. Clearly there are *a priori* arguments for expecting foreign expertise, public and private, to lie preferentially in these areas, but the empirical evidence does not provide strong support for this (except in cases where the process is helped by host-country policies which encourage such a link). It is difficult in practice to distinguish any such tendencies from the choice-of-sector or the marketing effects discussed above (Turner, 1990; Collas-Monsod, 1991). Most investment in developing countries, and especially flows to Africa, is still in primary sectors or to meet local demand, so that a foreign propensity to export would not be relevant or apparent. At a minimum, however, foreign investors or donors are less likely to ignore external implications and opportunities altogether.

By providing additional capital, foreign capital alters the balance between capital and labour (and other factors of production) in the host country, and it alters the demand for different types of labour. At a macro level, the returns to labour should rise and those to capital fall, but the importance of the sectoral distribution of the foreign inflow, and therefore of distribution effects on different types of labour, is likely to be greater. There is evidence that different investing countries prefer different sectors. (This is explored further in the next section, p.68.)

The reason why it is important to distinguish among the effects of the different flows is that most are, from the point of view of the developing country, largely exogenous, rather than demand-driven. Given exogenous investments, largely determined by specific opportunities, any choice is in practice likely to be whether or not to take them, not which advantages to seek.

Official flows are, as discussed in the next section, by far the most important for most African countries. Their purpose is normally seen in terms of one of the first three macro-economic objectives discussed above. The actual allocation among projects or uses within countries, however, will affect the other properties of external capital. As different donors do have different priorities and conditions, a change in the donor composition may, therefore, have effects additional to any stemming directly from a change in the absolute level.

For direct investment, the position is reversed. Although it will necessarily have at least the first two, more long-term, macro-economic effects, these are not its motive, and in the case of African countries, the quantities are so small that these are unlikely to be its most important effect. Given the small scale of the economies as a whole, and the small number of firms likely to be present in the same industry and service sectors, foreign investment may make a significant difference to the sectoral composition of output, to the share of exports or imports, and of particular products within this, and to relative labour incomes. For this reason it is necessary to examine how investors from different areas differ in these respects. But the practical importance for African countries is small. Only a handful (perhaps a dozen) of all developing countries attract significant quantities of foreign investment for motives other than natural resources, local import substitution, or services directly associated with trade flows, and few African countries are possible current candidates for this group.

Other types of commercial flow, through bank loans or portfolio type investments, are more like official flows in their non-sector-specific nature, but they have the highest fixed costs of the three. Their supply is likely to be determined more by conditions in the lending countries and by general perceptions of the risk of lending to all developing countries, or a particular region, than by either the macro or the micro opportunities discussed above. The demand for them by developing countries will depend on their macro-economic needs. This demand, however, will also be determined by their cost, especially for the reasons outlined above of the difficulty of securing a direct return to service them. Thus effectively the demand depends on conditions in the developed country home of the lender.

Trends in Private Investment and Official Capital Flows from Western Europe to Africa

The EU countries are the major source of official capital flows to Africa, 36 per cent in 1992, although this was less than the 40 per cent in 1989 (see Table 3.1). They are the major source of direct investment (probably about 70 per cent in 1989, see Table 3.8, although that was exceptionally high).[2] Africa also receives a large share of EU official and direct investment flows compared with other developing countries: sub-Saharan Africa received 47 per cent of EU official flows (Table 3.2) and the Middle East and North

[2] The data in Table 3.8 are only for the major suppliers of foreign investment, but the OECD figures for total DAC direct foreign investment in developing countries, $30 billion in 1989, are not very different (within the uncertainties of capital flow data) from the $37 billion estimated here for five major investors. French investment in Africa was about $1 billion a year in the early 1980s, and very much lower, with periods of disinvestment, in the late 1980s.

TABLE 3.1
Official flows: shares and importance (%), 1992

	Shares in flows to Africa[b]	Shares in EC flows to Africa[b]	Share of EC in total	ODA as % of GNP[a]	ODA as % of ODA+FDI
Developing countries	–	–	56.27	1.5	54.2
Africa	40.79	26.35	36.36	–	89.1
Sub-saharan Africa	31.07	26.5	47.99	13.4	92.12
Algeria	1.66	3.28	71.88	–	97.63
Angola	1.3	1.6	44.96	–	52.79
Benin	1.08	0.04	1.48	–	99.63
Botswana	0.45	0.15	12.03	–	64.94
Burkina Faso	1.79	2.41	48.99	31.3	100
Burundi	1.27	1.16	33.1	–	99.68
Cameroon	2.92	5.31	65.95	5.8	98.64
Cape Verde	0.48	0.24	17.75	–	100.84
Central African Republic	0.72	0.83	42.09	–	101.7
Chad	1.00	1.02	37.13	–	95.02
Comoros	0.19	–	–	–	97.96
Congo	0.46	1.02	80.08	4.8	96.64
Côte d'Ivoire	3.07	6.08	71.97	7.7	97.2
Djibouti	0.47	0.32	24.83	–	100
Egypt	14.23	12.99	33.17	11.2	88.52
Equatorial Guinea	0.25	0.22	31.68	–	75.9
Ethiopia	5.23	5.42	37.67	19.3	100
Gabon	0.28	0.76	100	–	209.09
Gambia	0.47	–	–	–	95.08
Ghana	2.52	2.16	31.16	10.2	96.46
Guinea	0.43	2.06	40.23	–	95.86
Guinea-Bissau	0.43	0.18	15.37	–	94.69
Kenya	3.14	3.13	36.22	9.7	99.62
Liberia	0.47	–	0.06	–	100.85
Libya	0.09	–	–	–	12.79
Lesotho	0.57	0.03	2.18	12.8	97.93
Madagascar	1.44	1.76	44.31	14.5	94.47
Malawi	2.1	1.19	20.58	–	100.58
Mali	1.77	1.43	29.34	–	101.86
Mauritania	0.84	0.83	35.88	–	100
Mauritius	0.19	–	–	–	75.81
Morocco	4.01	6.62	60.08	2.6	70.14
Mozambique	5.6	7.95	51.58	93.4	98.24
Namibia	0.56	0.64	41.51	–	71.43
Niger	1.46	1.96	48.41	–	100
Nigeria	1.07	0.49	16.72	0.9	22.81
Rwanda	1.42	1.16	29.75	18.7	99.44
São Tomé	0.22	0.14	23.8	–	100
Senegal	2.71	3.53	47.37	10.4	98.68

TABLE 3.1 cont.	Shares in flows to Africa[b]	Shares in EU flows to Africa[b]	Share of EU in total	ODA as % of GNP[a]	ODA as % of ODA+FDI
Seychelles	0.08	–	–	–	48.78
Sierra Leone	0.54	0.4	27.1	–	78.36
Somalia	2.32	0.38	5.91	–	100
Sudan	2.45	2.14	31.77	16.1	100
Swaziland	0.19	–	0.15	–	51.65
Tanzania	5.41	4.73	31.79	96.2	99.85
Togo	0.91	–	–	–	100.9
Tunisia	1.64	3.68	81.73	2.8	51.78
Uganda	2.89	2.35	29.55	42.7	99.58
Zaïre	1.08	2.69	90.25	–	100.75
Zambia	4.09	4.06	36.11	–	95.31
Zimbabwe	2.96	1.49	18.26	9.3	96.97

a For some countries OECD, 1994 gives two different figures. b Africa is % of all developing; countries are % African total. EU figures differ from other table because of different defination of EU programme.
Source: Tables 5 and 7; OECD (1994).

Africa 20 per cent, compared to the 34 per cent and 26 per cent respectively these areas received from all donors. While 14 per cent of the EU's investment in developing countries may not seem high, it is more than twice Africa's share in other OECD countries' investments in less-developed countries. Two conclusions follow from this summary: anything that affects the total official flows of the EU is likely to affect its flow to Africa. Any change in its flows from the EU will have a major effect on Africa.

There are two other points from Table 3.1 which indicate how important identifying any changes in official flows in particular will be. The first is the contrast between Africa's receipts of official and of direct investment flows. Ninety per cent of the inflow of official plus direct investment in 1992 was official. Translated into values, in 1992 (an exceptionally good year for foreign investment), Africa received about $3 billion in direct foreign investment and about $25 billion in official flows. The second is that official flows make a much more important contribution to the macro-economic performance of African countries than of other developing countries; they were equivalent to about 13 per cent of GDP in sub-Saharan Africa in 1989 compared to 1 per cent for all developing countries. Combining these with the shares in Table 3.2, EU development flows are equivalent to about 6.5 per cent of sub-Saharan GDP (up from 5 per cent in 1989).

OFFICIAL FLOWS

Although its share in EU flows is exceptionally large, Africa has a high share in total Official Development Assistance (ODA). Its share increased

TABLE 3.2
Regional distribution of ODA by individual DAC donors and multilateral agencies,[a] share of SSA and Middle East and North Africa in total for each donor

	Sub-Saharan Africa			Middle East and North Africa[b]		
	1981/2	1985/7	1991/2	1981/2	1985/7	1991/2
United States	17.0	15.5	12.8	47.3	47.2	58.9
Japan	10.1	10.6	16.1	6.9	6.8	12.3
EU Countries						
France	50.7	53.4	62.3	18.0	16.0	17.6
Germany	34.6	33.8	33.0	16.6	16.4	32.2
Italy	66.9	71.3	41.9	14.2	8.6	24.5
United Kingdom	38.5	41.1	53.5	4.7	4.8	5.5
Netherlands	31.5	39.8	40.5	4.5	5.6	6.7
Spain	n.a.	n.a.	15.4	n.a.	n.a	24.1
Portugal	n.a.	n.a.	99.9	n.a.	n.a.	0.0
Denmark	51.6	60.1	62.3	6.2	4.7	6.1
Belgium	67.6	77.8	60.7	10.1	4.4	16.4
Ireland	96.7	96.2	68.9	0.3	0.1	26.1
Luxembourg	n.a.	n.a.	55.0	n.a.	n.a	21.1
Total	42.0	48.4	47.3	12.7	12.1	20.3
Nordic Countries						
Sweden	53.4	58.1	63.9	1.5	2.0	5.0
Denmark	51.6	60.1	62.3	6.2	4.7	6.1
Finland	61.7	63.8	56.4	4.9	5.5	15.2
Norway	57.8	64.4	66.9	0.9	0.7	0.9
Total	54.5	60.7	63.1	2.6	2.7	5.9
Other Countries						
Canada	39.3	40.5	43.3	6.2	2.8	9.3
Switzerland	43.5	58.2	45.7	6.7	2.8	10.8
Australia	5.7	6.0	14.3	1.9	1.0	2.0
Austria	9.4	9.8	21.9	44.4	75.1	35.3
New Zealand	2.5	1.1	3.7	0.0	0.0	0.5
Total	22.5	29.0	35.2	9.0	11.9	11.9
DAC countries	30.4	30.3	31.2	19.3	28.7	28.7
EU	62.6	69.3	67.4	8.8	7.5	15.6
IFIs[c]	21.6	32.3	46.2	4.8	3.0	1.4
UN agencies[d]	34.4	43.0	46.7	17.5	10.7	21.9
Overall total	30.8	32.1	34.2	17.5	19.5	26.0

a Excluding non-specified amounts by region.
b Includes small amounts to Southern Europe.
c International financial institutions. Includes IDA, regional banks' soft windows and IFAD.
d Includes UNDP, UNICEF, UNRWA, WFP, UNHCR and UNFPA.
Source: OECD (1994).

throughout the 1960s and 1970s, from about 10 per cent in 1960 to 28 per cent by 1980 and 41 per cent in 1992 (Table 3.1). Most forecasts expect this increase in share to continue. If there is little change or a small reduction in OECD growth rates or the ratio of ODA to GDP, giving a total increase of 2–3 per cent in real terms per year, aid to sub-Saharan Africa could continue to rise at 4 per cent a year, 3 per cent from the general rise and 1 per cent from a rising share, only slightly below the average for the 1980s. Other areas would also receive rises although these would be smaller. If, however, aid flows continue to stagnate as they have in the last two years, and if flows to Eastern Europe and the former Soviet Union continue to rise (Table 3.3), then in order for Africa to see an increase, aid to all other areas would need to fall.

The increase in the 1980s was a real increase, although most of it came in the first half of the decade. Since then, overall, the increase in OECD aid has only slightly more than balanced the disappearance of the Organization of Petroleum Exporting Countries (OPEC) aid. In 1987–90, the real value of flows to sub-Saharan Africa remained roughly flat (see OECD 1991a), although there was an increase to Egypt which affected the total Africa figure in 1990. In the years immediately before that, the shift from OPEC to OECD donors meant a shift from North to sub-Saharan Africa.

The share of Africa in EU aid (Table 3.1) also increased in the early 1980s, although by much less than for other donors, and it has fallen slightly since 1987. This explains why the EU is now marginally less important among donors. This contrasts sharply with the rise in the EU's share of total aid to all developing countries. The EU's share was particularly low in the late 1970s and early 1980s, recovering during the 1980s from about 30 per cent to about 40 per cent in the late 1980s and more than 50 per cent in 1992. The major switches in aid to Africa among the bilateral donors came from the US (by the early 1980s) and Japan (in the late 1980s). There was also a major swing by the multilateral institutions (excluding those of the EU) (Table 3.1). All these changes suggest that the EU has not shared in the general move to increase the priority given to aid to Africa, and may therefore be particularly vulnerable to any influences which would redirect or even reduce it.

Table 3.1 shows how EU and total aid are distributed among the African countries, and its relative importance in individual countries. Table 3.4 shows how these flows were allocated in 1980 and 1989. Overwhelmingly, it is the francophone and lusophone countries which have the highest rate of dependence on EU countries (on France and Portugal in particular). Table 3.5 gives flows by country. The East and Southern African countries in contrast take a high share from non-EU donors as well. This was true in 1980 as well, and is largely confirmed by the distribution figures. The latter show clearly that Egypt had a special position in non-EU donors' aid (Table 3.6). Although this had diminished by 1989, it recovered in 1990 and even more in 1991. It has become increasingly true of EU aid, including EU joint aid.

TABLE 3.3
Official aid disbursements and direct investment flows to Eastern Europe and the former Soviet
Union ($ million)

| | Official aid | | | Direct investment |
	1990	1991	1992	1992
EU	1076.3	4955.9	5607.7	1545.3
Belgium	20.7	274.4	134.7	n.a.
Denmark	14.7	65.1	83.3	17.1
France	75.6	457. 5	365.5	167.2
Germany	473.2	2771.8	3874.9	988.0
Greece	5.2	31.6	52.0	n.a
Ireland	4.7	15.3	10.3	n.a
Italy	133.4	672.4	460.1	n.a
Luxembourg	0.7	4.5	5.7	5.2
Netherlands	61.6	152.7	162.8	364.6
Portugal	3.6	21.6	17.5	0.3
Spain	24.1	162.4	102.4	2.9
United Kingdom	258.8	326.6	338.5	n.a
Total OECD	1719.8	7821.9	8052.7	2365.6

Note: Data for 1990 exclude aid to the former Soviet Union and are, therefore, not fully comparable. Data refer to EU aid and
EBRD capital subscription. Incomplete data.
Source: OECD (1994).

TABLE 3.4
Distribution of ODA and foreign direct investment in 1989 and 1980

| | 1989 | | | | 1980 | |
| | ODA | | FDI | | ODA | |
	All	EU+ Members	All	EU + Members	All	EU+ Members
Africa % LDCs	38.8	43.5	5.7	13.5	30.0	44.4
by country as % Africa						
Algeria	0.8	1.1	5.9		1.7	2.4
Angola	0.8	0.8	0.0		0.5	0.3
Benin	1.4	2.1	0 0		0.9	1.0
Botswana	0.9	0.6	0.8		1.0	1.1
Burkina Faso	1.5	2.2	0.0	0.9	2.1	2.7
Burundi	1.1	1.4	0.6		1.1	1.4
Cameroon	2.6	5.0	3.0		2.6	3.4
Cape Verde	0.4	0.4	0.0		0.6	0.7
CAR	1.1	1.3	30.9		1.1	1.9
Chad	1.3	1.9	0.0		0.3	0.5
Comoros	0.2	0.4	0.0		0.4	0.4
Congo	0.5	1.0	9.9		0.9	1.3

TABLE 3.4 cont.	1989				1980	
	ODA		FDI		ODA	
	All	EU+ Members	All	EU + Members	All	EU+ Members
Côte d'Ivoire	2.3	4.6	0.0	1.6	2.0	3.5
Djibouti	0.4	0.8	3.7		0.7	0.7
Egypt	8.6	5.6	1.8		13.4	4.9
Equatorial Guinea	0.2	0.3	0.0	2.3	0.1	0.0
Ethiopia	4.1	3.8	2.1		2.1	1.5
Gabon	0.7	1.5	1.2	1.7	0.5	1.1
Gambia, The	0.5	0.6	5.2		0.5	0.5
Ghana	3.0	2.4	0.0		1.9	1.7
Guinea	1.9	2.6	0.1	3.6	0.9	1.0
Guinea-Bissau	0.6	0.6	0.1	−2.0	0.6	0.7
Kenya	5.3	4.8	0.0		3.8	3.5
Liberia	0.3	0.3	0.0		0.9	0.4
Libya			0.1			
Lesotho	0.7	0.6	0.8	0.6	0.9	0.8
Madagascar	1.8	2.4	−0.2		1.9	1.7
Malawi	2.2	2.0	0.0		1.4	1.6
Mali	2.5	3.3	0.0	1.8	2.4	2.8
Mauritania	1.3	2.3	4.5		2.1	1.0
Mauritius	0.3	0.5	0.0		0.3	0.4
Morocco	2.5	3.4	0.0		6.8	3.8
Mozambique	4.2	4.2	0.0		1.6	1.2
Namibia			0.7			
Niger	1.6	2.0	0.0		1.6	2.1
Nigeria	1.9	1.8	1.2	63.5	0.3	0.4
Reunion			0.0		4.8	10.6
Rwanda	1.3	1.5	−2.3		1.5	2.1
São Tomé and Príncipe			0.0		0.0	0.0
Senegal	3.6	5.0	−0.4		2.5	3.4
Seychelles	0.1	0.1	1.1		0.2	0.4
Sierra Leone	0.3	0.8	0.0	0.5	0.9	0.8
Somalia	2.3	3.1	0.0		4.3	2.3
Sudan	4.1	3.9	1.3	0.6	6.0	5.4
Swaziland	0.2	0.1	1.3		0.5	0.6
Tanzania	5.0	5.2	1.2	0.5	6.4	6.6
Togo	1.0	1.1	0.0		0.9	1.2
Tunisia	1.3	1.8	0.0		2.3	2.8
Uganda	2.2	1.0	0.0	0.1	1.1	1.1
Zaïre	3.5	4.3	0.0	0.8	4.1	6.0
Zambia	2.1	2.0	0.0	3.7	2.9	2.9
Zimbabwe	1.5	1.6	0.0	5.9	1.6	1.7
Total	87.9	100.0	74.6	86.1	100.0	100.0

All data = $ Millions.
Totals may not add to 100 because only major flows are given in source.
Source: OECD (1990) 1991b,

In 1970, the major individual recipients of total Development Assistance Committee (DAC) flows were Asian countries (the top five were India, Indonesia, Vietnam, Pakistan and Korea, with the top African country Algeria, in ninth place, followed by the other North African countries, Morocco and Tunisia, then Nigeria. By 1980, Egypt was in first place, Sudan ninth and Kenya tenth. In 1991/2, Egypt was still first, with Mozambique and Tanzania eighth and ninth. This is in sharp contrast to EU aid, both by countries (as indicated in Table 3.2) and joint (Table 3.6). For the latter, nine out of ten of the top places were already African in 1970; 1980 saw this reduced to eight (Bangladesh joined India); in 1991/2 there were still eight African, but with Turkey and Jordan the fifth and sixth, and Egypt now the first.

Among the EU donors to all developing countries (Table 3.5), France and Germany are the largest, followed by Italy, the UK and the Netherlands. The pattern for Africa is similar, except that the position of France is dominant. Although French ODA is still predominantly directed to the francophone countries, there are substantial flows to others as well. German flows are very concentrated on Egypt. There are some countries which receive their aid overwhelmingly from one member of the EU, including (from France) Algeria, the Central African Republic, Chad, Côte d'Ivoire, Gabon, Guinea, Madagascar, Mauritania, Morocco, Niger, Senegal; from the UK, Malawi, Nigeria; from Germany, Egypt and Zaïre, and from Italy, Somalia. Kenya, Tanzania, Zimbabwe and Mozambique had particularly widespread support.

The high value of aid relative to African countries' GDPs makes them particularly vulnerable to any changes in ODA flows. The share is high partly because the countries are low-income countries, but it is higher than the average for low-income countries in other areas, and high in comparison with low-, middle-, and high-income countries across the different areas, and this would be true even if the exceptionally low figures (for their income) of India and China were removed from the averages. The ratio was increasing at the end of the 1980s and in the early 1990s.

FOREIGN INVESTMENT

Over the last decade, the pattern of changes in direct investment flows to African countries, even if the sub-Saharan countries are distinguished from the rest, has perhaps not been very different from that for all developing countries. There was a sharp drop in mid-decade and a rebound at the end. Taking five-year averages, it has increased its share of total investment, with a particularly high estimate for 1992 (Table 3.7).[3] A crucial difference is that the values are very much smaller, not only in absolute terms but in relation to other capital flows to Africa (Table 3.1).

[3] Given the lags in the data, the 1992 figure must be an estimate by the United Nations Conference on Trade and Development (UNCTAD).

TABLE 3.5
Official flows, total and by EU countries, 1992 ($ million)

	All OECD	EU+ Members	EU	Belgium/ Luxembourg	Denmark	France	Germany	Italy	Netherland	Portugal	Spain	UK
Developing countries	60934	34290	3955	918	1324	8372	8352	3632	2836	257	1174	3398
Africa	24855	9036.31	1656.35	243.27	300.55	2957.34	1394.78	912	397.04	193.78	299.37	662.61
SSA	18935	9087	2200	238	305	2856	1164	696	611	200	122	682
Algeria	412	296.15	59.33	22.95		200.93		21.79			50.48	30.52
Angola	322	144.78						39.95			14.91	
Benin	269	3.97			3.97							
Botswana	113	13.59										13.59
Burkina Faso	444	217.53	51.42	41.31	9.27	125.58			31.2			
Burundi	316	104.59	63.28	6.43							19.96	
Cameroon	727	479.451	126.561	4.59		326.51				16.71		
Cape Verde	120	21.3										
CAR	179	75.35				75.35						
Chad	248	92.09				92.09						
Comoros	48	0										
Congo	115	92.09				92.09						
Côte d'Ivoire	763	549.12	130.52			418.6						
Djibouti	117	29.06						29.06				
Egypt	3538	1173.52	181.93		22.51	234.42	567.94	112.59	25.52		23.79	
Equatorial Guinea	63	19.96									19.96	
Ethiopia	1301	490.15	225.44		3.97		125.28	61.74	28.36		7.04	37.38
Gabon	69	69				69						
Gambia	116	0[a]										
Ghana	626	195.04	55.37		5.3		100.22		28.36			61.16
Guinea	463	186.25			5.3	125.58						
Guinea-Bissau	107	16.45								16.45		
Kenya	780	282.54	55.37	13.77	26.48		58.46	18.16	45.38			64.56
Liberia	118	0.07										

TABLE 3.5 cont.

	All OECD	EU+ Members	Belgium/ Luxembourg	Denmark	France	Germany	Italy	Netherland	Portugal	Spain	UK
Libya	22	0									
Lesotho	142	3.1									
Madagascar	359	159.07			159.07						
Malawi	521	107.23	51.42							4.7	50.97
Mali	439	128.82			100.46			28.36			
Mauritania	210	75.35			75.35						
Mauritius	47	0									
Morocco	996	598.36	54.58	17.44	276.28		116.22			133.84	
Mozambique	1393	718.56	94.92	23.83	92.09	83.52	188.86	51.05	132.87	10.57	40.78
Namibia	140	58.11	51.42	6.62							
Niger	362	175.26	47.46	10.59	117.21						
Nigeria	265	44.32									44.17
Rwanda	352	104.73	51.42	53.24							
São Tomé and Príncipe	54	12.85							12.85		
Senegal	673	318.83	7.34		267.9		43.58				
Seychelles	20	0									
Sierra Leone	134	36.32					36.32				
Somalia	577	34.11	4.59	6.62			4	25.52		30.58	
Sudan	608	193.19	114.7					39.7			
Swaziland	47	0.07									
Tanzania	1344	427.3	79.1	94	66.82		76.27	5.67			84.95
Togo	225	0									
Tunisia	407	332.65	11.93		108.84	66.82	138.02		7.04		
Uganda	718	212.17	33.97	34.42				19.85		15.26	47.57
Zaïre	269	242.77	94.92								
Zambia	1016	366.9	4.59	27.8		116.93	25.42	36.87			84.95
Zimbabwe	735	134.23	4.59	19.86				31.2			78.15

a. Too small to appear in lists of major recipients.
Note: Inconsistencies result of using 1991/2 and 1992 data. Only major recipients for each country are covered in data.
Source: OECD (1994), ODI calculations.

This means that single investments in any year can greatly distort the series. It also means that the rise since the late 1980s from an average of $2 billion in 1982–5 and 1986–7, to an average of $3 billion in 1988–91 (and estimated for 1992), although large in percentage, is still small relative to other flows. Most ($2 billion) goes to the oil-exporting countries and half of the rest to Morocco, leaving less than half a billion for other countries. For this reason, the poor prospects suggested in this section, although clearly discouraging, can have only small practical effects.

Table 3.8 gives more detailed data by investing country. African countries receive only about 6 per cent of the investments in developing countries. To take the example of the Netherlands, Africa accounted for about 6 per cent of its stocks of capital in developing countries in 1988 (Langhammer, 1991). (This is, however, not much lower than its 12 per cent share in their trade.)

Although, as indicated above, direct investment is not and has not been a major source of capital inflow compared to public sector flows, it has been the principal private flow, excluding export credits. The fall in private investment inflows was accompanied by falls in other private flows (although for Africa the drop in export credits has been much less than for developing countries as a whole). It is only the increase in the value of official flows which has held the total resource flow to sub-Saharan Africa constant. In other areas, official flows have been at best constant, so that in Asia and in Latin America it was the changes in non-official flows which brought about changes in total resources.

The principal increases in foreign investment in developing countries in recent years have come from outside the EU, notably from Japan, but also from Switzerland, the US and Australia. Within the EU, the increases have been from the United Kingdom and Germany, and also Italy. France, the other traditional major investor, has declined in share. With the exception of the rise for the UK, the increases have thus come from countries which traditionally have not invested heavily in Africa. The fall came in a country which has invested extensively there. Each of the major areas has reduced the share of its investment going to Africa (both North and sub-Saharan, although the fall to the latter has been sharper). Although this can be explained partly by the general trend towards more investment in Asian countries, which have been the fastest growing economically, it is a sharp contrast with Central and South America. Central America is also an area which mainly exports primary foods. It saw a sharp rise, in total investment and in European investment. South America, which did have a fall from its traditional sources, the US and Japan, gained investments from Europe. Sub-Saharan Africa had falls from both its traditional and other foreign investors. This situation was substantially worse in relative terms than its performance in the 1970s had been (Page, 1990: 312–13). Then, its share in total investment in developing countries did not rise, but it did remain roughly flat, with only the Côte d'Ivoire suffering a sharp fall (from 1.8 per cent of total

TABLE 3.6
Major African recipients of DAC members' aid (% of total)

	Total DAC bilateral			EU programme (not including members' aid)		
	1970–1	1980–1	1991–2	1970–1	1980–1	1991–2
Algeria	1.5	Egypt 4.4	Egypt 9.0	Cameroon 9.0	Sudan 4.1	Ethiopia 5.7
Morocco	1.4	Tanzania 2.1	Mozambique 1.5	Zaïre 8.4	Egypt 3.6	Egypt 4.6
Tunisia	1.3	Sudan 1.3	Tanzania 1.3	Senegal 8.2	Senegal 3.4	Côte d'Ivoire 3.3
Nigeria	1.3	Kenya 1.2	Morocco 1.1	Madagascar 6.1	Somalia 3.1	Cameroon 3.2
Zaïre	1.0	Zaïre 1.1	Zambia 1.1	Côte d'Ivoire 4.9	Ethiopia 3.0	Sudan 2.9
Egypt	0.8	Morocco 0.9	Kenya 1.0	Burkina Faso 4.2	Zaïre 2.8	Mozambique 2.4
Kenya	0.8	Zambia 0.8	Côte d'Ivoire 0.8	Niger 3.5	Mali 2.7	Uganda 2.4
Ghana	0.7	Senegal 0.7	Cameroon 0.8	Mali 3.3	Tanzania 2.6	Tanzania 2.0
Tanzania	0.6	Tunisia 0.7	Ethiopia 0.7	Gabon 3.0	Kenya 2.4	Zambia 1.7
		Burkina Faso 0.6	Ghana 0.7	Chad 3.0	Zambia 1.9	Burundi 1.6
			Senegal 0.7	Togo 2.7	Madagascar 1.9	Mali 1.5
				Algeria 2.2	Guinea 1.7	Angola 1.5
				Benin 2.2	Rwanda 1.6	Guinea 1.4
				Congo 1.9	Morocco 1.6	Kenya 1.4
				Egypt 1.9	Côte d'Ivoire 1.6	Rwanda 1.3
				Burundi 1.8	Burundi 1.5	Namibia 1.3
				Somalia 1.8	Uganda 1.4	Malawi 1.3
				Rwanda 1.5	Malawi 1.4	Morocco 1.3
				Central African Republic 1.4	Burkina Faso 1.2	Burkina Faso 1.3
					Mauritania 1.2	Niger 1.2

Source: OECD (1994).

TABLE 3.7
Foreign direct investment, 1992

	Inflows ($ m)	Shares in Total Africa	Share of foreign total investment (%)			
			1980–5	1986–90	1991	1992
Developing countries	51480	–	2.4	2.7	4	7.8
Africa	3042	5.91[a]	2.5	3.7	4.7	10.5
Sub-saharan Africa	1620	–	–	–	–	–
Algeria	10	0.33	-0.1	–	0.1	–
Angola	288	9.47	28.5	13.1	–	–
√Benin	1	0.03	0.2	0.2	5.1	–
Botswana	61	2.01	16.3	19.7	–	–
Burkina Faso	–	–	0.3	0.2	0.1	–
Burundi	1	0.03	2.1	0.7	0.4	0.3
Cameroon	10	0.33	8.7	0.3	-1.1	–
Cape Verde	-1	-0 03	–	0.5	1	–
Central African Republic	-3	-0.1	9.8	2.4	-2.8	–
Chad	13	0.43	–	–	–	–
√Comoros	1	0.03	–	6.4	5.4	–
Congo	4	0.13	4.6	4.2	1.8	–
Côte d'Ivoire	22	0.72	2.7	4.3	1.5	–
Djibouti	–	–	0.1	0.3	–	–
Egypt	459	15.09	7.7	5.4	3	5.3
√ Equatorial Guinea	20	0.66	9.5	15.8	79.8	–
Ethiopia	–	–	0.1	0.1	0.1	–
Gabon	-36	-1.18	5.1	6.8	-9.4	–
√ Gambia	6	0.2	–	9	20	–
Ghana	23	0.76	1.1	1.3	2.3	2.5
Guinea	20	0.66	–	1.1	–	–
Guinea -Bissau	6	0.2	1.9	1.6	3	–
Kenya	3	0.1	1.4	2.4	1.2	0.5
Liberia	-1	-0 03	–	–	–	–
Libya	150	4.93	-3.1	0.1	1.7	–
Lesotho	3	0.1	3.4	4.5	1.7	–
Madagascar	21	0.69	0.7	3.3	8	–
√ Malawi	-3	-0.1	4.5	5.6	4.4	-0.9
Mali	-8	-0.26	2.4	-0.3	0.6	–
Mauritania	–	–	4.7	1.9	0.9	–
Mauritius	15	0.49	–	–	–	–
√ Morocco	424	13.94	1.5	1.9	5.2	6.3
√Mozambique	25	0.82	0.2	3.9	15.8	–
Namibia	56	1.84	–	–	–	–
Niger	–	–	0.6	3.6	0.2	–
√✶ Nigeria	897	29.49	4.5	27.5	19.3	23.3
Reunion	–	–	–	–	–	–
Rwanda	2	0.07	6.8	4.8	2	0.9
São Tomé	–	–	–	–	–	–
Senegal	9	0.3	2.3	0.2	–	–
Seychelles	21	0.69	25.8	33.6	–	–
√ Sierra Leone	37	1.22	- 5	115.4	58.3	–
Somalia	0	0	-1.7	–	–	–
Sudan	–	–	0.7	–	–	–

TABLE 3.7 cont.	Inflows ($ m)	Shares in Total Africa	Share of foreign total investment (%)			
			1980–5	1986–90	1991	1992
Swaziland	44	1.45	6	39.5	–	–
Tanzania	2	0.07	0.7	–	0.3	0.2
Togo	–2	–0.07	2.4	2.1	2	–
Tunisia	379	12.46	8.3	3.4	4.2	9.6
Uganda	3	0.1	–0.1	–0.2	0.3	–
Zaïre	– 2	–0.07	–10.2	–1.4	3.2	–
Zambia	50	1.64	10.7	35.6	–	–
Zimbabwe	23	0.76	–	–1.1	–	–
Total	3042	100	–	–	–	–
South Africa	–5	–0.16	0.4	–	–	–

a Investment in Africa as proportion of investment in developing countries.
Source: UNCTAD (1991).

investment in developing countries in 1969–73 to 0.2 per cent by 1983–5). Africa as a whole showed a very strong rise, entirely explained by increased investment in Egypt (whose share rose from close to 0 to 11 per cent in the same period). Asia's share was already rising sharply in that decade, but this was at the expense of Latin America. The same pattern can be seen in UK data, with Africa keeping its share, or even slightly increasing it in all investment in developing countries through the 1970s, and with a particularly good performance in manufacturing and in new investment. (Much of UK investment in developing countries at that time was merely reinvestment of earnings [Page, 1986]). Although it is true that Africa's growth was slow in the 1980s, the deterioration in this relative to the 1970s was not exceptional.

The sharp, unexplained, change in Africa's relative performance in the 1980s in attracting investment from all the major investors, aggravated by actual withdrawals from some areas and, notably by the traditional investors, the UK and France, from some of their ex-colonies, makes it risky to indicate what could be expected in the light of current projections for foreign investment in the 1990s, even in the absence of any special 1992 effects. The extremely (and unexpectedly) good performance of foreign investment in some developing countries in the late 1980s has led to a surge of optimism for the 1990s. The World Bank (Page, 1991a) in its forecasts published in summer 1991 expected a growth rate of 10 per cent per annum in 1990–5, which would be about 6 per cent even after allowing for inflation. This was lowered later in the year, but only to 9 per cent (World Bank, 1991b). The United Nations Conference on Trade and Development (UNCTAD) took a more cautious view, as did the IMF, but the data for 1991 and 1992, and estimates for 1993 show a strong rise. Such a rise would reverse the 1980s shift from mainly private to more public financing of developing countries as a whole. But, given the

TABLE 3.8
Direct investment flows 1989

	USA 1989	USA 1990	Japan 1989	Japan 1990	Germany 1989	Germany 1990	Netherlands 1989	Netherlands 1990	UK 1989	EU 1989	All 1989	EU% of all
Total investment	33338	33437	67540	56911	14079	14865	50727	38532	35336	100141	201069	49.8
LDCs	11598	12175	14474	11526	537	533	6250	3631	3717	10504	36576	28.7
Africa	−20	−182	671	551					1420	1420	2071	68.6
SSA	−150	24									−150	
Algeria	9	9									9	
Angola	−20	−5									−20	
Benin												
Botswana												
Burkina Faso												
Burundi	0	0										
Cameroon	72	−34							13	13	85	15.4
Cape Verde												
CAR												
Chad	11	5									11	
Comoros												
Congo	−5	6									−5	
Côte d'Ivoire	9	−4									9	
Djibouti												
Egypt	93	−221							23	23	116	19.8
Equatorial Guinea												
Ethiopia												

TABLE 3.8 cont.	USA 1989	USA 1990	Japan 1989	Japan 1990	Germany 1989	Germany 1990	Netherlands 1989	Netherlands 1990	UK 1989	EU 1989	All 1989	EU% of all
∨ Gabon	-35	318							33	33	-2	
Gambia	0	0										
∨ Ghana	72	21							25	25	97	25.5
Guinea		1										
Guinea-Bissau												
∨ Kenya	18	-14							51	51	69	73.8
Liberia	38	-35	643	531					-28	-28	653	
Libya	-5	-7									-5	
Lesotho												
Madagascar	-3	-3									-3	
Malawi	1	2							8	8	9	89.1
Mali												
Mauritania	-1	-1									-1	
∨ Mauritius	1	1							26	26	27	96.3
Morocco	3	5									3	
Mozambique	-2	-2									-2	
Namibia	0	0										
Niger	-1	-2									-1	
∨ Nigeria	-184	-222	1	1					902	902	719	125.5
Reunion												
Rwanda	-1	-1									-1	
São Tomé & Príncipe												
Senegal	2										2	
Seychelles												

TABLE 3.8 cont.	USA		Japan		Germany		Netherlands		UK	EU	All	EU%
	1989	1990	1989	1990	1989	1990	1989	1990	1989	1989	1989	of all
Sierra Leone	-9	17							7	7	-2	-268.7
Somalia	10	-2										
Sudan									8	8	18	45.1
Swaziland	-1	7										
Tanzania									7	7	6	118.0
Togo	30	-30										
Tunisia											30	
Uganda									2	22	2	100.0
Zaire	7	16							11	11	18	62.1
Zambia	9								52	52	61	85.4
Zimbabwe	7	8							84	84	91	92.3

polarization which has occurred between the public and the private funding recipients, it is not clear that it would do so for individual areas, and for Africa in particular. It is more likely to mean that the middle- to high-income recipients of private funding can expect more capital inflows and the poorer, officially funded countries will see, as indicated above, smaller or no rises in total inflows. As we have seen above, although there was an increase in investment flows from some countries to Africa in 1989–92, the rises seem to be heavily concentrated in the oil countries.

The northern African countries, and those with an important mineral resource, account for most of the exceptions to the pattern of African dependence on official flows. Egypt, Libya, Tunisia and Nigeria are the major examples (see Table 3.1) with Botswana, Mauritius, Morocco, Namibia and Swaziland also receiving above average shares of their inflows from private investment. Kenya did receive inflows until 1991–2. Among these, Mauritius and perhaps Kenya are probably the only ones which can be considered examples of the 'more advanced developing country' pattern of investment in other sectors, notably in manufactures or other new products for export. In 1980, there had been markedly more countries with significant inflows of private investment, including Cameroon, Côte d'Ivoire, Gabon, Mauritania, Rwanda, Senegal, Togo and Zambia.

Some of these are also oil and mineral producers. But among the rest, there is a clear pattern of fall for the francophone countries, with a change for all of these from an inflow of $1 billion in 1980 to one of $0.4 billion in 1989. This pattern corresponds to the reduction noted in the total French flows to the continent over the decade. This change over the last decade indicates how important changes in one country's flows can be for small economies which are likely to be dependent on one or a small number of investing countries, and therefore suggests why some African countries are concerned by Single Market effects if they are dependent principally on European investors.

Although the international sources for aggregate data on which the tables are based normally use year by year flow data, the figures for individual countries' investments are a combination of flows and stocks. The figures for stocks of foreign capital, the current value of all past investment, have the advantage of smoothing out the notoriously irregular pattern of foreign investment (this is particularly serious for countries with a single, mineral, sector or with a small number of investors where averaging will not occur from large numbers), but the disadvantage that the numbers are even more subject to differences in estimation methods and whatever adjustments are made for price and exchange rate changes, and even more delayed in publication.[4]

---

[4] There is also the practical point that the preferences of individual investing countries for flow or stock data determine the care with which they are collected and presented. German and Japanese data for stocks are probably better; the US and the UK probably have better data for flows.

TABLE 3.9
Foreign capital stocks, 1992

	Value ($ million)			Shares in total for Africa		
	1980	1990	1992	1980	1990	1992
Developing countries	124974	340928	431233			
Africa[a]	37626	50990	56699	30.11	14.96	13.15
Sub-saharan Africa excluding South Africa	16678	23842	27581	44.33	46.76	48.64
Algeria	1320	1315	1337	3.51	2.58	2.36
Angola	61	1024	1977	0.16	2.01	3.49
Benin	32	36	50	0.09	0.07	0.09
Botswana	266	819	920	0.71	1.61	1.62
Burkina Faso	18	31	31	0.05	0.06	0.05
Burundi	7	29	31	0.02	0.06	0.05
Cameroon	330	1161	1150	0.88	2.28	2.03
Cape Verde	0	3	3	0	0.01	0.01
Central African Republic	50	96	88	0.13	0.19	0.16
Chad	123	243	254	0.33	0.48	0.45
Comoros	0	15	19	0	0.03	0.03
Congo	309	564	573	0.82	1.11	1.01
Côte d'Ivoire	650	1060	1102	1.73	2.08	1.94
Djibouti	3	5	5	0.01	0.01	0.01
Egypt	2256	11039	11751	6	21.65	20.73
Equatorial Guinea	0	23	85	0	0.05	0.15
Ethiopia	110	116	117	0.29	0.23	0.21
Gabon	809	1458	1320	2.15	2.86	2.33
Gambia	21	41	57	0.06	0.08	0.1
Ghana	288	375	418	0.77	0.74	0.74
Guinea	2	24	30	0.01	0.05	0.05
Guinea-Bissau	0	8	16	0	0.02	0.03
Kenya	666	393	668	1.77	0.77	1.18
Liberia	1230	2257	2535	3.27	4.43	4.47
Libya	–	–	–	–	–	–
Lesotho	9	69	79	0.02	0.14	0.14
Madagascar	36	103	138	0.1	0.2	0.24
Malawi	100	210	227	0.27	0.41	0.4
Mali	13	29	25	0.03	0.06	0.04
Mauritania	0	51	53	0	0.1	0.09
Mauritius	20	162	196	0.05	0.32	0.35
Morocco	305	1035	1779	0.81	2.03	3.14
Mozambique	15	42	90	0.04	0.08	0.16
Namibia	0	51	212	0	0.1	0.37
Niger	188	260	262	0.5	0.51	0.46
Nigeria	2404	8022	9631	6.39	15.73	16.99
Reunion	–	–	–	–	–	–
Rwanda	54	213	219	0.14	0.42	0.39

TABLE 3.9 cont.	Value ($ million)			Shares in total for Africa		
	1980	1990	1992	1980	1990	1992
São Tomé	–	–	–	–	–	–
Senegal	360	304	336	0.96	0.6	0 59
Seychelles	37	194	237	0.1	0.38	0.42
Sierra Leone	77	0	64	0.2	0	0.11
Somalia	29	28	28	0.08	0.05	0.05
Sudan	0	12	11	0	0.02	0.02
Swaziland	149	427	517	0.4	0.84	0.91
Tanzania	154	11	16	0.41	0.02	0.03
Togo	182	249	254	0.48	0.49	0.45
Tunisia	548	2708	3212	1.46	5.31	5.67
Uganda	9	4	8	0.02	0.01	0.01
Zaïre	440	277	287	1.17	0.54	0.51
Zambia	414	593	677	1.1	1.16	1 19
Zimbabwe	7023	2483	2567	18.67	4.87	4.53
Total excluding South Africa	21107	39939	45660	56.1	78.33	80.53
South Africa	16519	11051	11039	43.9	21.67	19.47

a Stocks in Africa as proportion of stocks in developing countries.
Source: UNCTAD (1994).

The declining share of Africa in total stocks of investment in developing countries (Table 3.9), and the fact that this share is still substantially higher than its share of current flows, is further evidence of its declining share in new flows since 1980, although as with flows, this trend seems to have at least paused in the early 1990s. The change in South Africa is striking, because of the practical ending of inflows in the mid-1980s, and its share is now below that of Egypt. Nigeria is the only other country at a similar level. Rises in share can be seen for Angola, Morocco, and Tunisia, and a sharp fall for Zimbabwe.

The discussion of stocks focuses attention on the major continuing providers of foreign investment. In the EU, this means the UK, Germany and the Netherlands (now that French investment has declined sharply). For the rest of the world, it is the US and Japan. Although, in general, the EU has invested less in developing countries than other foreign investors, the stock data confirm that this does not hold true in Africa. Table 3.10 shows that the share in 1989–90 of the EU in estimated stocks of foreign investment was only 17 per cent for all developing countries, and about 30 per cent for all countries. For Africa, however, it was 33 per cent. All these shares are lower than in 1980 (Table 3.11), when they were 26 per cent, 37 per cent, and 48 per cent respectively.[5] The fall for Africa was greater than the average; this confirms that African host countries have suffered not merely from a decline in the total flows of their major investor, but also from a fall in their share in these. As a comparison of Tables 3.10 and 3.11 shows, the share of Africa in total EU investment in developing countries has fallen from 25 per cent to 11 per cent, while for all major industrial country investment its share has fallen from 13 per cent to 6 per cent. For the most recent available years, the EU share going to Africa has recovered slightly (on both these measures, Tables 3.4 and 3.8), but this is the result of some exceptionally high inflows to individual countries, notably from the UK to Nigeria.

The countries which have been most dependent on EU sources, as shown by the most recent stock data in Table 3.10, include some of those identified as the major recipients of all foreign investment, but there are important exceptions (in both directions). The major recipients which do not depend on the EU are Egypt and Liberia. Algeria, Botswana, Kenya, Mauritius, Morocco, Nigeria, Swaziland and Tunisia do depend principally on the EU, but so do some small recipients: Ethiopia (although the numbers are too small to be meaningful), Ghana, Malawi, Zambia and Zimbabwe. In 1980, those dependent on French investment also fell into this category. Recent flow data by country (Table 3.8) suggest that this pattern is continuing.

Within the EU, the UK is probably now the most important investor in Africa. Flows from Germany and the Netherlands are irregular, in response to specific opportunities. For both of these countries, Africa has never represented more than about 10 per cent of their stock of investments in developing countries. Germany and the UK were among the countries whose total foreign investment increased most during the second half of the 1980s (Rutter, 1991). But this has been principally within Europe and to the United States, not to developing countries, and even more clearly not to Africa. Both German and UK stocks in Africa fell (even in current value terms) in the 1980s (Tables 3.10 and 3.11). By 1989, the value of German stocks was 8 per cent of total capital in developing countries (Table 3.10), but of this most was in North Africa: Libya, a third; Egypt, a fifth; and Algeria, Morocco and Tunisia, together almost another fifth, leaving approximately another third for sub-Saharan Africa, or 2.4 per cent of total German investment in developing countries. The major recipients in sub-Saharan Africa were the oil producers, Nigeria and Gabon.

The African fall in both value and share of investment in developing countries was much sharper in the UK figures. In 1980, Africa was almost 30 per cent of the total, while in 1989 it was about 12.5 per cent (Tables 3.10 and 3.11). The decline was irregular, but took place throughout the

[5] Comparing changes is probably more valid than comparing levels because of the different methods of valuation used. This is one reason that Japanese stocks exceed those of the UK, although the flows are and have been lower.

TABLE 3.10
Direct investment stocks, 1989–90

	USA (1990)	Japan (1990)	Germany (1989)	UK (1989)	EU[a]	All[b]	EU as % of all	Share by Country All	EU
Total investment	421494	310808	108936	203176	312112	1044414	29.9		
								Africa as % of LDCs	
LDCs	105721	98369	12800	28687	41487	245577	16.9	5.8	11.2
Africa	3780	5826	1057	3608	4665	14271	32.7		
SSA	1940					1940			
								Country as % of Africa	
Algeria	56		87		87	143	60.9	1.0	1.9
Angola	380			16	16	396	4.1	2.8	0.3
Benin									
Botswana				14	14	14	100.0	0.1	0.3
Burkina Faso									
Cameroon	277		21	24	45	322	13.9	2.3	1.0
Cape Verde									
CAR									
Chad	36					36		0.3	
Comoros									
Congo	27		7		7	34	20.7	0.2	0.2
Côte d'Ivoire	143		19		19	162	12.0	1.1	0.4
Djibouti	2					2		0	
Egypt	1451		200	225	424	1875	22.6	13.1	9.1
Equatorial Guinea									
Ethiopia	2		4		4	6	67.3	0	0.1
Gabon	463		88	88	88	551	15.9	3.9	1.9
Gambia									

TABLE 3.10 cont.	USA (1990)	Japan (1990)	Germany (1989)	UK (1989)	EU[a]	All[b]	EU as % of all	Share by Country All	Share by Country EU
Ghana	173		1	98	99	272	36.4	1.9	2.1
Guinea	85					85		0.6	
Guinea-Bissau									
Kenya	99		31	395	426	525	81.1	3.7	9.1
Liberia	58	4832		-24	-24	4866		34.1	-0.5
Libya	246		333		333	579	57.5	4.1	7.1
Lesotho									
Madagascar	6					6		0	
Malawi	4			122	122	126	96.8	0.9	2.6
Mali									
Mauritania	-2					-2		0.0	
Mauritius	6				92	98	93.8	0.7	2.0
Morocco	36		55		55	91	60.6	0.6	1.2
Mozambique	-9					-9		-0.1	
Namibia									
Niger	-2					-2		0	
Nigeria	210	159	88	1026	1114	1483	75.1	10.4	23.9
Reunion									
Rwanda									
São Tomé and Príncipe									
Senegal	34					34		0.2	
Seychelles									
Sierra Leone	56			10	10	66	14.7	0.5	0.2
Somalia									

TABLE 3.10 cont.	USA (1990)	Japan (1990)	Germany (1989)	UK (1989)	EU[a]	All[b]	EU as % of all	Share by Country All	EU
Sudan	-110			34	34	-76		-0.5	0.7
Swaziland	-1			37	37	36	102.8	0.3	0.8
Tanzania	-17		2	16	18	1		0	0.4
Tunisia	52		68		68	120	56.6	0.8	1.5
Togo									
Uganda	60			22	22	22	100	0.2	0.5
Zaire	63	282	32	19	51	393	13	2.8	1.1
Zambia	58	142		156	156	361	43.2	2.5	3.3
Zimbabwe			10	729	739	797	92.7	5.6	15.8

All data = $m.
a Germany, UK
b EU, USA, Japan.
Source: US, 1991; Germany, 1991; Japan, 1991; ODI estimates and calculations.

1980s, starting in 1981 and intensifying after 1983 (Bennell, 1990). The distribution of UK investment is very different from the German: almost all has gone to sub-Saharan Africa. Egypt received 6 per cent of the total on 1989 figures, but the major recipients were Nigeria, Zimbabwe and Kenya, followed by Ghana, Mauritius and Malawi. The same three countries were most important in 1980, and remained so in 1989 (Table 3.8). And it is the UK which was their major source of foreign investment.

All foreign investment in developing countries tends to be concentrated in the hands of large companies,[6] but UK investment in Africa is exceptionally concentrated, and there is some evidence that this is increasing because the decline in the 1980s occurred through the withdrawal of smaller investors (Bennell, 1990: 160). This could mean that the remaining investment is less likely to be reduced as the marginal investors have gone. Large companies have a tendency to have more stable investment patterns.

Thus within the total EU investment in Africa, North African countries would be most likely to be affected by any changes which strongly affected Germany, and sub-Saharan African countries by those which affected the UK. The oil producers would be affected by either, but are more likely to be affected by special oil market conditions. Those with UK investment may be less vulnerable to future changes because the least committed investors have already gone, while those dependent on French investment have also suffered a major fall already. Table 3.12 indicates which sectors are particularly important for different investors.[7] UK investment (not surprisingly in view of the predominant position of Nigeria) is mainly in energy industries, but there are also significant flows into some manufacturing industries. That its investments in manufactures are lower than is the case in its foreign investment in other areas is not surprising in view of the structure of most African economies, but UK investment in services is low in relation to that of other foreign investors in Africa. The most recent stock figures also show high past investment figures in agriculture, followed by financial services. Transport equipment, chemicals, and food have been the principal manufacturing sectors in the past. An alternative set of data (see Table 3.9) indicates that in terms of stocks it was the only major investing country for which Africa's share in its total manufacturing investment in developing countries was greater than its share in non-manufacturing investment. German investment is principally in mining

---

[6] Some new investment by the NICs within Asia seems to be an exception to this and there are also some counter-examples in Japanese investment. So far, however, this change appears not to have spread significantly to other countries' investments or to other developing regions.

[7] The figures do not add to the totals because countries normally give only the major sectors (as they do for destinations) and the UK in particular avoids giving individual sector data if fewer than three firms are involved in order to preserve confidentiality, and then omits another sector to make it more difficult to reconstruct the data.

(which includes oil in German data), but with a higher proportion in manufacturing and also (although the data are not complete) apparently in services. The manufacturing investment in the late 1970s and early 1980s included outward processing in textiles and clothing in the North African countries (Cantwell, 1988).

The high Japanese investment specified as transport is presumably associated with its high share to Liberia. Excluding this, Japan is also mainly involved in mining, but with a high share for services, and a spread of investments in manufactures. Although the US data for 1990 show disinvestment in oil, this has also been the traditional direction of its investment in Africa. French investment was predominantly in the traditional, primary activities, agriculture and mining (Cantwell, 1988).

OTHER CAPITAL FLOWS

Non-Governmental Organization (NGO) finance has gained in importance in the 1980s, although for most developing countries it is still a very small source of external finance. Much of it is now derived from official sources (especially if the value of tax and other concessions is included) so this trend can be related to the increase in the share of official flows.[8] For Africa, this increase and the fall in the role of foreign investment have meant that NGO finance may now be more important than foreign investment. For Africa, this funding also probably comes mainly from the EU countries, with the UK and Germany as the most conspicuous providers.

International bank lending was important at the beginning of the decade, but virtually disappeared in the early 1980s, and has not revived significantly since then. There appears to have been no net borrowing after 1989, on either flows or stock of debt data, with net repayments in 1990–2 (World Bank, 1993). Nigeria, the largest borrower, reduced its liabilities in the late 1980s and early 1990s (Bank for International Settlements (BIS), 1991; World Bank, 1993).

Bonds were only important to a few developing countries even before the early 1980s, and these did not include African economies. Algeria did use them from 1985 to 1989, borrowing up to $500 million a year (IMF 1991a), but except for Tunisia in one year, the only other African developing country to use this source was South Africa in 1991 and 1992. In 1994, however, Congo and Tunisia both had issues, of $0.6 and $0.3 million (IMF, 1994a). Morocco had a small equity issue in 1993.

In summary, the principal flows of capital to Africa have been official, and recent trends suggest that the official share is increasing, although there are now signs of new private flows. Both public flows and direct investment are predominantly from the EU. Although France has become a less important investor, it remains the major official donor, with Germany and the UK important for both. Because the private flows are so

[8] It is not clear why it is classified as wholly private in the OECD data.

TABLE 3.11
Stock 1980

	USA	Japan	2385	UK	1959	Germany	EU	All	EU % All	All Africa	EU Africa
										Africa as % of LDCs	
Total	213468	36497	43956	104837	84485	43127	147964	397929	37.2	13.5	25.4
LDCs	52684	22948	8155.4	19451	12789	6528	25979	101611	25.6		
Africa	5663	1445	2317.2	5527	2124	1084	6611	13719	48.2		
SSA	1933				988	504	504	2437	20.7		
										Country as % of Africa	
Algeria					304	155	155	155	100	1.1	2.3
Angola											
Benin											
Botswana											
Burkina Faso											
Burundi											
Cameroon					14	7	7	7	100	0.1	0.1
Cape Verde											
CAR											
Chad											
Comoros											
Congo					11	6	6	6	100	0	0.1
Côte d'Ivoire					72	37	37	37	100	0.3	0.6
Djibouti											
Egypt	1029				278	142	142	1171	12.1	8.5	2.1
Equatorial Guinea											
Ethiopia					5	3	3	3	100		
Gabon					30	15	15	15	100	0	0
Gambia, The										0.1	0.2

TABLE 3.11 cont.	USA	Japan	2.385	UK	1.959	Germany	EU	All	EU % All	All	EU
Ghana					5	3	3	3	100	0	0
Guinea											
Guinea-Bissau											
Kenya	278		235.1	561	47	24	585	585	100	4.3	8.8
Liberia					69	35	35	313	11.2	2.3	0.5
Libya	577	791			137	70	70	1438	4.9	10.5	1.1
Lesotho											
Madagascar					4	2	2	2	100	0	0
Malawi											
Mali											
Mauritania											
Mauritius											
Morocco					38	19	19	19	100	0.1	0.3
Mozambique											
Namibia											
Niger											
Nigeria	27	153	653.8	1559	629	321	1880	2060	91.3	15	28.4
Reunion											
Rwanda											
São Tomé and Príncipe											
Senegal					7	4	4	4	100	0	0.1
Seychelles											
Sierra Leone											
Somalia											

TABLE 3.11 cont.	USA	Japan	UK	1,959	Germany	EU	All	EU % All	All	EU
Sudan										
Swaziland										
Tanzania				18	9	9	9	100	0.1	0.1
Toga				19	10	10	10	100	0.1	0.1
Tunisia				75	38	38	38	100	0.3	0.6
Uganda										
Zaire		243	28	69	35	63	306	20.7	2.2	1.0
Zambia		11.8		14	7	7	7	100	0.1	0.1
Zimbabwe		547.9	1307	9	5	1311	1311	100	9.6	19.8

All data = $m.
Source: US, 1983; Japan, 1991; Germany, 1984; UK, 1984; ODI estimates and calculations.

TABLE 3.12
Direct investment flows and stocks by sector, 1990 (unless otherwise indicated)

	USA Total	USA in Africa	Japan total	Japan in Africa	Germany total	Germany in Africa	Netherlands total	UK total	UK in Africa
By industry				Stocks '90	Stocks '89	Stocks '89			
Metal Manufacture	1349	11	1047	127	2861	68		90	0
Chemical	2116	1	2292	24	23143	6	889a	0	0
Mech. engineering	464	1	1454	1	8957	19		0	0
Electrical	1324	11	5684	8	11606			0	0
Transport	-183	11	1872	17	10978			0	0
Food, drinks	1638	17	821	8	576		1904	0	0
Paper					266			0	0
Textiles			796	39	1526			0	0
Lumber & pulp			314	1	1152				
Other Manufacture	3455	2	1207	109	4933		563	0	0
Total Manufacture.	10164	54	15486	231	66838	256	3366	0	0
Agriculture			214	7	82		-9		
Mining			1328	582	4522	324	1082b	0	0
Energy					1144				
Petroleum	4483	-216			422				
Construction			300	23	820		115	0	0
Distribution	2275	7	6156	15	4567	5	1013	0	0
Transport			2169	3233			208	0	0
Financial services	10448	-50	8047	37	20648		2346	0	0
Other services	1642	-1	11292	725	19961	2	3445	0	0
Property			11107	69					
Total non-manufacturing	23273	-236	40620	5591	54822	802	7012	0	0
Total	33437	-182	56911	5828	121660	1057	11566	0	0

a Metals and electrical engineering
b Mining and quarrying, oil and chemicals
Source: US, 1991; Germany, 1991; Japan, 1991; Netherlands, 1991; UK, 1991.

small, it is often the case that countries are overwhelmingly dependent on just one source. There are some examples of this in official flows as well. In foreign investment, there are also clear differences in the sectoral allocation of different investors. There are, therefore, some countries which would be particularly vulnerable to effects of the Single European Market which influenced the flows of one country more than the others, or which led to any convergence in aid or investment flows or policies.

Current Intentions and Determinants of Official and Investment Flows

As was indicated above in the second section, the types of motive which lie behind official and private flows tend to be very different, with the former seen, on both sides, principally in terms of altering the macro-economic performance of an economy, even if the means may be through specific projects to improve individual sectors or activities, while the latter look at identifiable opportunities with capturable returns, with any benefits to the economy coming through the normal mechanisms of increased demand and supply. From the capital-providing country's point of view, therefore, the motivations of the two types of flow may be seen as basically independent, except to the extent that the improvements intended from public sector intervention are seen as necessary require-ments for the individual private sector investments.

As long as these general distinctions, on motives and on timing, hold, no obvious conflict arises from attracting the two types of inflow. Potential conflict may arise from two sources. From policy: if the official flows are conditional on specific policy measures (for example on industrial policy, including import controls) or policies for particular sectors, either of these could affect an investment decision directly. From performance: if the private flows are for investment to meet local demand, they depend on the general performance of the economy; this may be adversely affected if policies which restrain demand in the short term are a condition to obtain official flows. Potential conflict only becomes actual, however, if a country is in fact trying to attract both types of inflow at once, instead of following the traditional sequence of first official, then private. Current trends suggest that the potential conflict may well have arisen increasingly frequently in the 1980s, in Africa and other developing countries, stemming from both policy and performance, and this is continuing in the 1990s. The attempt to attract both official and private flows simul-taneously, however, is less common. Countries tend to divide into the poor recipients of public finance and the middle- to high-income recipients of direct investment. It is, of course, very possible that the first set of conflicts helps to explain why this polarization has occurred.

INFLUENCES ON OFFICIAL FLOWS

The shift of official flows to Africa in the 1980s, especially by the multi-lateral organizations for which traditional ties or foreign policy and defence motivations are likely to be less important than for bilateral donors, was clearly associated with the perceived greater needs of the low-income countries in that region. The shift was not a change in trend: the figures for the previous 20 years showed the same shift, and in pro-portional terms it could be said that 'the increase in the increase' was actually less. But the evidence on dependency ratios and the fact that the shift was stronger for African low-income countries than for other regions suggest that Africa came to occupy a special place in donors' conscious-ness. This may help to explain why the shift continued in spite of Africa's better growth performance in the 1980s than, for example, Latin America.[9] Among African countries, the aid flows are in general explicable by size and relative income, but the usual disadvantage for large countries is observed (although Nigeria may also be perceived as helped by the oil price rises) and there is some evidence of a tendency for the multilaterals to increase flows to those countries which follow their policy pre-scriptions.

The bilateral flows, taken individually, including those from the individual EU countries, have been less predictable from general criteria. The introduction of new criteria of 'governance' and other conditions related to countries' political or legal systems is too recent to appear in the data. Other new influences are the reduction in East–West conflict, which has clearly reduced aid from the former centrally planned economies (and the rise in European flows to these countries suggests a further fall for other countries), and the desire by EU countries to discourage immigration from African countries (as well as actively restricting it) by reducing the income gap and hence the incentive to move. The latter may help to explain increased flows to North Africa.

INFLUENCES ON FOREIGN INVESTMENT

The general criteria governing the determination of foreign investment can explain why investment should be relatively low in Africa, and they provide at least a partial explanation of why it should have declined.[10] Foreign investors are looking for an opportunity which their company has some special advantage in exploiting. It may be an international

[9] From 1982 to 1990 African output is estimated (IMF 1991b) to have increased by 17 per cent; Latin American by 12 per cent and from 1988 to 1990 it grew faster in each year. The 'usual' (pre-1982) pattern of more rapid Latin American growth returned in 1992–3, but these were years of drought..

[10] The relative growth figures for Africa and Latin America, however, make the EU shift in investment from Africa to Latin America seem difficult to explain, unless investors shared the international financial institutions persistently over-optimistic expectations.

advantage, in extracting a particular natural resource, or it may be an advantage relative to local firms, in supplying a particular product for local sale. The small markets, in population and income, in most African countries have meant that the first type of investment has been much more important, as was seen in the sectoral composition analysed in the third section (p. 68). In Africa, this has meant principally exploitation of a traditional natural advantage: oil, metals, diamonds or certain agricultural products. In Asia, it has developed into treating a large labour force, of a certain minimal level of skills, as the 'natural material' which certain companies use as an input in processing, whether of textiles and clothing or electrical and electronic goods. There are some examples of this in Africa, but both the size of the labour force and the level of infrastructural development, physical and human, have prevented such a processing-based foreign investment sector from emerging, except in a few cases in North Africa.

In the 1980s, the low and often falling prices of many raw materials reduced the attraction of this type of investment, and affected Africa disproportionately because of the pattern of its foreign investment. The increase in the share of Japanese investment, which might have favoured Africa because of the high share of primary exploitation traditional for Japanese investors, was at last going into different types of investment, and therefore into different geographical areas. The increase in total UK investment abroad came at least partly because of the removal of the restraints on investment after the 1979 abolition of exchange controls, and simultaneous reforms of domestic capital markets. As investment in developing countries (particularly reinvestment) had been less constrained in the past, it could gain less from the boom. France, which had followed the traditional pattern in Africa, was also perhaps more attracted by new freedoms to invest in other developed countries, and in developing countries outside the franc zone.

The slow growth in Africa, relative to Asia and to developed countries, reinforced the traditional hesitation to invest there to meet local demand. It is here that the policies of adjustment required in order to increase receipts of official capital could have militated against promoting private capital inflows, but it is not clear that such flows would have materialized under any circumstances. It is only in North Africa that there appears to have been a deterioration from an existing position of attracting investment. There is, however, some evidence that the policies of severe contraction as well as certain specific types of policy (reduction or removal of import controls, for example) led to the withdrawal of British firms from African countries (Bennell, 1990). This was mainly in the manufacturing rather than the primary sector.

It is important to recognize that small domestic markets may hinder not only investment to satisfy them but also more export-oriented investment in processes which (unlike large-scale mining, for example) can be used for both markets. A foreign investor does not see production for export and production to replace imports as separate activities, as they may appear to be to an analyst. If a company can begin production for a local market, perhaps following successful exports to it, and then expand to export from it the same goods, and then perhaps move on to processing specifically for export, it will be exploiting three different opportunities on the basis of one 'fixed cost' of entry and establishment in a new market. Countries which can only offer one or two of these possibilities are at a permanent disadvantage relative to those which can offer all three (as did the NICs and new NICs of Asia). In periods of extremely high growth or in the presence of some other strong influence (perhaps market familiarity for the French investors in North Africa), these disadvantages may be overcome, but the 1980s and early 1990s, in most African economies, have offered very few exceptions.

The influence of familiarity and the greater freedom or complete exemption from the exchange controls which restricted most capital outflows could help to explain the high investment in Africa by the UK and France until the early 1980s. If this reason has any force, one should consider the level in the 1970s as unusually high, rather than seeing the level in the 1980s as low, with discouraging implications for the 1990s.

Impact of '1992' on Official Capital Flows and Investment

OFFICIAL FLOWS

The prospects for official flows, as we have indicated, are not very good in aggregate. At best, on past trends, Africa could expect a rate of rise of 2–3 per cent, but any increase in available funds is increasingly likely to be diverted to the former centrally planned economies. This did not happen in 1990–1, partly because of the alternative diversion to the Gulf War and the countries affected by it (most spectacularly, Egypt), and also because of the severe disruption (and in some cases military conflict) within Eastern Europe and the republics of the former Soviet Union, which reduced their capacity to absorb funds. Although these problems may continue (imposing other threats to industrial country government spending and hence to aid allocations), the spectacular increases in 1991 and 1992 by bilateral and multilateral donors to the former centrally planned economies reduced funds available for developing countries. OPEC and Soviet aid have now disappeared. The 1 per cent real growth forecast by the World Bank for the 1990s can be taken as the maximum for total aid to developing countries.

The multilaterals at least are still increasing the share of their total developing country aid going to Africa, so the prospects from them are for a higher rise than this average, although not as high as in the 1980s. The diversion of incremental flows to the Eastern European countries, however, has been greatest from the Western European countries, which are important for Africa. They account for $4.5 billion of the $6.3 billion increase from 1990 to 1992. But, as indicated above, only if there is no diversion to new demands, and no rise to other areas, can a 1 per cent rise in the total yield 2 per cent for Africa.

The direct effects of '1992' on aid are on tying and on formal policies. There is some increase in the share of aid through the EU. Although such EU aid is still mainly to African countries, the Middle East has been increasingly important. The indirect effects may include greater informal coordination or questioning of apparently anomalous flows.

Under the SEM, rules for opening public procurement should open any public purchases to suppliers in all member countries on an equal basis. There are two reasons for expecting this to be of limited importance. First, it is at least arguable that the previous provisions for non-discrimination in procurement already restricted tying, and this was not implemented except by two of the smaller donors. The informal reciprocal pressures that supplemented legal regulation are likely to remain, although increased public questioning could gradually lead to a change. Second, many aid projects are funded through giving the recipient government the formal right to issue contracts. These governments are not bound by Single Market regulations; the project documents may not be public; the informal pressures are again available.

If (as assumed in Davenport and Page, 1991), 57 per cent of EU aid is tied, and removing the tie increases its value by 20 per cent, and if all the 57 per cent is untied, this would give a (probably maximum) estimate of an increase of $2 billion on total EU aid and $0.9 billion on its aid to Africa, or about 5 per cent in its total aid receipts. This could increase the rate of growth of aid by 1 point a year over a five-year period (to allow for the gradual implementation of new contracts). This extra one point could raise the annual increase for Africa from the optimistic 2–3 per cent estimated at the beginning of this section to 3–4 per cent, approaching past rates. The actual effect is likely to be at best half of this because of the practical constraints and also because of the high share of aid to Africa accounted for by technical assistance. Although this should also be 'untied', this is even more unlikely to happen in the short term than the untying of other forms. Taking the more realistic 1–2 per cent and adding a half point for untying makes 2 per cent a possible, if optimistic prospect. The rise is thus likely to be less than that in population.

Export credits should also be untied. This could reduce costs to developing countries, but competition and international pressure have already brought some standardization. Some countries have privatized their export credit agencies (in the case of the UK to a Netherlands buyer) so that effects should appear.

The political settlements agreed in December 1991 do increase the EU responsibility for development policy, with an objective of ensuring 'that the policies of the Community and of the Member States bilaterally are

consistent and coherent'. At least on such issues as political conditionality there has in practice been growing consultation and coordination.
This could reduce variance among aid flows to different donors' 'special
clients'. The coordination of EU aid to the associated African, Caribbean
and Pacific (ACP) countries under the current Lomé agreement has also
been increased. Any standardization here could affect the francophone
countries most severely, although French resistance could delay or miti-
gate any change, plus a few of those which receive large inflows from the
UK. The gainers might be other African countries, but it seems increasingly
likely that the EU will continue its slight move away from Africa. This
would be consistent with its increased trade arrangements with other
areas, notably Latin America. The francophone countries could also be
affected, especially now that their access to automatic short-term
financing of deficits has been reduced because of the devaluation of the
CFA franc.

There is one direct cost arising out of the Single Market diversion in the
form of the introduction of a series of information activities to explain the
implications of the SEM to different areas. The benefits could outweigh
the costs for those with extensive trading interests at stake. On this count,
African countries could be gainers.

A final effect is from the increase expected in aggregate growth in the
EU as a result of increased efficiency and, perhaps, dynamic gains from
the SEM. It is estimated that this will add between 4 and 7 per cent to its
output (by the EU itself, Cecchini, 1988) or twice this (Baldwin, 1989). This
effect is implicit in the forecasts of output used above to estimate total
industrial country growth, and should not therefore be re-added here.[11]

EFFECTS ON NGOS

NGOs are also increasingly coordinating themselves and being co-
ordinated at the EU level. As with aid, the principal effect is likely to be
reduced divergence in the distribution of their efforts where this arises
purely from traditional linkages, and possibly increased pressure to
operate common criteria of need or acceptability.

EFFECTS ON FOREIGN INVESTMENT

Investors have been aware of the SEM since the mid-1980s, and therefore
acted in anticipation of its effects well before 1 January 1993. Since many

---

[11] This may account for 0.5 to 1 point on the industrial country growth rate, and
therefore, at a constant ratio, on aggregate aid flows. Thus 0.5 of the expected 2.5 per cent
growth in aid to Africa (or 1 point of the optimistic estimate, 3–3.5 per cent), may be
attributed to the 1992 impact on growth, in addition to the special factors like tying
already cited.

of the influences and effects are similar to those which arose from the expansion of the EU to include the Southern European economies (Greece, Portugal, and Spain) in the early 1980s, some of the effects which can be identified for the SEM may explain existing trends in the data rather than signal new ones.

The SEM could be affecting investment flows through a variety of routes, acting on both the aggregate and the sectoral influences. Most of the potential aggregate effects appear to be negative. It increases total world growth, increasing total investment, but within this, if successful, it increases the relative growth and attractiveness of the EU. The principal objective of the SEM was to improve the economic performance of the EU by increasing its competitiveness against the rest of the world. It was thus intended explicitly to increase the incentives to trade and invest within the Union relative to all other countries. The mechanisms used for the SEM concentrate on lowering costs, so the costs of supplying this improved market from investment within the EU are reduced, especially in the case of goods for which the location is relatively flexible.

Both through the direct effects and through the widespread dissemination of the 1992 programme within the EU, knowledge of other members' markets is being increased for all companies. The marketing advantages given by such knowledge have thus been improved for investors within the EU compared to those outside.

The increase in total investment demand should, other things being equal, increase the cost of investment in order to induce the required increase in savings: in other words, raise world interest rates. There is a clear recent illustration of how large such an effect can be. The extra demand for German investment funds as a result of the reincorporation of eastern Germany, and the resulting need to finance investment there, occurred at a precisely identifiable point in 1990. In the two quarters which followed, German interest rates rose relative to dollar rates from slightly below in the second quarter of 1990 to a one point premium, and then to a three point premium by the second quarter of 1991. This occurred at a precise time, with a rapid response from capital (and from monetary policy). The more widely spread and gradual effect of a '1992' impact is more difficult to identify, but world investment has been high since the late 1980s, and particularly in the EU. During this period, real interest rates have been high in historic terms, especially in the initial period of recession. Within this, European interest rates, even before German reunification, were relatively high, and they have remained so. The effect of higher interest rates on countries with large debts (and some official debt as well as commercial is linked to market rates) is obvious and severe. For an outstanding African debt at $174 billion (World Bank 1991), the effect of a 1 per cent change in interest rates is of the same order of magnitude as a high estimate of the benefit of untying aid, or of a year's inflow of investment from the EU.

There are some potentially favourable indirect effects. If one reason for relatively low European investment in outward processing and other 'world industry' types of activity in developing countries was that European companies lacked experience in behaving as continental industries, the experience which EU firms gain within Europe could eventually make them better able to compete with US firms at this type of investment. There was a significant expansion in cross-border mergers and other arrangements within the EU (compared with other areas) in the late 1980s (Gittelman, 1990), and informal evidence suggests that it is continuing.

The increase in European income and growth, and any standardization of working conditions within the EU, could increase labour costs there, and thus give EU investors the same type of incentive to transfer production abroad which US firms have had. Against this is the probability that the industries of the 1990s will be different from those of the 1970s and 1980s, and therefore that labour costs will not necessarily be as important a determinant of location. For Africa, they never were an important factor so it has the least to gain.

The advantages of investment to take advantage of particular opportunities will be altered, depending on what happens to demand and alternative supplies within the EU. The effects on trade of the SEM, discussed in Chapter 2, clearly in turn feed back on the prospects for profitable investment in the affected countries. Estimates of the effects on different countries, based principally on their trading patterns and the changes in demand which will result from the SEM, suggest that primary producers, particularly oil producers, will benefit most because they suffer least from trade diversion to other countries in the EU (Davenport and Page, 1991). This suggests that at least some of the African countries may do well, or less badly, relative to the rest of the world. This is, however, likely to reinforce the present pattern of EU investment in Africa, which emphasizes energy at the expense of manufactures. Some of the most recent shifts observed in investment may already reflect this.

Foreign investment into the EU did increase its share in total foreign investment after 1985 (Rutter, 1991); this did not occur in other European countries, and there was a smaller increase to the US. This represented an increase by EU countries themselves, investing in other EU countries; by the US and Japan; and, to a limited extent, by some of the Asian (and other) NICs. The US increase, however, subsequently diminished (Gittelman, 1990), suggesting that it was principally European firms (possibly including US firms already established there) which could reap the advantages of the SEM. The question of interest for Africa is whether any of these flows were or will be at its expense. If it is principally European firms which are affected, this could lower the risk of diversion of non-European firms to Europe, but increase the risk to Africa relative to other developing areas because it suggests that European investors' destinations are more affected than those of other industrial countries. The increase in Japanese investment in Europe suggests that its alternative destinations will also be affected. This will mainly affect Asian countries. It is only NICs with a substantial industrial (and technological) base of their own which have themselves invested in the EU (including Brazil, South Korea, Taiwan and, potentially, India). African investment in the EU has been and remains negligible.

The evidence is difficult to disentangle from the other influences on foreign investment, but, like the arguments, it tends not to support a view that any decline, past or expected, in Africa is a SEM share effect. The fall in investment in Africa (and in developing countries as a whole) predated the SEM programme. Investment has revived there but by less than in Asia and Latin America. Its performance, however, has also revived less, and the local and export prospects remain poor. The political obstacles to investment in South Africa are less great, but economic and political uncertainties remain and growth has not resumed. Most African investment is not in the industries which should be particularly vulnerable to investment and trade diversion (the services and manufactures which can now be obtained more cheaply or more efficiently within the EU), but rather in the primary products, including oil, which should suffer least, or even gain. Exceptions could be found in German investment in North Africa, although there it may be the admission of the Southern European states, rather than the further effects of '1992', which has been important: '1992' could postpone or prevent any move towards manufacturing and other new investment, however, by offering new opportunities in the EU. This delay could be prolonged further by investment in the Eastern European economies as these are restructured. EU investment there is still lower than in Africa. The impetus to growth from the SEM in the EU could increase the contrast between European growth and the slow growth required by structural adjustment programmes in Africa. This would discourage investment related to host country performance, but the effect, as stressed above, could be significant only if these countries had a realistic prospect of attracting inward-looking foreign investment, whatever their policies.

The most important opportunities for increased foreign investment in Africa in recent years have come from quite particular local opportunities, whether from a natural resource or some other unique condition, which a foreign investor could only exploit by making a particular investment in a particular country at a particular time (Page and Riddell, 1989). Clearly more favourable world conditions affect any of these at the margin, but the types of aggregate change expected from the SEM are unlikely to be sufficient to do so. Examples of investment which took place even in the depressed conditions of the early 1980s include many in minerals: gold in Zimbabwe, Guinea and Ghana; diamonds in Botswana, Ghana, Namibia and Zaïre; and oil even in the disrupted conditions of Angola and the Sudan. Other opportunities came from privatization policies or moves out of South Africa. The former are difficult to predict and even more difficult for a country to encourage by creating opportunities. The latter are also difficult to predict. For some Southern African countries, changes resulting from the political changes in South Africa and the eventual reversal of flows out of it could outweigh changes in Europe. Other new investment in Africa has frequently been in agriculture: here the opportunities may come from the new international trade policies after the Uruguay Round or in technological advances, but again are not related directly to economic conditions or policies in either the host or the investing country, and therefore will not be affected by SEM changes.

Conclusion

The discussion in the second section (p. 65) suggested that some of the structural or micro-economic benefits of foreign capital flows were heavily dependent on their form (public or private), their allocation by sector, or their nationality of origin. Given that only some types and sources appear to be readily available to African countries, a strategy of promoting foreign flows must be realistic about what types of benefit can be expected from the sources for which there is a potential supply. If, as has been argued, that supply is predominantly European, frequently from the multilateral organizations, normally in the form of official finance, with private foreign investment normally in the primary sector (especially mining and agriculture), the specific gains which can be hoped for will not include the contributions to technology to be expected, for example, from direct Japanese investment in electronics, or direct US investment in consumer goods for export. Gains will come instead from certain types of public sector expertise and infrastructure provision.

It seems likely that the SEM is having a small effect on direct investment in Africa, compared with either investment in other developing countries or investment in industrial countries, although for a discouraging reason: investment in Africa has been low, and mainly in primary industries for which there was no obvious alternative, so that Africa had little to lose. For UK investment in sub-Saharan Africa, this conclusion is strengthened by the withdrawal which already appears to have occurred in the most vulnerable investments by mobile investors in manufacturing sectors. One area which is still vulnerable could be German investment in North Africa. Both the relatively favourable effects for primary investment and the unfavourable implications for processing, however, could retard Africa's move into more advanced investment and industrial structures. There is also the knowledge and familiarity effect, which means that investors' search for new opportunities has been diverted first to other EU countries, and then to Eastern Europe.

The indirect effects on investment could be important, and probably negative, with the principal one identified being the effect on the cost of capital. This could be balanced by the real increases in trade demand from a higher EU growth, and this balance would apply at country level (the oil exporters are also the most indebted). And even a 100 per cent change in

EU direct investment would only be equivalent to about a 20 per cent change in its official flows to Africa. This suggests that it is official flows on which promotion efforts, and in particular efforts to prevent diversion, should be concentrated.

Current policy preferences by some international organizations, however, present a possible paradox. If they are setting promotion of foreign investment as a criterion for their own lending, and are even encouraged to divert some of their lending to support private sector investment, then promoting private sector investment, however unpromising the evidence may suggest such a policy would be, may become in itself a way of securing greater official finance. Any such policy diversion would be particularly serious for Africa, which combines high dependence on official flows with low immediate appeal to private investors.

Although this is a policy prescription from the multilaterals, not the EU, this problem may serve as an example of one of the risks identified for Africa from the SEM: the increased coordination of EU countries' policies, and thus the reduced freedom to obtain official finance from a variety of (reasonably) independent sources with different criteria. The increased donor coordination within Europe will bring new donors' views to bear on governments which previously had to please only one. Again this risk is increased by Africa's unusually high dependence on official flows. It is also, perhaps, affected by its high share in total EU aid flows. How aid money is used there must be a major concern of any active donor in Europe, as it is of the multilateral agencies following their shift in flows to Africa.

The fact that it was Africa's major donors in the EU which tended not to join in the shift to Africa in the 1980s may also illustrate the risk which stems from being a previously favoured area. More immediately, it is important to ensure that whatever explanations lie behind this shift are not strengthened by the SEM programme. One cause which might be intensified by the SEM is a shift from relying on traditional relationships to determine aid flows.

This is also a factor which could affect changes among African countries. It is the countries which have been most favoured on public sector inflows, and therefore have most to lose, which are most vulnerable. The opportunities from official capital flows arise for countries which have not benefited from 'special relationships' in the past. They can press for any rationalization of flows to be used as an opportunity to increase total flows and the flow to them, and can oppose attempts to cut the total by reducing unjustified flows without using the funds for other development purposes.

As a principal international policy consequence of the SEM is the formation of a large country from 12 small to middle-sized ones, with obvious consequences for its bargaining power, one suitable response would be for present and potential recipients to do the same, although it must be recognized that inevitably there will be conflicts of interest among them. There are, however, informational advantages in exchanging experiences of dealing with different donors which may balance at least some of the competition among potential recipients. (The obvious analogy in the context of this chapter is with the linking among subsidiaries to bargain with head office which is feared by many multinational companies.) On questions like aid-tying, which will increasingly survive only by consent, such links and coordination could have a major impact.

It would be possible for the formation of the SEM to have very little impact, or a small negative one, on African countries. One of these outcomes is likely in the absence of any active response. But there are opportunities to be found in any establishment of new mechanisms. What is important is to identify which types of flow are large and which are most likely to be susceptible to influence. Aid flows from major donors which are changing their aid programmes for both the SEM and other reasons are the obvious first target.

References

African Development Bank (1991), *Annual Report*, Abidjan.

Baldwin, R. (1989), 'On the growth effects of 1992', *Economic Policy*, 9, pp.248–81.

Bank for International Settlements (1991), *International Banking and Financial Market Developments*, Basle, November.

Bennell, Paul (1990), 'British industrial investment in SSA', *Development Policy Review*. 8, 2, pp. 155–77.

Cantwell, John (1988), 'The role of foreign direct investment in development in Africa', paper produced by Department of Economics, University of Reading.

Cecchini, Paolo (1988), *European Economy: The Economics of 1992*, Brussels: European Commission .

Collas-Monsod, S. (1991), 'Report on foreign direct investment and development: a brief survey', paper prepared for an inter-parliamentary conference on Economic Cooperation in the Asia–Pacific Region, January.

Davenport, Michael with Page, Sheila (1991), *Europe: 1992 and the Developing World*. London: Overseas Development Institute.

Germany (1991), (1984) *Statische Beihefte zu den Monatsberichten der Deutschen Bundesbank*.

Gittelman, Michelle (1990), 'Transnational corporations in Europe 1992: implication for developing countries', *The CTC Reporter*, Vol. 29, Spring, pp.35–42.

International Monetary Fund (IMF), *International Financial Statistics*, monthly, and yearbook.

International Monetary Fund (1991a), *International Capital Markets. Developments and Prospects*. Washington, DC.

International Monetary Fund (1991b), *World Economic Outlook October 1991*. Washington, DC.

International Monetary Fund (1992), *World Economic Outlook May 1992*. Washington, DC.

International Monetary Fund (1994a), *International Capital Markets: Developments, Prospects and Policy Issues*. Washington, DC.

International Monetary Fund (1994b), *World Economic Outlook May 1994*. Washington,DC.

Japan (1991), Data from Ministry of Finance, supplied by JETRO.

Langhammer, R.J. (1991), 'Competition among developing countries for foreign investment in the Eighties', *Review of World Economics*, 127, 2, pp.390–403.

Moran, T.H. et al. (1986), *Investing in Development: New Roles for Private Capital?*. New Brunswick and Oxford: Transaction Books.

Netherlands (1991), *Quarterly Bulletin*. De Nederlandsche Bank.

Organization for Economic Cooperation and Development (OECD) (1984), *Geographical Distribution of Financial Flows to Developing Countries: 1980–1983*, Paris.

Organization for Economic Cooperation and Development (1990), *Development Cooperation: 1990 Report*, Paris.

Organization for Economic Cooperation and Development (1994), *Development Cooperation: 1993 Report*, Paris.

Organization for Economic Cooperation and Development (1991a), *Financing and External Debt of Developing Countries: 1990 Survey*. Paris.

Organization for Economic Cooperation and Development (1991b), *Geographical Distribution of Financial Flows to Developing Countries. 1986–89*, Paris.

Page, Sheila (1986), 'Relocating manufacturing in developing countries: opportunities for UK companies', *Economic Working Papers*. London: NEDO.

Page, Sheila (1987), 'The structure of foreign investment: implications of recent changes for Europe and the Third World', in Christopher Stevens and Joan Verloren van Themaat (eds), *Europe and the International Division of Labour*. London: Hodder and Stoughton.

Page, Sheila (1990), *Trade, Finance and Developing Countries: Strategies and Constraints in the 1990s*. London: Harvester Wheatsheaf.

Page, Sheila (1991a), 'Europe 1992: views of developing countries', *The Economic Journal*, 101, November, pp.1553–66.

Page, Sheila (1991b), *Economic Prospects for Developing Countries: Changing Patterns of Industrial Production and Developing Country Trade, the 1991 Forecasts*. London: Overseas Development Institute.

Page, Sheila and Riddell, R.C. (1989), 'FDI in Africa: opportunities and impediments', *The CTC Reporter*, 27, Spring, pp. 6–11, 15.

Rutter, J.W. (1991) 'Trends in international direct investment', Staff Paper No. 91–5, July, US Department of Commerce: International Trade Administration.

Turner, P. (1990), *Foreign direct investment in the developing world: the experience of the 1980s*, Bank for International Settlements, Switzerland.

United Kingdom (1991), (1984) *Overseas Transactions, Business Monitor MA4*, Central Statistical Office, London.

United Nations Conference on Trade and Development (1994), *World Investment Report*. Geneva: UNCTAD.

United States (1991), (1983) *Survey of Current Business*, August, Department of Commerce, Washington, DC.

World Bank (1991a), *Annual Report*, Washington, DC.

World Bank (1991b), *World Debt Tables 1991–92. External Debt of Developing Countries*. Washington, DC. World Bank.

World Bank (1993), *World Debt Tables 1993–94: External Debt of Developing Countries*, Washington, DC.

4

The CFA Franc Devaluation and the Future of Monetary Cooperation in Africa

OLADEJI O. OJO

One of the more enduring legacies of French colonialism in Africa is the CFA franc zone. This is an arrangement whereby a group of independent African states peg their exchange rates at a common level, to the French franc (FF). These African states are grouped in two monetary unions – the Union Monétaire Ouest Africain (UMOA) and the Banque des États d'Afrique Centrale (BEAC).[1] The main features of the unions are the free convertibility of the CFA franc, maintenance of a fixed parity with the French franc, and common management of external reserves. The convertibility of the CFA franc is guaranteed by an operations account, which is an overdraft facility located in the French Treasury. Apart from serving as a reservoir of pooled external reserves, it also absorbs, at the existing exchange rate, whatever supply of CFA francs exists on foreign exchange markets. Until January 1994 when it was devalued by 50 per cent, the parity between the CFA franc and the French franc had been maintained since 1948, despite differences in the structures of the economies of the zone.

The rules of the CFA franc zone are designed to ensure that credit creation and aggregate demand are contained at levels consistent with exchange rate stability and minimum drawings on the operations account facility (Berg and Berlin, 1993: 2). The level of net foreign assets for each zone is taken as the principal target of the central bank. Limits on rediscounting of private sector borrowing and statutory limits on advances to governments are the main instruments used to achieve stability in foreign asset holdings. The maintenance of stable exchange rates within the union requires joint adherence to fiscal and monetary discipline as fiscal or monetary excesses by any one member would have to be financed by the more prudent members.

---

[1] The members of the UMOA are Benin, Burkina Faso, Côte d'Ivoire, Mali, Niger, Senegal and Togo. The members of the BEAC are Cameroon, Chad, the Central African Republic, the Congo, Equatorial Guinea and Gabon.

Since its inception, and in particular since the decade of the 1980s (the so-called decade of adjustment), this monetary arrangement has been subject to critical evaluation. It is not the intention here to go into the benefits and costs of membership of the zone – these are abundantly documented in the literature.[2]

After 1986, however, the economic situation of the African members of the CFA franc zone deteriorated significantly. The strong export expansion which had been the engine of growth during the period 1970–85 declined by more than half between 1986 and 1992. During this period, too, the purchasing power of exports declined by about 5 per cent per year as import prices rose and export earnings declined. Real *per capita* incomes fell while real investment levels fell by the same amount. Thus, on the eve of the devaluation, the countries of the CFA franc zone faced, jointly and individually, serious economic difficulties in the form of declining GDP growth rates, declining and worsening standards of living, and loss of external competitiveness brought about largely by the gross over-valuation of their common currency – the CFA franc. It became obvious that in order to restore these economies to the path of sustained growth, some policy reforms – further-reaching than those hitherto implemented, and this time involving exchange rate adjustment – were inevitable. Thus on 12 January 1994 the parity was changed to FF1= FCFA100, after a period of prolonged negotiation. This chapter discusses some theoretical issues involved in the currency devaluation, and analyses the prospects and strategies for monetary integration in Africa.

The CFA Devaluation: Theory and Empirical Evidence[3]

THE BALANCE OF PAYMENTS

A useful starting point for analysis derives from the view that balance of payments disequilibria are mainly due to overvalued exchange rates which put domestic costs out of line with those of competitors – distorting relative prices and reducing production efficiency. A country faced with such a deficit has two remedies: either to undertake deflationary policies,

[2] J. Boughton, 'The CFA franc zone: currency union and monetary standard', IMF Working Paper, December 1991, and 'The economics of the franc zone', in Paul Masson and Mark Taylor (eds), *Policy Issues in the Operation of Currency Unions* (Cambridge University Press, 1993); E. Elbadawi and N. Majd, 'Fixed parity of the exchange rate and economic performance in the CFA zone', World Bank Working Paper, January 1992; S. Devarajan and J. de Melo, 'Evaluating participation in African monetary unions: a statistical analysis of the CFA zone', in *World Development*, 15, 4 (1987), pp. 483–96; same authors, 'Membership in the CFA zone: Odyssean journey or Trojan horse,' World Bank Working Paper, August 1990; S. Devarajan and D. Roderik, 'Do the benefits of fixed exchange rates outweigh their costs: the franc zone in Africa', World Bank Working Paper, October 1991; P. and S. Guillaumont, 'Participating in African monetary unions: an alternative evaluation,' *World Development*, 16, 5 (1988), pp. 569–70.
[3] This section on theory (pp. 112–17) is drawn from unpublished internal documents of the Bank.

and/or to devalue its currency. The economic logic of contemporary balance of payments adjustment theories tends to favour the second remedy. This is not only because deflationary policies are viewed as costly in terms of output and employment losses, but mainly because of the downward rigidity of prices which undermines the effectiveness of deflationary policies. The situation may be corrected by currency devaluation supported by strong anti-inflationary demand management policies.

The CFA devaluation is expected to increase the demand for the devaluing country's exports and to decrease the demand for imports, with the aim of improving the balance of payments. It is expected to do this by causing an initial deterioration in the terms of trade (an increase in the price of imports relative to the price of exports). A positive impact on the balance of payments depends on whether the increase in the volume of exports is sufficient to outweigh the devaluation-induced deterioration in the terms of trade. On the supply side, exchange rate depreciation is expected to work on the balance of payments predominantly through encouraging the production of exportables and increasing the supply of exports. Whether viewed from the demand or supply side, the extent to which the conditions for a positive devaluation impact on the balance of payments are met by CFA countries is an empirical question. Nevertheless, some inferences might be drawn with reference to the inflationary mechanism in the franc zone and to the structures of exports and imports. The reference to the inflationary mechanism in the Franc-zone is important because if, following devaluation, all prices were to increase by the same amount as the devaluation, the price incentive which the devaluation was designed to achieve would be nullified. Consequently, the expected effect of devaluation on export and import volumes would not materialize; and what would remain of devaluation would be its adverse impact on income distribution via the devaluation-induced inflation. This points to the paramount importance of the supporting fiscal and monetary policies to the success of the CFA devaluation. The reference to the structures (including marketing arrangements) of exports and imports is also important because it determines the possible supply/demand responses to the devaluation.

The final outcome on the balance of payments would depend not only on total export earnings but also on total expenditure on imports. In this respect, the larger the share of imported raw materials, capital and necessary consumer goods (fuel and medicine, for example) in the total import bill, the smaller the reduction would be in the demand for imports, indicating a small elasticity of demand for imports. In general, the larger the total demand elasticities of imports, more positive the impact of devaluation would be on the balance of payments. Conversely, the smaller these elasticities, the more negative the effect of devaluation would be.

PRODUCTION AND SUPPLY RESPONSES

A devaluation generally raises the domestic currency price of imports and exports. On the side of imports, the effect is similar to that of a uniform tariff, whereas on the side of exports it is similar to a uniform subsidy, reducing their foreign currency value. It follows that, after a devaluation, those industries producing tradables are likely to become more profitable relative to those industries producing non-tradables. This change in relative profitability should lead eventually to the shift of resources into those sectors that produce tradables. Similarly, the higher prices of tradables will cause the pattern of domestic spending to shift away from tradables, thus inducing a cut in imports and making more goods available for export.

It is, however, important to bear in mind the following qualifications. Devaluation is likely to encourage excess demand for non-tradables and, hence, domestic inflation that may negate its initial favourable effect on the balance of payments. For the positive effect to dominate, therefore, there must be a fall in real expenditure unless there is initially excess capacity and unemployment, as is apparently the case in most CFA zone countries. Also, if the higher domestic prices of tradables brought about by the devaluation cause wages to rise, so as to compensate for the higher prices, then the favourable switching of production and consumption will be negated.

In the case where devaluation is effective in switching expenditure (that is not offset by wage and other inflation), it is likely to bring about an expansion of the production of import-competing goods. In other words, because of its protective effect, the devaluation could induce an expansion of the import-substitution sector. Similarly, devaluation will make the export sector more profitable. In this context, it is important to stress that devaluation endeavours to protect the tradable sector (whether agriculture or industry) relative to the non-tradable sector. This is a desired outcome in that it is supportive of an expansion in overall domestic production. In a situation where the economy is operating below capacity because of lack of demand, a devaluation might increase output by making tradables more profitable and by raising demand for non-tradables through the switching effect.

In a situation where the domestic economy is a leading producer of an export item, devaluation may induce an expansion of the production of this item as a result of the improvement in returns on the foreign exchange. Assuming that the demand of this export item is inelastic, as is the case of cocoa in Côte d'Ivoire, this is likely to lead to a deterioration in the terms of trade. To be effective, the devaluation thus has to be implemented in the context of the broad macro-economic policy framework. Where, for instance, the local content of intermediate inputs in the production process is very low or, alternatively, the foreign content is very high, devaluation could be accompanied by exemptions of imported inputs from import duties to encourage domestic production. Similarly where the domestic factor costs are high – as is the case with energy, tele-communications, wages and other costs in Côte d'Ivoire, for example – devaluation may need to be coupled with factor cost reduction measures and fiscal and other incentives.

SOME FISCAL IMPLICATIONS

The impact of devaluation on fiscal operations emanates directly from the devaluation-supporting measures and indirectly from the devaluation-induced inflation. Devaluation is usually accompanied by government expenditure ceilings, the purpose of which is to curb aggregate demand and hence, together with other measures, prevent inflation from eroding the price incentive of devaluation. Given the important role of government, the deflationary impact on output can be quite serious.

As the government is also a consumer of imported and local goods and services, government expenditures in the CFA zone will be affected by the inflation-induced devaluation, causing it to rise, as domestic prices of imported and local goods rise. If the expenditure ceilings are effective in containing such a nominal increase, the effect will be reflected in reductions in real government expenditure. Normally such ceilings are aggregate figures, however, and avoid specification of the items of expenditure that are to be curtailed. It has been observed that many African countries satisfy such ceilings, at the expense of budgetary allocations to education, health and wages. Under such circumstances, human disinvestment usually occurs, undermining the very long-run growth stimulus which devaluation is designed to achieve.

On the revenue side, inflation tends to widen the tax base, as nominal incomes rise, and redistributes income from the general public to the government through the inflationary tax and to public enterprises through price increases. The extent to which government revenue will increase as a result of devaluation depends, however, on the nominal income elasticity of tax and on the length of the time lag in tax collection. In most African countries, and the CFA zone is no exception, the nominal income tax elasticity is observed to be less than unity, indicating that tax revenue will rise by less than the devaluation-induced increase in nominal incomes. Also, there are long time lags in tax collection, due to inefficiencies in tax systems or tax evasion, which erode the real value of the collected revenue in the face of inflation.

THE IMPACT ON INFLATION

The devaluation of the CFA will raise consumer prices directly through higher local-currency costs of imported consumer goods. Indirectly, it will raise the local-currency cost of intermediate and capital goods to local producers and generate a round-effect between money wages and prices, on the one hand, and government expenditure and prices, on the other. These round-effects might spill over into government operations, causing an increase in the government deficit and hence the money supply. The question at stake is whether or not these effects are likely to initiate an inflationary process which will not only nullify the effect of devaluation but exceed that to produce an 'explosive' devaluation.

The actual impact of the devaluation of the CFA on prices depends on many factors, including the wage-price response to devaluation, the weight of imported goods in the Consumer Price Index, the import content of exports and import substitutes, the effect of devaluation on government expenditure relative to government revenue, the effectiveness of monetary and fiscal policies, and whether France will continue to uphold the convertibility of the CFA. Related to all these is the question of whether devaluation will create an inflationary mechanism driven by inflation psychology, with speculative and parallel market dealings in trade goods and in foreign currency.

Although these are essentially empirical issues, inferences drawn from the devaluation experiences of other African countries would suggest that in a majority of cases devaluation in African countries has been associated with unchanged or reduced inflation rates (at various times in Ethiopia, Nigeria, Tanzania and Uganda, for example). In most cases devaluations are only partially eroded by resulting inflation, which preserves the usefulness of the exchange rate as a policy instrument. Where devaluations have been neutralized by rapid inflation, as in Sierra Leone and Sudan, these have been accompanied by expansionary macro-economic policies. In view of the mechanisms they incorporate for fiscal and monetary control, which give CFA countries a superior anti-inflation record, the partial erosion of the price incentive of devaluation is more likely to be the case for CFA countries.

THE IMPACT ON INCOME DISTRIBUTION

Income distribution effects are caused by both currency devaluation and its supporting demand management policies. The devaluation-induced inflation is likely to redistribute income from those who have a higher marginal propensity to consume to those who have a higher marginal propensity to save (that is, generally at the expense of wages and in favour of profits). The supporting policies are expected to have additional distributional effects. The elements that give rise to these distributional effects can be classified into:

1 those resulting from measures which directly affect particular group activities, such as the abolition of subsidies, increases in taxes, the dismantling of price controls and control of wages; and

2 those which come indirectly, as a result of the curtailment of bank credit and the devaluation-induced inflation.

There is also a 'real money balance effect' which works to reduce aggregate demand. This effect is caused by the devaluation-induced inflation and results from the desire of some people to hold a constant proportion of their wealth in the form of real money balances. As the devaluation-induced inflation erodes the value of their real money balances, people will tend to hold more nominal balances to keep their real balances intact, which they do by reducing expenditure out of real income. The effect on output and employment would be deflationary.

THE EMPIRICAL EVIDENCE

It is perhaps too premature – partly because of data limitations and partly because of the time horizon involved – to assess the impact of the CFA franc devaluation and the policy reforms which accompanied it on the economies of the zone. But available indicators point to some favourable developments. The soaring inflation which was anticipated did not materialize and the annual inflation rate in 1994 averaged no more than 27 per cent (Table 4.1). The GDP grew, on average, by about 1 per cent, up from 0.2 per cent during 1990–3. The forecast for 1995 is that the GDP growth rate could be as high as 5 per cent. Import growth rate declined by 2.1 per cent while exports grew marginally from 9.7 per cent during 1990–3 to 10.9 per cent in 1994. External competitiveness, as measured by the real effective exchange rate, improved. During the first nine months of 1994, the CFA franc depreciated by about 33 per cent in real effective terms (Clement, 1995: 26).

TABLE 4.1
Selected economic indicators for CFA zone countries, 1985–94*

Economic indicator	1985–9	1990–3	1994
1 GDP (% growth rate)	0.2	−0.2	1.0
2 CPI (% growth rate)	1.4	−0.3	27.4
3 Budget deficits (as % of GDP)	4.8	6.4	6.1
4 Value of exports (% growth rate)	2.3	9.7	10.9
5 Value of imports (% growth rate)	5.8	8.7	−2.1
6 Money supply (M2) (% growth rate)	2.3	−2.5	31.5
7 Current account balance ($m)	−13,534	−11,971	−2,128
8 Balance of payments (overall) ($m)	−8,380	−13,870	−385

* Excluding Comoros
Sources: National sources, IMF International Financial Statistics and ADB Statistics Division estimates.

There is evidence that private capital which had fled prior to devaluation returned on a grand scale. For example, deposits in banks in Gabon, Côte d'Ivoire and Cameroon increased by 28 per cent to $2.7 billion in the first eight months of 1994. Services, such as tourism, have flourished by capitalizing on lower local prices. Perhaps much more encouraging, from the standpoint of regional cooperation, is that inter-regional trade has increased as import prices have soared. For example, in Côte d'Ivoire South–South trade is estimated to have grown by about 35 per cent in 1994. There is also evidence that the trade of the zone is being diversified gradually away from France.

These aggregate economic indicators mask variations across countries. Some countries have performed better than others. For example, Côte d'Ivoire is credited with the best performance (*The Economist* Intelligence Unit, April 1995). In 1994, consumer inflation averaged 32.5 per cent, well below the 35 per cent target set for 1994. The government expects this to level to single-digit in 1996. Wage pressures, which were expected in the wake of the devaluation, were contained by limiting the minimum wage hike set by the government to 10 per cent. Top public sector wage earners were restricted to 5 per cent, while lower wage earners received awards of up to 24 per cent to cushion the effect of rising consumer prices. In the case of essential services such as water and electricity, price freezes were imposed.

The GDP rose by nearly 2 per cent, while revenues and incomes have improved substantially. The devaluation has doubled the CFA franc-denominated value of earnings from agricultural exports, allowing the government to boost payments to farmers by 21–30 per cent. In the first half of 1994, there was a primary surplus (before interest payments) of some CFA102 billion. The return of flight capital and increased exports boosted market liquidity and, with inflation slowing down, the central bank was able to cut its discount rate from 14 to 12.5 and then to 10 per cent. The overall balance of payments registered a surplus of CFA120 billion, as against a deficit of CFA100 million in 1993. The country's external reserves increased to CFA390 billion in the first half of the year.

Overall, the trend is towards improvement in the performance of the CFA franc zone countries during the post-devaluation era, and this is best achieved within the context of African economic integration. Thus, the challenge before these countries is to consolidate the gains of the devaluation, and with other countries of the continent to examine how the coordination of economic policies (which existence of a common currency entails) could be used to advance the cause of African economic integration.

The Future of Monetary Integration in Africa

In the aftermath of the CFA franc devaluation, a fundamental question has arisen concerning the future of the entire monetary arrangement. Specifically, some commentators have wondered whether the interests of the participating African countries would not be served better by pursuing independent monetary and exchange rate policies, with each country having its own monetary authority, currency and administrative apparatus. Some observers have even revived the notion of an African Monetary Fund (AMF) that could provide balance of payments support for African countries along the lines of the International Monetary Fund (IMF).

As regards the first question, observers have noted that the change in the CFA exchange rate still implies a fixed value against the French franc. This means that the movement of the CFA franc against other currencies will continue to be determined by the movement of the French franc *vis-à-vis* other currencies. This further means that French monetary, fiscal and commercial policy will continue to determine the relationship between the CFA franc and other currencies. It is doubtful if the loss of control over monetary and exchange rate policies (which the arrangement implies) is the most desirable policy choice. This is because the arrangement continues to limit the freedom of those countries who may wish to explore trading opportunities outside France, particularly those in Africa. In addition, the continued fixed parity amounts to a lost opportunity to bring the currency into the new world of floating exchange arrangements of which many African countries are now a part. Had the currency been allowed to float, as a common currency or individual national currencies, with the guarantee of convertibility by France, a CFA zone Exchange Rate Mechanism similar to the European Exchange Rate Mechanism probably would have emerged. The developmental impact of the devaluation would have been enhanced, and, in addition, the rest of Africa would have found it easier to use such a mechanism as a basis for continental monetary cooperation.

With regard to an AMF which would be capable of providing balance of payments and exchange rate support, it will be recalled that the African Council of Ministers has examined this proposal before and found it unworkable. For one thing, a monetary fund in the context of the present negative balance of payments facing the vast majority of African countries is unlikely to be feasible. For another, it is unlikely that the required resources for establishing and operating such an institution would ever be mobilized. The question of monetary integration as envisaged by the Abuja Treaty remains unanswered, however, and is addressed in the rest of this chapter.

The rationale for integration is rooted in the view that countries participating in it could reap economies of scale (through cost reduction) and thereby enhance GDP growth. In the case of Africa, the argument for integration is further reinforced by the similar size of most economies – only five of 53 countries have populations of more than 30 million; 36 countries have populations of less than 10 million each; 15 are landlocked; and seven are small-island countries. Similarly, about 35 countries have a *per capita* income of less than US$500; another ten of between US$500 and US$1000; and only seven countries have a *per capita* income of more than US$1000 to support either modern industries of optional size or greater diversification of products and services. By contrast, an integrated African regional economy, with a potential market of over 600 million people, offers better investment and growth opportunities than fragmented and fragile national economies.

This general rationale for economic integration must have influenced African heads of state and governments when, in 1981, they adopted the

Lagos Plan of Action. In that declaration they called for African economic integration and directed that sub-regional blocs be established as a first step towards the eventual integration of the African economies. Since then, sub-regional economic institutions have been established in all the sub-regions of the continent.

Virtually all the sub-regional integration institutions see their mandate in terms of the development of intra-African trade. As a consequence, they have adopted the removal of institutional and other barriers to trade as their principal strategy. In spite of the various tariff reduction measures, however, intra-African trade has remained distressingly low at about 5 per cent of total trade. Many factors are said to account for this phenomenon. They include the inconvertibility of national currencies and inconsistent monetary, exchange rate and tax policies, including price policies (Ojo, 1988). All these have combined to reduce recorded intra-African trade, while correspondingly making unrecorded (illegal) transactions attractive. If a monetary union existed, it is argued, it would be capable of harmonizing various national economic policies, ensuring the convertibility of national currencies and thus enhancing the growth of recorded trade (Ojo, 1988).

Some form of monetary integration is usually recommended for a group or groups of countries which have made significant progress towards the integration of the real economy. Such countries must have achieved a substantial reduction in exchange rate variability and a high degree of convergence towards cost and price stability. This is far from being the case in Africa. Apart from the absence of convergence in policies, the economies are characterized by low intra-regional trade, external trade dependence, limited cross-border flows of capital, small market size and large disparities in the levels of income and development. Such countries obviously constitute neither optimal trade blocs nor optimal currency areas as defined by Mundell (Mundell, 1961) and others. In terms of orthodox theory no region of Africa, with the possible exception of the Common Monetary Area (CMA) comprising the Republic of South Africa, Lesotho, Swaziland and Namibia, would qualify as an optimal currency area. Monetary union in its pure orthodox form, therefore, should be ruled out of the question.

But a review of recent developments tends to modify this assertion. In many of the sub-regional integration schemes on the continent, tremendous progress is being made in the promotion of intra-community trade. In the Economic Community of West African States (ECOWAS), for example, a comprehensive trade liberalization scheme has been approved. Freedom of people and rights of residence are also guaranteed. In the Preferential Trade Area of Eastern and Southern Africa (PTA) progress has also been made towards trade liberalization. The PTA also has a travellers' cheque facility and a development bank. In the CFA zone countries, intra-community trade has expanded considerably, largely because of the use of a common currency. The zone has also enjoyed, until recently, relatively good economic performance and macro-economic stability. Similar experiences can be documented in other sub-regions of the continent. These developments tend to suggest some scope for monetary integration as an instrument for further advancing the integration of the real economy. Thus African monetary integration, which should theoretically follow the integration of the real economy, should be seen as a means of reinforcing the integration process that is already under way, and of ensuring macro-economic stability.

This view is being reinforced currently by the wave of the 'new regionalism' (Cobham and Robson, 1993). This new regionalism – which is taking place in the context of widespread reform which emphasizes trade liberalization and outward-oriented policies – is redirecting the attention of policy makers and analysts away from the orthodox domains of integration and towards the broader benefits that were hitherto not central to their concerns. These benefits require that the viability of a currency area be judged, not strictly on the criteria defined in the litera-ture, but, rather, on other criteria like the imperatives of macro-economic stability. It will be recalled that the relative price stability of the CFA franc zone has been attributed largely to the existence of the monetary union and the monetary and fiscal discipline which accompanies it.

Monetary integration, in all its forms, involves fixed exchange rates and full convertibility among the currencies concerned. But a distinction ought to be made between several types of monetary union – the informal exchange rate union, the formal exchange rate union and the full monetary union. Whereas the formal exchange rate union has a central agency coordinating the national central banks, and a monetary union has a single currency and a single central bank, the informal union does not have an adequate mechanism for policy coordination.

In the Abuja Treaty, African heads of state and governments have opted for a monetary union.[4] This option has several advantages. There would be improvements in domestic and international resource allocation. There would also be savings from the pooling of foreign exchange reserves. There would be reduction in transaction costs derived from replacing the various national currencies with a single currency. An additional benefit would accrue from the elimination of uncertainty normally associated with exchange rate movements. The coordination of economic policy which a monetary union entails would permit the centralization of investment decisions, and decisions about the exploitation of resources, such that the present uncomplementary production structures of the economies could be eliminated gradually. Finally, by restricting the option of issuing currency for the purpose of financing fiscal deficit, a monetary union would eliminate one of the sources of inflation on the continent as it would transfer monetary policy to an independent central bank regulated not merely by a single government, but by a number of

[4] See Annex 1.

governments bound together by a treaty (Ojo, 1988).

Against these benefits, one must balance the costs of a monetary union. These include the loss of the exchange rate as an instrument of adjustment by individual member countries, the initial cost of adjustment (mostly deflation) required to enter a monetary union, and the loss of seigniorage and inflation-tax revenue. On balance, however, the benefits of a monetary union would tend to outweigh the costs. Whether those net benefits, in the African case, would come close to the benefits of a monetary union in, say, Europe is a different question. Given the present structure of African economies, the benefits may be minimal, but if the criteria for evaluating a monetary union are widened to include the attainment of macro-economic stability and eventual GDP growth, then a monetary union as envisaged by the Abuja Treaty may be a desirable goal.

If a monetary union is the ultimate goal, the question of institutional arrangements remains unanswered. Where a political decision has been made to have a monetary union,

> monetary unification requires two stages: a preparatory period during which fiscal policy in each country is stabilized, the existing currencies are made convertible, the union-level central bank is established and the transformation of the existing national central banks into subordinate agencies is prepared; and a subsequent transitional period during which the old currencies would be phased out and the new one phased in, with monetary responsibility transferred to the new union-level central bank (Cobham and Robson, 1993: 10).

In the case of Africa, with its 40 or so currencies, it may be more desirable, operationally, to choose five or six of the sub-regional economic communities as building blocs for monetary integration. Each community should be required to take adjustment and convergence measures necessary to achieving monetary integration. When the stage is set for continental monetary integration, one would be dealing with convergence and adjustment issues among five or six (rather than upwards of 40) currencies. Here the advantage of retaining the two monetary unions of the CFA franc zone becomes evident. The two unions already have an elaborate institutional monetary arrangement and a culture of monetary discipline which could form the backbone of a future monetary union.

The timetable for achieving monetary integration is also important. Cobham and Robson have suggested five years, which they consider reasonable when viewed against the lifespan of a structural adjustment programme of the kind most African countries are implementing. The attainment of a monetary union in Africa falls within the sixth phase of the Abuja Treaty (see Annex). In that phase, a period of five years has been allocated to the establishment of a full monetary union. The Treaty is silent, however, on the institutional arrangements for the union: presumably these would be worked out as the integration process proceeds. It bears mentioning that if the monetary union is eventually established there would be a single currency, a single central bank and a single exchange rate. What is less certain is the relationship (if any) which the single currency would have with other leading world currencies. Will it be pegged to a particular currency or a basket of currencies? Or will it be autonomous?

If the objective of the monetary union is to enhance the integration of the real economy and contribute to macro-economic stability, there is an obvious need for a strong and independent central bank which would be capable of removing monetary policy from the hands of politicians. If such a central bank could be established, it would be a most desirable step as it would guarantee African control over monetary and exchange rate policies. As of now, none of the central banks on the continent can lay claim to the type of independence required to run the monetary union.

In the absence of such a central bank, Africa could consider the option of pegging its currency to another currency or basket of currencies. The choice of a peg is not a particularly easy exercise. In recent years, however, the choice of an optimal peg has been determined largely by the direction and volume of trade of a country, and by the currency composition of its external reserves, among other things. On the basis of these criteria, some commentators (Cobham and Robson) have proposed that since the CFA franc/French franc arrangement has worked well particularly in guaranteeing macro-economic stability, it could be extended to the rest of Africa, albeit with some modifications. The modification being proposed is that partly because of the move towards European monetary integration (of which France is a part), and partly because of the diversification of African trade to other countries of Europe, the appropriate peg could be the European Currency Unit (ECU), which is likelier to emerge as Europe's currency than the French franc. Under this kind of arrangement, it is hoped that greater independence and credibility might be gained with this 'extra-African' involvement (Cobham and Robson, 1993: 13).

Several advantages are expected to derive from this arrangement. To start with, an ECU peg is likely to be close to the optimal peg for most African countries. Secondly, the ECU could be expected to generate low inflation over the medium term as this is a requirement under the Maastricht Treaty (which establishes the European monetary and economic union). Furthermore, a peg to the ECU could be simple and transparent, and at the same time guarantee EU support necessary to compensate for any deviation from the optimal in the cases of a few individual countries (Cobham and Robson, 1993: 18).

The major argument against this kind of arrangement is largely political and to some extent economic. On political grounds, an ECU peg would amount to a return to the colonial era during which Europe held sway in Africa. The control over the determination of money supply by a European central bank, which an ECU peg would imply, would amount to loss of sovereignty and political independence. It may be recalled that control over national currency has always been viewed as a symbol of political independence. On economic grounds, an ECU peg would carry with it loss of control over monetary and exchange rate policies, leaving the countries effectively with only one weapon – fiscal policy. From the standpoint of the theory of economic policy (Mundell, 1961), this would tend to violate the principles governing the assignment of policy instruments to policy problems, and would therefore be less than optimal.

In addition to this major criticism, there are others which run very much along the lines of those levelled against the CFA franc zone and the currency boards of the former British colonies. The CFA zone and the currency boards, it is argued, did not provide opportunity (for Africans) to acquire experience in monetary management. Secondly, the currency boards in particular imposed a burden on the former colonial economies through the maintenance of a buffer stock of sterling reserves. This burden derived from the permanent immobilization of a large part of a country's foreign exchange reserves which the system entailed (Ajayi and Ojo, 1981: 78).

Perhaps a much more beneficial arrangement is a peg to a broader basket of currencies, where the weight of each currency in the basket is determined by the relative share of the country (owing the currency) in the total external trade of Africa, and the currency composition of external reserves, among other things. This has the advantage of including two of the world's leading currencies – the US dollar and the Japanese yen – along with the ECU in the basket. A peg to a basket of currencies has the advantage that the continental central bank would also be able to conduct an active exchange rate policy. In a world of generalized floating, it would be the responsibility of the central bank to select an optimal basket of currencies against which to peg. The rule governing such a choice could be determined, for example, by the method suggested by Lipschitz and Sundararajan (1980). This rule assigns weights to the currencies in the basket, in order to minimize variations of the real exchange rate around its equilibrium level over some reference period, and ensures that the mean value of the real exchange rate remains close to its equilibrium level over the same period. This rule has the advantage of guaranteeing the stability of the real exchange rate under conditions of generalized floating of exchange rates.

This arrangement has several other advantages over an ECU peg. First, the establishment of a strong and independent central bank, which would accompany a monetary union, would imply full control by that central bank over money supply and monetary policy. Secondly, a peg to a basket of currencies would overcome the political and economic arguments against an ECU peg, and it would at the same time, guarantee African control over monetary and exchange rate policies. The only disadvantage would be the loss of control over monetary matters by individual countries, but this may well be the price for monetary stability on the continent.

An African central bank which would be capable of neutralizing the influence of individual national governments may be difficult to establish and manage in the present political atmosphere. But then, this may well be one of the many challenges which Africa has to address in its quest for economic integration and accelerated development. Needless to say, detailed studies would be required on the nature of the monetary union, including the powers of the central bank, the suitability of the alternative forms of external anchor, and the other various issues relating to monetary integration before a formal decision can be made on an African monetary union.

Conclusions

The combination of the devaluation of the CFA and the movement towards a monetary union has exposed the fragility of the CFA franc monetary arrangement. A source of stability in the past, the arrangement has entered a phase where its efficacy is being called into question. For example, it is not clear if France would be willing or able to provide the necessary financial accommodation required for the system to continue to function properly. This uncertainty creates the opportunity to use the experience and the institutional framework provided by the monetary arrangement partially as a basis for wider monetary integration in Africa. Although Africa is not yet close to monetary union, as it pursues that objective it needs to reflect on the appropriate form of monetary integration. This chapter has offered a proposal – full monetary union, with a continental central bank and a continental currency pegged to a basket of key international currencies. The modalities of this or any other arrangements would, need to be carefully studied, of course, before an eventual decision is taken.

Chapter 4 ANNEX

• •

Modalities for the Establishment of the Community

1 The Community shall be established gradually in six (6) stages of variable duration over a transitional period not exceeding thirty-four (34) years.

2 At each such stage, specific activities shall be assigned and implemented concurrently as follows:

a) *First Stage:* Strengthening of existing regional economic communities and, within a period not exceeding five (5) years from the date of entry into force of this Treaty, establishing economic communities in regions where they do not exist;

b) *Second Stage:*

(i) at the level of each regional economic community and within a period, not exceeding eight (8) years, stabilizing Tariff Barriers and Non-Tariff Barriers, Customs Duties and internal taxes existing at the date of entry into force of this Treaty; there shall also be prepared and adopted studies to determine the time-table for the gradual removal of Tariff Barriers and Non-Tariff Barriers to regional and intra-community trade and for the gradual harmonization of Customs Duties in relation to third States;

(ii) strengthening of sectoral integration at the regional and continental levels in all areas of activity particularly in the fields of trade, agriculture, money and finance, transport and communications, industry and energy; and

(iii) coordination and harmonization of activities among the existing and future economic communities.

c) *Third Stage:* At the level of each regional economic community, and within a period not exceeding ten (10) years, establishment of a Free Trade Area through the observance of the time-table for the gradual removal of Tariff Barriers and Non-Tariff Barriers to intra-community trade and the establishment of a Customs Union by means of adopting of a common external tariff.

d) *Fourth Stage:* Within a period not exceeding two (2) years, co-ordination and harmonization of tariff and non-tariff systems among the various regional economic communities with a view to establishing a Customs Union at the continental level by means of adopting of a common external tariff.

e) *Fifth Stage:* Within a period not exceeding four (4) years, establishment of an African Common Market through:

(i) the adoption of a common policy in several areas such as agriculture, transport and communications, industry, energy, and scientific research;

(ii) the harmonization of monetary, financial and fiscal policies;

(iii) the application of the principle of free movement of persons as well as the provisions herein regarding the rights of residence and establishment; and

(iv) constituting the proper resources of the Community as provided for in paragraph 2 of Article 82 of this Treaty.

f) *Sixth Stage:* Within a period not exceeding five (5) years:

(i) consolidation and strengthening of the structure of the African Common Market, through including the free movement of people, goods, capital and services, as well as, the provisions herein regarding the rights of residence and establishment;

(ii) integration of all the sectors namely economic, political, social and cultural; establishment of a single domestic market and a Pan-African Economic and Monetary Union;

(iii) implementation of the final stage for the setting up of an African Monetary Union, the establishment of a single African Central Bank and the creation of a single African Currency;

(iv) implementation of the final stage for the setting up of the structure of the Pan-African Parliament and election of its members by continental universal suffrage;

(v) implementation of the final stage for the harmonization and coordination process of the activities of regional economic communities;

(vi) implementation of the final stage for the setting up of the structures of African multi-national enterprises in all sectors; and

(vii) implementation of the final stage for the setting up of the structures of the executive organs of the Community.

3 All measures envisaged under this Treaty for the promotion of a harmonious and balanced development among Member States, particularly, those relating to the formulation of multi-national projects and programmes, shall be implemented concurrently within the time period specified for the attainment of the objectives of the various stages outlined in paragraph 2 of this Article.

4   The transition from one stage to another shall be determined when the specific objectives set in this Treaty or pronounced by the Assembly for a particular stage, are implemented and all commitments fulfilled. The Assembly, on the recommendation of the Council, shall confirm that the objectives assigned to a particular stage have been attained and shall approve the transition to the next stage.

5   Notwithstanding the provisions of the preceding paragraph, the cumulative transitional period shall not exceed forty (40) years from the date of entry into force of this Treaty.

References

Ajayi, S.I. and O.O. Ojo (1981), *Money and Banking*, George Allen and Unwin, London.

Berg, Elliot and Philip Berlin (1993), *Exchange Rate Issues in the African Countries of the Franc Zone*, Development Alternatives Inc. USA.

Clément, J.A.P. (1995) 'Aftermath of the CFA franc devaluation' *Finance and Development*, June 1995.

Cobham David and P. Robson (1993) 'Monetary integration in Africa: a deliberately European perspective'. Mimeo, University of St. Andrews.

De Cecco M. and A. Giovannini (eds) (1989) *A European Central Bank?* Cambridge University Press, New York.

The Economist Intelligence Unit, (1995), *Business Africa*, London.

Frimpong-Ansah, J.H. (1984), *Report on Proposals for an ECOWAS Monetary Zone*. ECOWAS Lagos.

Lipschitz, L. and V. Sundararajan (1980), 'The optimal basket in a world of generalized floating' IMF Staff Papers, 27, 1, March.

McKinnon, R.I. (1963) 'Optimum currency areas' *American Economic Review*, September.

Mundell, R.A. (1961) 'A theory of optimum currency areas' *American Economic Review*, September.

Nana-Sinkam, Samuel (1978), *Monetary Integration and the Theory of Optimum Currency Area in Africa*, Marton Publishers, New York.

Ojo, O.O. (1988) 'Monetary and other financial obstacles to intra-African trade' *Nigerian Journal of Economic and Social Studies*, 30, 1, March.

5

Recent Changes in the Former Soviet Union and Eastern Europe: Opportunities and Challenges for Africa

OLADEJI O. OJO
CHRISTOPHER STEVENS

In addition to the movement towards greater integration in Western Europe, embodied in the Single European Act, another major development in Europe is the collapse of the former Soviet Union as a political and economic power. The collapse has permitted the unification of East and Western Germany and the emergence, in the place of the Soviet Union, of successor states loosely referred to as the Commonwealth of Independent States (CIS), comprising the Russian Federation and eleven other republics. In Eastern Europe, the following countries hitherto under the control of the Soviet Union have emerged as independent and democratic states: Bulgaria, the Czech Republic, Hungary, Poland, Romania, the Russian Federation, Slovakia, and the former Yugoslavia. Until the collapse of the Soviet Union, these countries were organized into a monolithic economic and political relationship called the Council for Mutual Economic Assistance (CMEA) with the Soviet Union at its apex. The aim of this chapter is to describe briefly the events that led to the collapse of this economic and political arrangement, and the economic opportunities and challenges which that collapse could make available to Africa.

Eastern Europe: Economic and Political Background

The end of the Second World War saw the Soviet Union impose its rule on those states of Eastern Europe which it overran in its march against Germany. Economically, these states were bonded together in a Soviet Union-dominated bloc generally referred to as the Council for Mutual Economic Assistance. The Soviet Union also imposed its economic doctrine of central planning on these states. This ideology relied on state apparatus for regulating the economy. Politically, one-party rule – the Communist Party – was also imposed by the Soviet Union. As these regimes were not democratically elected, they were sustained in power by the military might of the Soviet Union.

The year 1985 was a watershed in the history of the Soviet Union and, in retrospect, of the world. In that year, the Soviet Communist Party had been in power continuously for nearly seven decades. The year 1985 also marked the conclusion of the eleventh of the series of five-year plans which the government had initiated in 1928. Rather than having surpassed the economy of the United States, as envisaged under these plans, the Soviet economy was in great difficulty in 1985. According to official figures, the average annual rate of net material product (NMP) of members of the CMEA declined from 9.6 per cent in the 1950s to 6.7 per cent in the 1970s, and to 3 per cent during 1981–8 (Wolf, 1991: 46). In 1985 *per capita* consumption of the Soviet Union was 28.6 per cent of the United States and somewhat below that of Portugal (Bergson, 1991: 30). Portugal had the lowest *per capita* consumption among all the OECD countries except Turkey. Ericson (1991: 88) also estimated that Soviet output *per capita* in 1985 was about 28 per cent of the United States.

While the strategy of extensive economic development on the basis of centrally directed mobilization of resources permitted the centrally planned economies to achieve relatively high rates of growth in the early years of planning, over time the scope for further rapid growth on this basis diminished. Structural problems surfaced, further casting doubt on the capacity of the planning apparatus to direct an increasingly complex economy. In 1985 it became obvious to Mikhail Gorbachev, then Soviet President, that the system of centralized planning was limiting economic performance. Similarly, Communist ideological and political constraints on free and full participation of the people in the development process were also limiting the performance of the Soviet economy. In an attempt to shake off these constraints, Gorbachev in April 1985 announced his plans for reform at a meeting of the Communist Party. The new strategies for economic and social transformation were summed up in *perestroika* (restructuring), *glasnost* (openness) and *uskorenie* (acceleration). By these new strategies, the Soviet economy was to be restructured along market lines; the society was to be democratized and opened up, and economic and social progress was to be accelerated.

The process of reform inside the Soviet Union set the stage for similar demands in the Soviet-dominated states. The wave of reforms inside the Soviet Union itself meant that the Soviet Union could not interfere in those states demanding similar reforms. In the process, authoritarian regimes were swept aside in Romania, Czechoslovakia, East Germany and Bulgaria. Before then, Hungary, Poland and Yugoslavia had embarked upon their own processes of reform. In retrospect, it is now obvious that it was the failure of the centrally planned economy to deliver a steady improvement in the standard of living of the people, the demonstration effect of the success of free enterprise in the West, and the inevitable human reaction to authoritarian rule that ushered in the process of economic and political reform within the Soviet bloc.

Since the revolution started in 1989 a series of events have taken place:

East Germany has been united with the rest of Germany; central planning has been replaced by market-oriented economies in all these states; the Russian rouble has become convertible and the European Bank for Reconstruction and Development has been established by the Western European countries as a mechanism for financing private enterprises in the East. In many of these countries, state-owned enterprises are being privatized. In effect, these countries, hitherto a monolithic and tightly controlled economic and political system, are being opened up both politically and economically. This opening up has implications for the world economy, including Africa.

Initially, the events in Eastern Europe were greeted with optimism. Observers thought that the establishment of free markets in the East would provide a new growth pole for the world economy. Since the political transition also meant the end of the Cold War, it was thought that the world economy would reap some peace dividends inasmuch as funds that would have been earmarked for defence would now become increasingly available for more productive investments. As available records show, the transition from central planning to a market economy, and from authoritarian rule to multi-party democracy, has not been easy in these countries. While progress has been made towards political pluralism, progress on the economic front has been slow. Quoting a 1991 World Bank study, Killick and Stevens (1991) have argued that Poland, Czechoslovakia and Hungary are unlikely to regain their 1989 income levels until 1996. This assessment is true of all the countries, including Russia.

In its own assessment, the United Nations predicted a period of protracted austerity, with either sharp downward adjustments or stagnating levels of sustainable absorption as well as output. This, according to the UN, owes a good deal to the inability of former Eastern bloc countries to divert their trade to Western markets without incurring sizeable terms of trade and/or export-revenue losses. In the absence of balance of payments support from the West, there could be a sharp cut in aggregate demand. This could derail the reform process and damage the expectation of beneficial effects of the reform process on the world economy. In the short to medium term, therefore, the import potentials of these countries as well as their ability to provide official development assistance (ODA) and direct foreign investment to developing countries could be reduced considerably. If, however, the reform process succeeds, particularly in the long run, world economic growth and trade could increase. But some diversion of capital from developing countries could also occur as economic and social progress makes the East increasingly attractive.

In response to the global trend towards regionalism, the CIS has been making moves recently that could lead to greater economic integration among them. At a recent meeting of the leaders of these states, it was agreed to form an Inter-State Economic Committee. Arrangements on forming a payments union – which might require a curtailment of national control over monetary policy if it is formed – and a customs union were also signed. If these moves succeed, they will have far-reaching implications for world trade and payments, similar to the effects of a United Europe on the world economy.

Relationship between Africa and Eastern Europe

Until 1989, the relationship between Eastern Europe and Africa largely reflected the ideological differences between Western and Eastern Europe. Politically, Eastern Europe supported and aided African countries which embraced socialism, while the West provided support (military and economic) to those African countries which embraced the free-market economy and were seen as capable of containing the spread of communism. Thus trade and financial flows to Africa were dictated mainly by these considerations.

TABLE 5.1
Share of Africa in the trade of Eastern Europe and the Soviet Union: (US$m)

EXPORTS TO	1980	1985	1986	1987	1988	1989	1990	1991	1992	1993
USSR (former)	656	499	536	499	491	534	495	455	411	–
Bulgaria	23	25	18	33	99	42	41	48	70	56
Czechoslovakia	30	37	48	67	56	52	39	233	245	–
Eastern Germany	19	158	119	103	121	119	43	–	–	–
Hungary	30	19	17	29	63	27	14	36	17	13
Poland	89	60	66	62	72	54	43	43	482	563
Romania	176	71	76	69	89	55	45	35	21	25
Yugoslavia	229	546	276	198	211	341	404	221	234	–
Total	1252	1415	1156	1060	1202	1224	1124	1071	1480	657

IMPORTS FROM	1980	1985	1986	1987	1988	1989	1990	1991	1992	1993
USSR (former)	458	523	539	503	476	631	609	410	900	–
Bulgaria	37	53	56	72	84	63	73	54	64	60
Czechoslovakia	66	86	100	133	118	199	187	135	180	–
Eastern Germany	88	240	247	183	168	140	106	–	–	–
Hungary	57	176	117	105	117	136	110	70	36	27
Poland	129	141	136	149	158	171	248	287	277	295
Romania	66	172	273	173	157	201	98	66	89	100
Yugoslavia	173	299	279	280	291	302	507	487	547	–
Total	1074	1690	1747	1598	1569	1843	1938	1509	2093	482

Source: *Direction of Trade Statistics Yearbook*, various issues.

TABLE 5.2
Shares of Africa in the trade of Eastern Europe and the Soviet Union (%)

EXPORTS TO	1980	1985	1986	1987	1988	1989	1990	1991	1992	1993
USSR (former)	1.23	0.81	1.19	0.98	0.95	0.93	0.67	0.65	0.57	–
Bulgaria	0.04	0.04	0.04	0.06	0.19	0.07	0.06	0.07	0.10	0.08
Czechoslovakia	0.06	0.06	0.11	0.13	0.11	0.09	0.05	0.33	0.34	–
Eastern Germany	0.04	0.25	0.26	0.20	0.23	0.21	0.06	–	–	–
Hungary	0.06	0.03	0.04	0.06	0.12	0.05	0.02	0.05	0.02	0.02
Poland	0.17	0.10	0.15	0.12	0.14	0.09	0.06	0.06	0.67	0.81
Romania	0.33	0.11	0.17	0.14	0.17	0.10	0.06	0.05	0.03	0.04
Yugoslavia	0.43	0.88	0.61	0.39	0.41	0.60	0.55	0.32	0.33	–
Total	2.35	8.28	2.57	2.08	2.32	2.14	1.53	1.53	2.06	0.94

IMPORTS FROM	1980	1985	1986	1987	1988	1989	1990	1991	1992	1993
USSR (former)	0.98	0.96	1.00	0.93	0.78	1.01	0.79	0.55	1.08	–
Bulgaria	0.08	0.10	0.10	0.13	0.14	0.10	0.09	0.07	0.08	0.07
Czechoslovakia	0.14	0.16	0.19	0.24	0.19	0.32	0.24	0.18	0.22	–
Eastern Germany	0.19	0.44	0.46	0.34	0.27	0.22	0.14	–	–	–
Hungary	0.12	0.32	0.22	0.19	0.19	0.22	0.14	0.09	0.04	0.03
Poland	0.28	0.26	0.25	0.27	0.26	0.27	0.32	0.39	0.33	0.34
Romania	0.14	0.31	0.51	0.32	0.26	0.32	0.13	0.09	0.11	0.12
Yugoslavia	0.37	0.55	0.52	0.52	0.48	0.48	0.66	0.66	0.65	–
Total	2.30	3.09	3.24	2.94	2.57	2.95	2.51	2.04	2.51	0.56

Source: Direction of Trade Statistics Yearbook., various issues.

One major feature of that trade (indeed, of Eastern European trade with developing countries) is that it was 'marginal, rather unstable, heavily concentrated on a few partners and dominated by quite traditional forms of exchange, overwhelmingly manufactures exported by the planned economies in exchange for food stuffs, fuels and industrial raw materials' (UN, 1991: 136). Eastern Europe and the Soviet Union accounted for only 5 per cent of all African exports and imports.

Eastern Europe and the Soviet Union had limited or insignificant trade with Africa before the end of the Second World War. After 1945, however, this trade developed rapidly, largely as a result of East–West rivalry. The trade was mostly with the socialist countries of Africa, and was dictated largely by political considerations. Because the trade was, in most cases, in terms of military hardware, it was reported inadequately. Available information points to the fact that exports to Africa were dominated, apart from military hardware, by exports of machinery and some light manufactures. In return, Africa exported mostly agricultural raw materials to the Eastern European countries. Table 5.1 shows the share of Africa in the trade of Eastern Europe and the Soviet Union in value terms, while Table 5.2 provides the same information in percentage terms. The two tables indicate that the share of Eastern Europe and the Soviet Union in Africa's trade has never been significant – exports range from a high of 2.3 per cent in 1980 to a low of 0.91 in 1992. As for imports, 1985 recorded the highest percentage (3.5 per cent) while the lowest figure was recorded for 1980.

Several factors account for this low volume of trade. Perhaps the most important is the absence of colonial relationships between these countries and Africa. Africa's trade has tended to flow, until recently, to those countries with which it had a previous colonial relationship. The rigid control over trade and payments for trade in Eastern Europe and the Soviet Union was another important factor. It was thus difficult for the African private sector to engage in trade in these countries; what trade existed was mostly government-to-government. In some cases payment for this trade was by barter, as happened during the Nigerian civil war when the government bartered its oil exports for arms.

The tables also reveal an important feature of this trade: since the revolution in the Soviet Union and Eastern Europe in 1989, exports to Africa have been declining whereas imports from Africa have either stagnated or shown some slight increase. What this point underscores is that there is considerable scope for Africa to penetrate these emergent markets. The opening up of these economies thus presents Africa with an opportunity to establish trading relations founded on market mechanisms rather than on ideological considerations. These issues, and those relating to capital flows from Eastern Europe, are discussed in the rest of this chapter.

The Former Soviet Union and Eastern Europe: Opportunities and Challenges

The countries of Eastern Europe face many obstacles in their path from centrally planned to free market economies. Their success in overcoming them, and the pace of the transition, are uncertain. While, in the long term, growth in Eastern Europe is likely to be a positive-sum game benefiting most parts of the world, in the short to medium term there are likely to be both positive and negative effects. These will include both trade creation and trade diversion, increased global demand for savings, and a potential diversion of OECD resources that may affect developing countries, whether or not this is dubbed as 'aid'. The trade creation and diversion effects are likely to be the most pervasive and complex in the early stages. They may include increased competition on OECD markets (especially the European Union) from Eastern European exports, increased demand in Eastern Europe for primary products from developing countries, and a shift in demand in Eastern Europe away from imports from those developing countries which used to engage in barter trade in favour of other sources, possibly other LDCs.

TRADE

Trade Diversion
There are two reasons to anticipate some diversion of trade away from developing countries towards Eastern Europe. The first is that economic reform is expected to increase the competitiveness of some of Eastern Europe's exports. The second is that, in responding to the political changes in Eastern Europe, the OECD states are in the process of elevating some countries in the region in their hierarchy of trade preferences. Whereas generalized trade liberalization may be a positive-sum game, partial liberalization tends to be a zero-sum game since it largely redistributes the economic rent arising from a protectionist restriction of supply.

Competitiveness
On the whole, Eastern Europe's exports to the European Union stagnated or declined during the second half of the 1980s. Only Hungary and Poland saw their exports increase in current value terms at an average annual rate that was faster than the growth of total EU imports from outside the Union (by 16 per cent and 12 per cent respectively compared to the extra-EU average of 8 per cent).

Because of the gross distortions which occurred during the centrally planned era, it is far from clear which existing East European exports will remain competitive and what new exports may emerge. However, on the basis of past flows and current expectations of competitiveness, it would appear that, within the industrial and manufacturing sectors, the sub-sectors in which Eastern Europe's continued competitiveness is most in doubt are machinery and equipment and other capital goods; those in which the outlook is more promising include light manufactures and assembly.

The distribution of exports between broad commodity groups varies among the countries, although manufactured goods classified by material is the most important category for both Czechoslovakia and Poland, and the second most important for Hungary. Czechoslovakia's top three categories are all manufactured goods, whereas for both Hungary and Poland food is also significant. In terms of market shares the picture is broadly similar. Czechoslovakia's share of EU imports is greatest in manufactured goods classified by material, which is also the commodity group in which Poland has the second highest import share after food. Hungary's share of EU imports is also highest for food, followed by two of the manufactured good categories.

At this highly aggregated level, the region's main competitors on the EU market are largely developing countries from outside the African region: they include Brazil, Argentina, Thailand, India, China, Turkey, Taiwan and South Korea. These are all significant suppliers in the product categories of most importance to Eastern Europe. The picture becomes clearer if data on imports are disaggregated to more specific product categories (Table 5.3). Of the 30 most important Eastern European exports to the EU in 1989, the top seven were relatively unprocessed raw materials and of the remainder five were basic engineering products and five were in the clothing/footwear categories. For clothing/footwear, Eastern Europe's principal competitors were the countries of the Mediterranean (including North Africa) and East Asia, while sub-Saharan Africa has also begun to export clothing.

An Eastern European challenge to developing country dominance in these products is not imminent. Much can happen over the coming years that could lead to a reduction rather than an increase in such import shares. However, third parties should observe the process of restructuring in Eastern Europe with such possibilities in mind, in order to monitor progress and to identify both sources of future potential competition and opportunities for investment.

Trade policy
Trade policy changes in EU markets will be important because Eastern Europe's exports have tended to be of goods for which protectionist tariffs are high, and because the region has been near the base of the hierarchy of trade preferences in Western markets. Hence, there is scope for changes in Western trade policy to result in significant improvements in the competitiveness of Eastern European exports.

The task of assessing the incidence of protection on Eastern European exports is not straightforward. Attempts have been made to compare the tariff rates applying to Eastern European exports with those applicable to imports from other countries. The figures suggest that, overall, the barriers faced by Eastern Europe are higher than those faced by developing countries, although the disparity is not great. However, these figures apply only to the common external tariff of the EU and do not take account of preferential trade arrangements. Since the latter are highly complex (see, for example, Mishalani *et al.*, 1981; Pomfret, 1986), it is not practical to make detailed comparisons between Eastern Europe and developing countries except on a product-by-product and country-by-country basis, but their general effect will have been to increase the relative barriers facing socialist exports.

Moreover, Eastern European exports of sensitive goods face a range of non-tariff barriers in the EU market. The socialist countries generally faced more NTBs than did developing countries, with the disparity being particularly marked in relation to the Mediterranean states, including North Africa. Furthermore, these country group averages conceal a wide range. The proportion of Eastern European imports to the EU subject to special EU-level NTBs in 1987 ranged from 12 per cent for Poland and

TABLE 5.3

The 30 most important industrial products[a] imported by the EC from Eastern European countries and their main competitors,[b] 1989

CN	Product	% Share of imports[c]	Three most important competitors
2710	Petroleum oils other than crude	19.83	Kuwait, Libya, Algeria
2709	Petroleum oils; crude	14.02	Libya, Saudi Arabia, Iran
4407	Wood sawn lengthwise; thickness exceeding 6 mm	4.09	Canada, USA, Malaysia
2711	Petroleum gases and other gaseous hydrocarbons	2.97	Algeria, Saudi Arabia, Libya
7502	Unwrought nickel	2.90	Canada, Zimbabwe, USA
7403	Refined copper and copper alloys; unwrought	2.30	Chile, Zambia, Zaïre
2701	Coal; briquettes and solid fuels made from coal	2.19	USA, Colombia, Canada
8703	Motor cars etc. for the transport of persons	2.19	USA, Brazil, Yugoslavia
9403	Other furniture, parts thereof	1.64	Yugoslavia, Taiwan, USA
7102	Diamonds; not mounted or set	1.60	India, Liberia, Israel
7208	Flat-rolled products of iron; hot rolled	1.36	USA, Brazil, Turkey
7601	Unwrought aluminium	1.25	Ghana, Yugoslavia, Brazil
6204	Women's/girls' suits, breeches, shorts, etc.	1.13	Hong Kong, Yugoslavia, Turkey
6203	Men's/boys' suits, breeches, shorts, etc.	1.11	Hong Kong, Yugoslavia, Tunisia
7204	Ferrous waste and scrap	1.03	USA, Yugoslavia, Canada
5201	Cotton; not carded or combed	0.97	USA, Pakistan, Turkey
2902	Cyclic hydrocarbons	0.95	USA, Canada, Brazil
7108	Gold (unwrought/semi-manufactured/powder form)	0.94	Canada, USA, Zimbabwe
4703	Chemical wood pulp; soda; non-dissolving	0.94	Canada, USA, Brazil
9401	Certain seats	0.80	Yugoslavia, USA, Taiwan
6403	Footwear with uppers of leather	0.71	South Korea, Brazil, Taiwan
2844	Radioactive chemical elements and isotopes	0.68	USA, Niger, Canada
2707	Oils; other products of high temperature coal tar	0.63	USA, Libya, Yugoslavia
7216	Angles, shapes, etc. of iron/non-alloy steel	0.54	Yugoslavia, Turkey, Egypt
7202	Ferro-alloys	0.45	New Caledonia Dominican Rep., Yugoslavia
6202	Women's/girls' overcoats, wind-jackets, etc.	0.45	Yugoslavia, South Korea, China
6201	Men's/boys' overcoats, wind-jackets, etc.	0.43	Hong Kong, S.Korea, China
3102	Mineral or chemical fertilizers; nitrogenous	0.40	USA, Nigeria, Yugoslavia
7207	Semi-finished products of iron/non-alloy steel	0.39	Brazil, Mexico, S. Korea
4412	Plywood, veneered panels and similar wood	0.39	Indonesia, USA, Brazil

a 4-digit positions of the goods classification of the Combined Nomenclature (CN).

b Only developing countries, USA and Canada.

c Share in total supplies of industrial goods by the respective country.

Source: Mobius and Schumacher, 1991.

Czechoslovakia to 17 per cent for Hungary (Möbius and Schumacher, 1991:11). Although this was a smaller proportion than applied to the most discriminated-against developing countries – such as Thailand (50 per cent), Hong Kong (38 per cent) and Pakistan (37 per cent) – it was much higher than applied to most African states.

The sectors most heavily protected in the EU were textiles and agriculture, those of great potential interest to Eastern Europe. Within agriculture, the heavily protected sub-sector of most interest to Eastern Europe was animals/animal products (with 37 per cent of Bulgaria's and 16 per cent of Hungary's exports covered). Other protected sectors included precision and optical instruments (12 per cent of Poland's and 22 per cent of Czechoslovakia's exports covered) and chemicals (12 per cent of Romania's exports covered) (Möbius and Schumacher, 1991). Several of these products are also of importance to Africa.

Eastern Europe's exports have also faced NTBs in some EU member state national markets. Quantitative restrictions especially have been common, and there is evidence that they have constrained the volume of exports (Möbius and Schumacher, 1991:16). Moreover, Eastern Europe has been a major target of EU anti-dumping action. Between 1980 and 1988, 34 per cent of all EU anti-dumping investigations were directed at Eastern Europe (including the GDR and the USSR), as against 25 per cent in respect of the Far East, the second most-affected region (Möbius and Schumacher, 1991: 17).

However, although the EU imposed an impressive array of quantitative restrictions on imports from Eastern Europe, many of these were not binding as the actual flow of competitive exports was too low. The analysis by Möbius and Schumacher concludes that constraints on supply were a more important factor affecting the volume of exports than constraints on demand. Even so, the removal of such demand constraints may affect Eastern Europe's competitiveness with unconstrained developing country supplies.

Until the revolutions, Poland, Romania, Czechoslovakia and Hungary, as signatories of the GATT, were supposed to benefit from most-favoured nation treatment (although they did not always do so), but only Romania (with Yugoslavia) benefited from the EU's Generalized System of Preferences (GSP). Following the revolutions, a renegotiation of the terms of access which had begun in the late 1980s has accelerated. For Hungary and Poland quantitative restrictions on EU imports of industrial products (except textiles and products covered by the European Coal and Steel Community) were reduced or abolished with effect from 1 January 1990 and the countries were admitted unilaterally into the GSP. By the middle of 1990 similar agreements had been reached with Czechoslovakia and Bulgaria. Then, in autumn 1991, following tortuous negotiations, the EU agreed to an association agreement with Poland which paved the way for rapid completion of similar agreements with Czechoslovakia and Hungary.

Eastern European imports
It is not only on EU markets that Africa may face some trade diversion as a result of the changes in Eastern Europe. During the centrally planned era, a significant trade developed between the countries of Eastern Europe and the Soviet Union, on the one hand, and a group of developing countries on the other. The latter included both socialist states and others, like India, which favoured barter trade. Most African states were not well represented in this trade. With the collapse of the CMEA and the shift towards trade in convertible currency, it is likely that there will be some diversion away from such traditional Third World suppliers. Beneficiaries may be EU states or other developing countries. They could include African states if the reform process in Africa succeeds, particularly in the medium to long term.

Eastern European imports from developing countries originated in four main groups of countries: CMEA members, CMEA associates, developing countries with formal arrangements and the newly industrializing countries. Of these, the most important source of Eastern European imports were the developing countries with formal arrangements. In 1989, this group supplied $2.2 billion of imports into Eastern Europe, which was equivalent to 48 per cent of Eastern Europe's imports from all four groups. Although imports from developing countries declined during the 1980s (being 23 per cent lower in current value terms in 1989 than in 1980), they still formed a substantial flow at the time of the revolutions.

In geographical terms the most important source of Eastern European imports has been Latin America, with 36 per cent of the 1988 total. Africa and the Middle East were the next two most important regions. There are insufficient data available on the commodity composition of this trade to determine the danger of diversion and the possible beneficiaries. However, there is some reason to suppose that imports from Africa, especially, and also from Latin America, included a high proportion of primary commodities. This trade might increase in the medium term as a result of growing incomes in Eastern Europe, rather than decline.

The countries at most risk of a decline in exports would seem to be those that had formal agreements with Eastern Europe under the centrally planned regimes; these are primarily countries in the Mediterranean (including North Africa) and Asian regions. They are vulnerable in the short term because of the region's declining import capacity, and in the medium term, when the volume of imports may rise again, for competitive reasons. The preference of centrally planned economies for barter trade gave those developing countries willing to supply on this basis an undoubted, but hard to quantify, competitive advantage over other suppliers. Now that trade is on a convertible currency basis, the former centrally planned economies may find alternative sources of supply more competitive.

Trade creation

In the longer term, Africa could benefit along with other regions from the fillip to world growth provided by a more buoyant Eastern European economy. Of more immediate interest is that Eastern European consumption of tropical products and imported consumer goods may rise. Under the twin forces of low incomes and administrative controls, Eastern European consumption of many tropical products was extremely low during the centrally planned era. *Per capita* import levels in 1989 in Western Europe were higher than those in Eastern Europe by a factor of 2 in the case of tea, 3 for cocoa beans, 4 for coffee, 5 for bananas and 370 for canned pineapple. As the market outlook for many of these commodities in the OECD is depressed, a rise in *per capita* Eastern European imports to Western levels could represent a significant improvement for the exporters. The benefits would tend to accrue mainly to Latin America and sub-Saharan Africa, with the latter gaining most relatively as it is still heavily dependent upon the export of traditional primary products.

More generally, growth in Eastern Europe would tend to improve the terms of trade of many countries. Global imports would increase, providing export opportunities for developed and developing countries alike. At the same time, Eastern European exports would tend to reduce world prices to the benefit of those countries which are net importers. To put the scale of such changes into perspective, if *per capita* GNP levels in Eastern Europe were to increase to the current average OECD levels, the effect would be an increase to world GDP equivalent to some 6 per cent of its 1989 level.

As such figures make clear, a great deal depends upon the speed with which the reformed economies of Eastern Europe start to grow. Until the transitional problems, which currently darken the outlook for all the countries of the region, are overcome in at least some of them, the long-run trade-creating potential of the Eastern European revolutions must remain an area for speculation.

COMPETITION FOR JOBS

If the Eastern European economies fail to grow sufficiently to satisfy popular aspirations there may be a marked increase in migration to Western Europe. Even though immigration tends to benefit the host economy, at least in the longer term, a resurgence of labour mobility of such magnitude would probably increase pressure on migrants from the Third World. This could happen both directly, through competition for jobs, and indirectly if it sustains xenophobic and overtly racist tendencies in Europe (such as have been evident in Germany in the second half of 1991). The dangers are the more serious because they arise at a time when, because of the Single European Market and the free movement of labour within the EU, the member states are being forced to reconsider their immigration policies. Any increase in labour movement from

Eastern Europe will occur against a background in which migration is already perceived to be a problem by EU officials.

The numbers wishing to migrate can only increase. This increased supply of potential migrants will face competition from other sources. After a decade in which the flow of new legal immigrants fell to very low levels (less than 0.1 per cent of the EU population), there has been an upsurge in the past three years. This has been due largely to inflows from Eastern Europe into Germany. Although this flow may have fallen off following the revolutions, the experience of population movements between the eastern and western parts of Germany suggests that there remains strong potential for economic migration from the east. If economic growth is slow (as is quite likely in the short term) the movement of people will continue. Moreover, one effect of post-1992 industrial rationalization could be an increase of unemployment on the EU periphery and, with the free movement of labour, greater intra-EU migration. Even without the undoubted racist pressures to exclude non-white migrants, this increase in potential supply is considered to be a source of concern by the EU. The response is likely to be to restrict immigration from developing countries.

FINANCE

Financial needs

Will Eastern Europe divert funds from Africa? There have been many estimates of the financial implications of reform in Eastern Europe. Some simulate the financing that Eastern Europe would require to achieve specified growth targets within a particular period of time. Others concentrate either on the absorptive capacity of Eastern Europe or on the volume of finance likely to be available.

Naturally, the bottom line of such calculations varies considerably according to the approach adopted. Estimates based on Eastern Europe's 'need' have tended to produce very large figures. One estimate, for example, suggested that global real interest rates could rise by 1–3 percentage points as a result of the increased demand for finance (Collins and Rodrik, 1991). This was based on the assumption that foreign capital inflows to the region would reach $55 billion annually, of which $18 billion would be destined for Eastern Europe (including Yugoslavia) and the rest for the states of the former USSR and (the bulk) for the former GDR. The rise in interest rates is on the assumption that there is no decline in flows to developing countries; if, by contrast, interest rates are to remain stable, these flows would have to fall by between 0.8 per cent and 2.3 per cent of their GDP. A review and analysis of seven such 'needs-based' estimates show a range of total costs required over a 10–15-year period of $770–2,800 billion, or an annual requirement of $56–171 billion (Colijn, 1991).

Whilst it is easy to see how such large figures have provoked fears of financial diversion among developing countries, it is perhaps naïve to assume that external finance, whether private or official, will be available to satisfy all of the region's needs or that the countries could actually absorb such large inflows. The alternative approaches, based on the likely level of supply or absorptive capacity, tend to produce much lower figures. One assessment of absorptive capacity has produced a figure of $14–15 billion per annum, whilst an assessment of likely supply produces an even lower figure of $6.8 billion per annum (Colijn, 1991). The evidence from flows in 1990 and 1991 noted below suggests that even this low figure of supply errs on the side of optimism.

An attempt has been made by the World Bank to marry estimates of need and availability. The Bank has estimated the external financing requirements of six Eastern and Central European countries at $9–10 billion a year. This is the financing required simply to achieve a moderate rate of growth sufficient for them to return to their 1989 levels of GDP *per capita* by the late 1990s. It also excludes scheduled amortization payments on debt, which average another $11–11.5 billion a year until 1995 (Qureshi, 1991:7). A more ambitious scenario, in which 1989 real *per capita* income levels are restored by 1995, would increase the financing requirement by about $5 billion per annum.

The World Bank estimates that there is a gap of at least $3 billion per year for the first half of the decade on the low growth scenario. Moreover, there is a pressing need to restructure and refinance the heavy burden of debt amortization payments. The Paris Club agreement with Poland reached in spring 1991 will reduce these payments by an average of $5.5 billion until 1995, but this will not remove the problem completely, even for Poland, and no relief has yet been negotiated for the other East European countries. Not all of them are seeking debt reduction – Hungary, for example, is reported to have chosen not to request a rescheduling, preferring to safeguard its existing access to the capital markets. However, Bulgaria faces a significant debt burden (as does Yugoslavia) which it is difficult to see being serviced without major disruption to economic recovery.

COMMERCIAL FLOWS

Investment
One source of external capital is foreign direct investment, and the countries of Eastern Europe have put great emphasis on encouraging investment from the OECD. Thus far, however, foreign investment inflows have been modest. The level of foreign direct investment into Czechoslovakia, Hungary and Poland (the three countries most likely to be favoured in this respect) was $400 million in 1990 and $1.2 billion in 1991 (Feinberg, 1991). It is not unreasonable to expect investment to begin slowly but to accelerate as the economic reforms start to take effect.

However, it is notoriously difficult to monitor foreign investment flows. Well publicized announcements of large investments, such as the Volkswagen stake in Skoda, may have provided a false impression of actual flows. It would be prudent, therefore, to wait until evidence is obtainable from balance of payments statistics before assuming that there has been a quantum leap from the 1990 level.

Commercial lending
Another source of external capital is commercial and semi-commercial lending from the banks and public sector institutions. Thus far, however, commercial bank lending has been very limited. Figures up to December 1990 from the Bank for International Settlements provide no evidence of a significant inflow: the stock of East European loans was barely higher (0.6 per cent) than a year earlier, indicating that any new loans have simply offset the repayment of old ones. Estimates for 1991 suggest a net outflow of funds by commercial creditors to the extent of $200 million from Czechoslovakia, $1,800 million from Hungary and $400 million from Poland (Feinberg, 1991).

Will the newly created European Bank for Reconstruction and Development, established specifically for Eastern Europe and oriented towards the private sector, provide the necessary finance? Although the bank will have an important function to perform, its impact in the early years of the transition should not be overestimated. For a start, it is relatively small. Its capital base has been described as less than half the cost of cleaning up Poland's power industry alone. Second, its loans will not be cheap. It will essentially be on-lending money which has been raised on the international capital markets. In this respect, its funding will be similar to that of the World Bank. To some extent its net impact may be more muted still because it may simply replace funds that would otherwise have come from the World Bank.

AID

In the absence of adequate commercial funds, will concessional finance fill the gap? This could be serious for sub-Saharan Africa. Figures for 1990, and estimates for 1991, suggest that inflows of official finance have been modest and have barely offset the outflows of commercial money. In 1990 the level of net transfers to the three more-developed Eastern European states ranged from a small positive flow for Czechoslovakia (of $200 million) to negative flows for Hungary (of $1.7 billion) and Poland (of $8.1 billion); the estimated position for 1991 is for a positive, but still modest, flow for Czechoslovakia (of $1.1 billion), a continued outflow for Hungary (of $600 million) and a marginal inflow for Poland (of $300ʼ million) (Feinberg, 1991). These figures exclude short-term capital movements and foreign direct investment but, as noted above, the latter has been modest thus far.

Food aid

Partly because of the past emphasis on emergency relief, food aid has formed a substantial part of the aid received so far by Eastern Europe, having increased significantly in volume during the past two years. When it substitutes for commercial imports food aid can be a form of balance of payments support as well as emergency relief, so it is expected that in the next five years much larger commitments will be made. As the scale of these actions increases resources could be diverted from Third World countries, although in the case of the EU at least there has been no such diversion thus far.

In 1989/90 Poland was the single largest recipient of EU cereals food aid, receiving 1.4 million tonnes compared to 300,000 tonnes granted to the second largest recipient, Ethiopia. In 1990/1 Poland and Romania looked set to be the third and fifth largest recipients of US food aid. Food aid to Eastern Europe in recent times began in 1980/1 when some 14,000 tonnes of cereals food aid was granted to Poland, which has since received food aid in some form in every year. In 1989/90 a record 1.6 million tonnes of cereals food aid, representing 13.3 per cent of the world total, was granted to Poland. In 1990/1, substantial additional food aid donations of around 1.0 million tonnes were made to Poland and also Romania. A further $133 million in food aid for Bulgaria and Romania was approved by the EU in early March 1991. There was, also, high-profile provision of 'emergency'-type food aid, partly privately funded, from Germany to the USSR during the winter of 1990/1. Meanwhile the EU was considering a $333 million food aid programme to the USSR until the August 1991 coup; the programme was later reinstated.

A sizeable volume of food imports at highly concessional rates has also been received by Eastern European countries and the USSR in recent years. For example, between the inception of the US Export Enhancement Programme, in 1985, and March 1990, Eastern Europe was approved the right to purchase 3.1 million tonnes of wheat and 1.1 million tonnes of barley under the scheme. During the same period, the USSR was given the opportunity to purchase 20.3 million tonnes of wheat (26.5 per cent of the world total). In Eastern Europe there are complaints that these concessional supplies have displaced their exports. The region has traditionally exported agricultural goods to the USSR which are of too low a quality to be redirected on to other markets. Despite the need for substantial food imports in some East European states, there is a continuing requirement to earn foreign exchange by exporting agricultural goods.

Financial aid

The total of official financial commitments by the 'Group of 24' rich countries to Eastern Europe was estimated as of April 1991 at ECU30 billion, plus contributions from the international financial institutions and debt reduction/rescheduling (UN, 1991b: 26). These sums are upper-limit commitments, with disbursements being spread over several years; in most cases the planned period is 1990–3, but some lag is likely. Thus far, almost all OECD donors have been meticulous in insulating transfers to Eastern Europe from their normal aid programmes. In the cases of both the UK and the EU, for example, aid to Eastern Europe is additional to development aid (and from a separate budgetary line). Only in the USA, Sweden and Italy (which often has difficulty spending all its pledged aid) is there believed to have been a diversion.

Whilst there may not have been significant diversion so far, in the medium term, the boundary between assistance to Eastern Europe and aid to middle-income states may become blurred. If it does, the scale of the diversion could be quite marked. Middle-income regions such as North Africa, the Middle East and Latin America currently receive levels of OECD aid that, when combined, are not greatly in excess of even the EU's lower estimate of Eastern Europe's balance of payments needs. Moreover, there could be a major diversion of technical skills towards Eastern Europe.

Conclusion

Given the high level of uncertainty, it is arguable that the most productive response for Africa is to construct scenarios that indicate the potential implications if Eastern Europe grows and if it stagnates. For the middle-income states of Africa, growth in Eastern Europe could give rise in the medium term to increased competition for commercial finance and foreign investment and on export markets, but little diversion of concessional aid. For the primary producers of Africa, the net impact of growth in Eastern Europe could be an increased demand for tropical products. On the stagnation scenario, by contrast, all parts of Africa would stand to lose from events in Eastern Europe. The poorer states of Africa would face competition for aid (and especially food aid) while the African countries of emigration to the EU would face increased pressure from migrants out of Eastern Europe.

References

Bergson, A. (1991), 'The USSR before the fall: how poor and why', *Journal of Economic Perspectives*, 5, 4, (Autumn).

Colijn, Leendert (1991), 'East Central European economies in transition: long-term performance, new aspirations and the costs of realizing them'. 'Background material for the Institute of East West Security Studies Task Force Workshop on Western Assistance, the European Studies Center at Stirin, Czechoslovakia, 27–29 September, Revised November (mimeo).

Collins, S. and Rodrik, D. (1991), *Eastern Europe and the Soviet Union in the World Economy*,

Washington: Institute for International Economics.

Ericson, Richard E., (1991), 'The classical Soviet-type economy: nature of the system and implications for reform' *Journal of Economic Perspectives*, 5, 4, (Autumn).

Feinberg, Richard E. (1991), 'Financial assistance to Central Europe : how real is it?' Paper presented as discussion material at the Institute of East West Security Studies Task Force Workshop on Western Assistance, the European Studies Center at Stirin, Czechoslovakia, 27–29 September (mimeo).

Howell, Jude (1994), 'The end of an era: the rise and fall of GDR aid', *The Journal of Modern African Studies*, 32, 2.

Killick, T.& C. Stevens, (1991), 'Eastern Europe: lessons of economic adjustment from the Third World' *International Affairs*, 67, 4.

Mishalani, P. Robert, A.; Stevens, C. and Weston, A. (1981), *The Pyramid of Privilege*, in Christopher Stevens (ed. *EEC and the Third World: A Survey*. London: Hodder & Stoughton, in association with the Overseas Development Institute and the institute of Development Studies.

Möbius, Uta and Schumacher, Dieter (1991), 'Eastern Europe and the EC: trade relations and trade policy with regard to industrial products'. Paper presented to Joint Canada–Germany Symposium, Toronto, 1–2 November 1990. Revised January 1991.

Pomfret, Richard (1986), *Mediterranean Policy of the EC*. London: Macmillan.

Qureshi, M. (1991), 'Sustaining the development of Central and Eastern Europe'. Speech to UK House of Commons All Party Group on Overseas Development; 3 July.

UN (1991), DIESA paper prepared for Special Meeting of the UN Economic and Social Council; 4–5 July.

Wolf, Thomas A. (1991), 'The lessons of limited market-oriented reform' *Journal of Economic Perspectives*, 5, 4.

6

The Uruguay Round
of Trade Negotiations:
Implications for Africa

TEMITOPE OSHIKOYA

In the aftermath of the Second World War, world leaders at the Bretton Woods Conference considered ways and means of strengthening international economic cooperation. There were proposals for strengthening surveillance over the international monetary system; for mobilizing resources for the reconstruction of war-ravaged economies; and for gradual liberalization and expansion of world trade. The first two proposals gave birth respectively to the International Monetary Fund (IMF) and the International Bank for Reconstruction and Development (IBRD), popularly known as the World Bank. Although the idea of an International Trade Organization, along the lines of the IMF and the World Bank, did not materialize as planned, the General Agreement on Tariffs and Trade (GATT) was nonetheless established on a provisional basis in 1946.

GATT operates in three ways: as a set of multilaterally agreed rules governing the trade behaviour of governments; as a forum for trade negotiations in which the trade environment is liberalized and made more predictable either through the opening up of national markets or through the reinforcement and extension of the rules themselves; and as an international court for the resolution of trade disputes among governments. Since its establishment, GATT has initiated seven rounds of trade negotiations (Geneva (1947); Annecy (1949); Torquay (1951); Geneva (1956); Geneva (Dillon Round, 1960–61); Geneva (Kennedy Round, 1964–67); Geneva (Tokyo Round, 1973–79); and Geneva (Uruguay Round 1986–94).

The present round – the Uruguay Round – was launched at a ministerial meeting in Punta del Este, Uruguay, in September 1986 and was, in part, a culmination of the work begun in Geneva in November 1982. It is the most ambitious of all trade talks to date. The objectives are to bring about further liberalization and expansion of world trade, strengthen the role of GATT and improve the multilateral trading system; increase the responsiveness of GATT to the evolving international economic environment;

and encourage cooperation in strengthening the interrelationship between trade and other economic policies affecting growth and development. After almost nine years of negotiations, the Uruguay Round Agreement was finally signed in April 1994 in the Moroccan city of Marrakech.

This chapter provides a preliminary qualitative assessment of selected aspects of the Uruguay Round Agreement which are of interest to African countries, with particular emphasis on its overall developmental impact, market access for tropical products, erosion of preferences, and the implications of the agreements for new issues such as services, intellectual property and investment for the region's developmental needs. The next section provides an outline of the Uruguay Round framework; an evaluation of the implications of the Agreement for the African economy follows in the third section (p. 151).Policy implications of the Round for Africa are assessed in the fourth section (p. 163).

Outline of the Uruguay Round Framework

The Uruguay Round agreement provides for a substantial improvement in the market access opportunities to the signatories of the Final Act, with world-wide tariff reduction of about 40 per cent. The agreement includes a set of new rules covering agriculture, services, intellectual property rights, government support for industry, anti-dumping, dispute settlement, safeguards, subsidies, countervailing measures, trade-related investment measures, and a proposal to establish a new World Trade Organization (WTO) to replace GATT.[1]

The Round aims at establishing binding commitments and disciplines in three key areas – market access, domestic support and export competition – which constitute the core of the agriculture trade liberalization programme to be implemented over a six-year period. The agreement seeks to achieve global commitment towards tariffication and the removal of quantitative import licensing and restrictions, voluntary export restraints and similar schemes from the provisions of the GATT; and the reduction in all commitments supporting agricultural producers which do not meet policy-specific criteria for exemption. The reduction of export subsidies applies at two levels of commitments – budgetary outlays and volumes of subsidized exports. The integration of agriculture into the multilateral rules is expected to create new market access opportunities for current and potential exporters of agricultural products by reducing distortions largely attributed to quotas, export subsidies and domestic market supports such as those inherent in the Common Agricultural Policy of the European Union. Total export subsidy outlays and domestic support to agricultural producers are expected to decline by 36 per cent

---

[1] This organization was established in January 1995.

and 18 per cent to US$13.7 billion and $162 billion respectively by the end of the transition period. Tariffs on agricultural products will be reduced on average by 24 per cent over a period of ten years and on average by 36 per cent over a six-year period by developing countries and developed countries respectively. More generally, these multilateral rules on trade in agriculture are expected to stabilize world food markets and reduce fluctuations in food import bills in the long term. Reflecting the concern that net food-importing countries may face higher import bills for food in the medium term, the agreements contain provisions on food aid and assistance for short-term financing of commercial food imports. Quantitative restrictions imposed under the Multifibre Agreement (MFA) in the textiles and clothing sector will be liberalized over a ten-year period.

The widening of market access for most industrial products will be achieved over a five-year period as the proportion of goods entering industrial country markets at zero duty increases from 20 to 43 per cent; as the average tariffs applied by industrial countries decline from 6.3 per cent to 3.9 per cent; and as orderly marketing arrangements and voluntary export restraints (VERs) are eliminated. Average tariffs on industrial products will be reduced by about 40 per cent and 30 per cent in developed and developing economies respectively. As duties in different production stages are harmonized, tariff escalation will also be reduced.

TABLE 6.1
Pre- and post-Uruguay Round scope of bindings for industrial products [1]
(Number of lines, US$ billion and %)

Country group	Number of lines	Import value	Percentage of tariff lines bound		Percentage of imports under bound rates	
			Pre-UR	Post-UR	Pre-UR	Post-UR
Total	249,573	1,089.0	43	83	68	87
By major country group:						
Developed economies	86,369	737.2	78	99	94	99
Developing economies	163,204	352.1	21	73	13	61
Transition economies	18,962	34.7	73	98	74	96
By Region						
North America	14,136	325.7	99	100	99	100
Latin America	64,136	40.4	38	100	57	100
Western Europe	57,851	239.9	79	82	98	98
Central Europe	23,565	38.1	63	98	68	97
Africa [2]	21,500	18.5	13	65	26	84
Asia	87,944	461.2	16	68	32	70

1 Imports of 44 participants in GATT's Integrated Database (excluding petroleum)
2 Covers imports of 2 IDB participants.
Source: GATT Secretariat (1994).

According to Table 6.1, however, tariff cuts for African products are uneven among industrial sub-sectors. Tropical industrial, and natural resource-based products, including furniture, paper, wood, metals and mineral products will attract the largest cuts in industrial country tariffs. More limited cuts were agreed for other products such as transport equipment, leather goods and footwear.

The General Agreement on Trade in Services (GATS) establishes a multilateral framework of principles and rules based on transparency, progressive liberalization and non-discrimination for the expansion of global delivery of services, including transportation services, professional services, financial services, tourism and the movement of people. The obligations under GATS, however, provide for flexibility in order to allow countries to adapt their regulatory practices to the new multilateral disciplines.

The GATS agreement includes increased protection for trade-related intellectual property rights (TRIPS) by setting binding standards with respect to copyright, trademarks, industrial designs and patents; through the establishment of rules to combat international trade in counterfeit goods; and by establishing dispute settlement procedures with multi-lateral sanctions for infringement. Developing countries have five years to introduce the necessary reforms, but most African countries have as long as 11 years, starting from 1995, to implement reforms on intellectual property systems. It has been pointed out that 'as net importers of knowledge, developing countries may face higher prices for protected products and the costs of displacement in "pirate" industries before the potential benefits of more domestic research and additional foreign direct investment materialize' (Primo Braga et al., 1994). Over the long term, however, TRIPS would significantly enhance the access of developing countries to foreign technology and foreign direct investment (FDI).

The trade-related investment measures (TRIMS) would limit the requirements on foreign investment of the use of local content and trade balancing, and promote more neutral trade and investment policies. All countries (developed, developing and least developed alike) are expected to eliminate the list of prohibited TRIMS on local content and trade balan-cing requirements within two years, five years, and seven years respectively.

Finally, the Uruguay Round agreement provides for the establishment of the WTO. This organization, which formally came into existence early in 1995, will serve as an umbrella institution for both old and new agreements under GATT and will be instrumental in the enforcement of the agreed rules and principles. It will have greater authority to adjudicate trade disputes and provide a permanent forum for negotiating trade relations on a multilateral basis among its members. The agreement also provides for greater clarification and strengthening of rules on subsidies and countervailing measures, safeguards, anti-dumping and dispute settlement. In general, developing countries will have to assume a higher level of obligations in trying to meet the requirements of the new WTO.

Implications of the Round for Africa:
A Preliminary Assessment

The criteria used for evaluating the implications for the African economies are as follows: overall developmental effects on Africa; the impact of improved market access in tropical and natural resource-based products; the extent of erosion of preferences under the trade agreements; provisions for compensating measures for net-food importing countries; and obligations with respect to new issues of services, TRIPs and TRIMs.

OVERALL GLOBAL EFFECTS

There have been few assessments of the quantitative impact of the Uruguay Round on global incomes and trade, and fewer still for developing countries. As a result of the increased access to export markets, strengthened rules providing greater security of market access, and more efficient use of resources, these estimates point to a permanent increase in global income (in constant 1992 dollars) arising from full implementation of the agreement of between $212 billion and $274 billion. This is equivalent to about 1 per cent of world GDP in 1992, out of which $80 billion a year would accrue to developing countries. This is also equivalent to about 1.7 per cent of their GDP in 1992 (Goldin *et al*, 1993). Annual exports from developing countries as a whole would increase by about 2.8 per cent, with Asia, Latin America and Africa likely to register export gains of 3.5, 1.5, and 0.5 per cent respectively. Africa's gains could arise from increased exports of diary products, textiles and clothing. But overall, African countries could incur losses of some $2.6 billion annually as net food importers face increases in world food prices, and preferential margins for traditional African exports are eroded. Against this background, African countries thus face the challenge of having to adjust to a new competitive global market environment in order to maintain the level of export earnings essential to their development. Their prospects of maintaining current market shares could worsen in respect of products where preferential margins are minimal or have disappeared completely as a result of Uruguay Round liberalization. Thus deliberate efforts to build long-term competitiveness through improvements in their supply capabilities, product and market diversification, marketing skills, quality control techniques, trade promotion and level of manufacturing technology are essential if they are to meet the challenges of the new competitive global trade.

Several African countries have undertaken trade policy reforms within the context of national adjustment programmes, and domestic policies will be further constrained by the strengthened GATT rules and commitments. Although African countries have been given differential and more favourable treatment in respect of all the areas of binding commitments, and flexibility in the implementation of the agricultural trade liberalization programme, several major commitments which they have to undertake include the liberalizing of agricultural tariffs and industrial policies with impact on the protection of agriculture, and the tariffication of non-tariff measures.

MARKET ACCESS

The multilateral trade negotiations are viewed by many African countries as a framework for consolidating and expanding favourable conditions of access to markets which are crucial to the recovery and expansion of their export earnings, and as an opportunity for the international community to give further concrete expression to the principle of differential and more favourable treatment in the market access area. Their effective participation in the world trading system should be seen in the light of their special financial, development and trade needs, and this would require improved trade opportunities for products of export interest to them. Tropical products, natural resource-based products (fishery and forestry products, minerals and metals), other agricultural products, textiles and clothing, and energy-related products are among the categories of goods that are of immediate export interest to African countries.

Seven tropical agricultural product groups formed the basis for negotiations in the Uruguay Round of multilateral trade negotiations (UNDP/UNCTAD, 1994): (1) tropical beverages; (2) spices, flowers and plants (including essential oils, cut flowers, plants, vegetable materials, lacs, and products thereof); (3) certain oilseeds, vegetable oils and oilcakes; (4) tobacco, rice and tropical roots (tobacco and tobacco products, rice, manioc and other tropical roots, and products thereof); (5) tropical fruits and nuts (bananas and banana products, tropical fruits and nuts, fruit juices and other products); (6) tropical wood and rubber (tropical wood and wood products, natural rubber and rubber products); and (7) jute and hard fibres. The share of the seven categories of tropical products in total exports ranges from 50 per cent to 100 per cent for the majority of these countries. Among the least developed countries such as Comoros and Equatorial Guinea, tropical products as a share of total exports rise as high as 95 per cent. The share of tropical products in total exports among the middle-income countries ranges from 6.8 per cent in Morocco and 23.4 per cent in Zimbabwe to 75.4 per cent in Kenya and 76.1 per cent in Côte d'Ivoire. The high dependence on tropical products for export earnings is limited, in several countries, to a few products. For example, coffee and related products constitute 91.7 per cent and 72.4 per cent of exports in Uganda and Ethiopia respectively; spices and essential oil represent 97 per cent of exports in Comoros; and the share of tropical wood in total exports is 74.3 per cent in Equatorial Guinea.

With respect to products of African countries, tariffs will be reduced on average by 35 per cent on coffee, tea and cocoa; by 40 per cent on oilseeds, fats and oils; by 36 per cent on tobacco; and by 48 per cent on other agricultural products. In general, tariff reductions on African tropical products are above the average cut of 37 per cent for tariffs of developed countries: 52 per cent on spices, flowers and plants; 46 per cent on tropical beverages; 40 per cent on oil seeds, oils, roots, rice and tobacco; and 37 per cent on tropical nuts and fruits (GATT Secretariat, 1994: 4).

African primary-producing countries are more likely to be among the last to benefit from the expected trade expansion and global income growth. This is partly because of their low income elasticities of demand for primary products, which mean that the demand for such products will not increase appreciably as a result of the expected increase in global income; and partly because the trade barriers on some primary products are already low. For instance, the barriers on most tropical products are already low in industrialized countries and a further reduction in tariffs resulting from the Uruguay Round is unlikely to lead to an appreciable increase in their exports.

The export products of interest to African countries among natural resource-based industrial products include fish and fishery products, textiles and clothing, forestry products and non-ferrous metals and minerals, which account for more than half the export earnings of about a quarter of the African countries. The export products of interest, however, vary considerably among countries (Table 6.2). For instance, mineral products and precious metals are of high interest to countries such as Lesotho, Botswana, Zaïre, and Zambia; and textiles and clothing to Morocco, Tunisia and Egypt; fish and fish products feature prominently among the exports of interest in The Gambia, Madagascar and Senegal; while wood, pulp and forestry products are of high interest in Côte d'Ivoire, Ghana, Cameroon, and Swaziland. This group of products, along with other natural resource products, such as energy and energy-related products, petroleum, gas, coal, uranium, petrochemicals, iron and steel, fertilizers, other non-ferrous minerals and metals – accounts for more

TABLE 6.2
Average tariff reductions on industrial products imported from Africa [1]
(US$ billion and %)

Country group	Value of imports	Trade-weighted tariff averages[2]		
		Pre-UR	Post-UR	Reduction
All participants	39.2	3.9	2.7	31
Developed countries	34.1	2.7	2.0	26
Developing economies	5.0	12.3	8.0	35
Transition economies	0.2	4.1	2.1	49

1 Imports of 44 IDB participants (excluding petroleum).
2 Covers tariff lines whose tariffs were reduced (excludes ceiling bindings).
Source: GATT Secretariat (1994).

than 50 per cent of the export earnings of over half of African countries.

For industrial products, developed countries have pledged to expand most-favoured nation (MFN) tariff treatment to cover 85 per cent of Africa's exports compared with 77 per cent before the Uruguay Round. Above-average tariffs will continue to apply mainly to fish and fish products, and textiles and clothing, although market access will be augmented for the latter through the integration of this sector in the multilateral rules by the progressive elimination of voluntary restraint agreements.

The manufacturing sector, rather than its primary counterpart, is expected to experience the fastest growth under the Uruguay Round. Hence, most of the benefit is likely to accrue to the more diversified economies of Asia and Latin America and the more prosperous African countries such as South Africa, which has a large industrial base. In many primary-producing African countries, the diversification and transformation into manufacturing to take advantage of the potential expansion of trade in manufactures is likely to be realized over the 10-year time horizon in which most of the negotiated measures are expected to take effect. For these African countries, the expected gain from trade liberalization will be small. For African countries to take advantage of the new arrangements, particularly for manufactured exports, a major reorientation in industrial strategy and programmes will be necessary. This must be designed to improve the industrial policy environment, competitiveness, product quality and standardization, private sector investment and the spirit of enterprise.

PREFERENTIAL MARGINS

Market access possibilities for African products could decline since the preferences to developing country exporters under the Generalized System of Preferences (GSP), the Lomé Convention and other preferential arrangements would be reduced by the cuts in MFN tariffs. The concern about the erosion of preferences is likely to be greatest among African countries with a narrow export base and high dependence on primary commodities. As Stevens and Kennan (1994) have shown. the impact of any preference erosion in the short term will be a function of the extent of any reduction in European Union MFN tariffs, and the importance of the producers from other developing countries for Africa.

The average overall reductions in MFN tariffs, weighted by the value of total dutiable imports from African countries, are as follows: 40.2 per cent, 28.2 per cent, and 15.7 per cent in Japan, the EU and the USA respectively. African exports to these markets affected by the tariff reductions have a value of about US$1.1 billion, US$ 12.7 billion, and US$0.7 billion, respectively (UNDP/UNCTAD, 1994: 9). The average loss in preferential margins for African countries implied by the MFN offer of reduction in tariffs, as calculated by UNDP and UNCTAD (1994), amounts to about 50 per cent in the GSP preferential margins in the three markets, with an

TABLE 6.3
Pre- and post-Uruguay Round MFN tariff treatment of developed country imports from Africa
(US$ million and %)

Importer	Value	Pre-UR			Post-UR		
		0%	0.1–3%	Over 3%	0%	0.1–3%	Over 3%
Total	33613.6	67.0	10.5	22.4	73.8	11.0	15.3
Australia	119.8	33.7	10.5	55.8	39.7	2.6	57.7
Austria	99.3	78.0	0.4	21.6	79.0	0.5	20.5
Canada	249.8	55.6	3.8	40.6	62.0	4.6	33.5
Finland	26.1	87.4	2.3	10.3	88.1	2.3	9.6
Japan	2761.7	59.2	5.3	35.6	71.4	19.4	9.2
Norway	843.8	98.9	0.1	1.0	99.0	0.1	0.9
New Zealand	18.6	48.9	0.0	51.1	65.2	0.0	34.9
Sweden	72.1	39.4	21.5	39.1	52.0	19.3	28.7
Switzerland	576.9	5.2	91.8	3.0	7.3	90.5	2.2
United States	2855.0	66.3	15.0	18.7	71.7	12.7	15.6
European Union	25990.5	68.6	9.2	22.2	75.2	8.6	16.2

Source: GATT Secretariat (1994).

overall loss of about 30 per cent on ACP preferential margins in the EU (see Table 6.3). On a sectoral basis, the loss in preferential margins for tropical products, industrial products and natural resource-based products respectively amounts to 80 per cent, 49 per cent and 60 per cent on a GSP basis; and 50 per cent, 47 per cent, and 16 per cent on ACP preferential margins. The loss of preferential margins on individual products enjoyed by African countries in the EU market under the Lomé Convention is even higher. There is, for example, a 100 per cent erosion of preferential margins on coffee beans, cocoa beans and meat; a 50 per cent erosion of margins on cut flowers, coffee extracts and veneer sheets; and an erosion of more than 30 per cent of margins on crustaceans, edible oils, cocoa butter/fat/oil, leather (pre-tanned) and fruits and nuts (UNDP/UNCTAD, 1994: 9).

African countries, therefore, are likely to suffer trade losses in the short to medium term due to the erosion of preferential margins in their principal markets – the European Union. In the longer term, there may be additional effects if African countries fail to diversify into non-traditional products and non-traditional markets. The region's exports are concentrated on a relatively small range of products, most of which face low or zero MFN tariffs with low preference margins. Some African states have started to diversify their exports into products where MFN rates and preferences are higher with a significant price advantage over their less preferred competitors (McQueen and Stevens, 1989). Geographically, Africa's exports are concentrated on Europe and, over the longer term,

TABLE 6.4

Tariff reductions on imports of industrial products (excluding petroleum) from African countries in the European Union, Japan, and the United States (US$ million and %)

Market	Value	Average tariff		Reduction
		Pre-UR	Post-UR	
European Union				
Industrial products	26,115,170	2.8	2.0	29
Wood, pulp, paper & furniture	1,379,856	1.6	0.5	69
Textiles & clothing[a]	2,222,510	11.8	10.0	15
Leather, rubber, footwear & travel goods	516,146	3.0	2.3	23
Metals	4,044,224	1.9	1.3	32
Chemicals & photographic supplies	1,047,613	6.9	2.1	70
Transport equipment	510,327	1.0	0.8	20
Non-electric machinery	156,302	3.7	1.1	70
Electric machinery	179,378	8.0	4.3	46
Mineral products, precious stones & metals	14,829,442	0.4	0.2	50
Manufactured articles	100,185	5.3	2.7	49
Fish & fish products	1,129,187	17.3	14.8	14
Japan				
Industrial products	3,095,216	3.4	1.8	47
Wood, pulp, paper & furniture	145,134	1.2	0.1	92
Textiles & clothing[a]	82,121	1.5	1.0	33
Leather, rubber, footwear & travel goods	10,437	7.8	6.0	23
Metals	1,302,820	4.2	2.1	50
Chemicals & photographic supplies	71,654	2.5	0.5	80
Transport equipment	41,318	0.1	0.0	100
Non-electric machinery	513	3.7	0.0	100
Electric machinery	564	0.6	0.0	100
Mineral products, precious stones & metals	903,394	0.3	0.0	100
Manufactured articles	4,491	1.3	0.8	38
Fish & fish products	532.770	7.6	5.2	32
United States				
Industrial products	2,876,509	2.3	1.9	17
Wood, pulp, paper & furniture	102,393	0.7	0.1	86
Textiles & clothing[a]	255,054	16.4	14.9	9
Leather, rubber, footwear & travel goods	108,080	1.0	0.8	20
Metals	892,190	1.5	1.4	7
Chemicals & photographic supplies	48,577	4.8	2.6	46
Transport equipment	8,011	2.7	1.7	37
Non-electric machinery	47,081	3.1	0.7	77
Electric machinery	17,348	4.6	0.9	80
Mineral products, precious stones & metals	1,316,854	0.2	0.1	50
Manufactured articles	37,406	5.1	1.4	73
Fish & fish products	43,515	0.9	0.4	56

a Figures understate the increase in market access because they do not take into account the phase-out of bilateral quotas imposed under the MFA.
Source: GATT Secretariat (1994).

TABLE 6.5
Tariff reductions on imports of industrial products (excluding petroleum) from least developed
African countries in the European Union, Japan and the United States (US$ million and %)

Market	Value	Average tariff		Reduction
		Pre-UR	Post-UR	
European Union				
Industrial products	3,711	1.4	0.8	43
Wood, pulp, paper & furniture	216	0.3	0.2	33
Textiles & clothing[a]	333	2.3	1.8	22
Leather, rubber, footwear & travel goods	118	0.9	0.7	22
Metals	1578	0.1	0.0	100
Chemicals & photographic supplier	341	4.9	0.6	88
Mineral products, precious stones & metals	779	0.0	0.0	0
Fish & fish products	156	15.8	11.0	30
Japan				
Industrial products	867	5.6	3.1	45
Textiles & clothing[a]	62	0.3	0.0	100
Leather, rubber, footwear & travel goods	17	0.2	0.0	100
Metals	474	5.4	2.5	54
Fish & fish products	275	8.2	5.6	32
United States				
Industrial products	592	1.2	1.1	8
Textiles & clothing[a]	27	16.1	14.5	10
Leather, rubber, footwear & travel goods	18	1.9	1.3	32
Metals	278	0.6	0.6	0
Mineral products, precious stones & metals	171	0.1	0.0	100

a Figures understate the increase in market access because they do not take into account the phase-out of bilateral quotas
imposed under the Multifibre Arrangement.
Source: GATT Secretariat (1994).

losses in the European market need to be set against potential gains in
other markets, such as the USA and Japan, where Africa could see its
competitors' preferential margins reduced.

NET FOOD IMPORTERS

While African countries are likely to experience losses on the export side
due to an erosion of preferential margins on most of their exports to the
major markets, the net food importers will also incur losses on the import
side through higher expenditure for basic foodstuffs. Most African
countries are highly dependent on exports of tropical agricultural

products and on imports of temperate agricultural products. Food imports as a percentage of the total value of exports averaged about 20 per cent for all African countries, with much higher value in some least-developed countries such as Cape Verde (673 per cent), Djibouti (450 per cent), Guinea Bissau (575 per cent), Mozambique (161 per cent) and Ethiopia (148 per cent). Of the net food imports of African countries, cereals top the list in value terms ($5.0 billion annually in 1987–9) followed by dairy products ($1.6 billion), edible oils ($1.1 billion) and sugar ($0.4 billion). A few African countries have a positive trade balance for all the products combined. In 1989, the gross food imports of African countries rose to nearly $14 billion (sub-Saharan Africa, $5 billion), with net food imports of $10.4 billion (sub-Saharan Africa, $2.7 billion).

African countries as net food importers are likely to face higher food import bills due to the agricultural liberalization programmes, with serious implications for balance of payments, debt repayments and food security. It has been estimated that a 20 per cent cut in domestic support and a 21 per cent reduction in export subsidies by OECD countries would result in annual net trade losses for African countries amounting to US$808 million, and net income losses of US$1,054 million (UNDP/UNCTAD, 1994: 11).

TABLE 6.6

Tariff treatment of imports from African countries by Japan, the European Union and the United States

	Value	Pre-UR			Post-UR		
		0%	.1–3%	Over 3%	0%	.1–3%	Over 3%
European Union's imports from:							
South Africa	13058.9	86	5	9	93	2	5
Other Africa	13056.3	43	13	44	49	15	36
Total Africa	26115.2	65	9	26	71	9	20
Japan's imports from:							
South Africa	1737.6	69	9	22	83	5	11
Other Africa	1364.9	18	7	75	24	40	35
Total Africa	3102.5	47	8	45	57	21	22
United States' imports from:							
South Africa	1501.9	71	17	11	75	15	10
Other Africa	1374.7	62	12	26	69	9	22
Total Africa	2876.5	67	15	18	72	13	15

Source: GATT Secretariat (1994).

TABLE 6.7
Export interests of African countries in industrial products (excluding petroleum)

	Share in exports	Export Interest			
		Low (6-10%)	Medium (11-20%)	High (21-50%)	Very high (51-100%)
Benin	25.2	Fish and fish products; textiles and clothing; electric machinery			Transport equipment
Botswana	86.8				Metals
Burkina Faso	40.5	Textiles and clothing			Mineral products, precious metals and stones
Burundi	31.4				Mineral products, precious metals and stones
Cameroon	44.5	Leather, rubber, footwear and travel goods		Metals	Wood, pulp, paper and furniture
Central African Republic	61.5		Wood, pulp, paper and furniture		Mineral products, precious metals and stones
Congo	93.6	Metals		Mineral products, precious metals and stones	Wood, pulp, paper and furniture
Côte d'Ivoire	30.7	Textiles and clothing; leather, rubber, footwear and travel goods	Fish and fish products; mineral products, precious metals and stones	Wood, pulp, paper and furniture	
Egypt	65.0	Chemicals and photographic supplies		Textiles and clothing; metals	
Gabon	98.5	Chemicals and photographic supplies		Wood, pulp, paper and furniture; metals and transport equipment	

TABLE 6.7 cont.	Share in exports	Export Interest			
		Low(6-10%)	Medium (11-20%)	High (21-50%)	Very high (51-100%)
Gambia	27.4			Mineral products, precious metals and stones	Fish and fish products
Ghana	60.1	Fish and fish products	Mineral products, precious metals and stones	Wood, pulp, paper and furniture; metals	
Kenya	20.1	Fish and fish products	Textiles and clothing; chemicals and photographic supplies; mineral products, precious metals and stones	Leather, rubber, footwear and travel goods	
Lesotho	91.7			Mineral products, precious metals and stones	Textiles and clothing;
Madagascar	33.8	Metals	Mineral products, precious metals and stones	Fish and fish products; textiles and clothing	
Mali	22.3				
Mauritania	99.3			Metals	Fish and fish products
Mauritius	64.9				Textiles and clothing
Morocco	80.2		Fish and fish products; chemicals and photographic supplies;	Textiles and clothing; mineral products, precious metals and stones	
Mozambique	83.6	Mineral products, precious metals and stones		Fish and fish products	Metals
Namibia	96.3			Chemicals and photographic supplies	Fish and fish products
Niger	98.6			Chemicals and photographic supplies	Chemicals and photographic supplies

TABLE 6.7 cont.	Share in exports	Export Interest			
		Low(6-10%)	Medium (11-20%)	High (21-50%)	Very high (51-100%)
Nigeria	42.2	Metals	Transport equipment	Leather, rubber, footwear and travel goods; mineral products, precious metals and stones	
Senegal	67.1			Mineral products, precious metals and stones	Fish and fish products
Sierra Leone	86.7	Fish and fish products		Mineral products, precious metals and stones	Metals
Swaziland	35.4	Textiles and clothing; transport equipment	Mineral products, precious metals and stones		Wood, pulp, paper and furniture
Tanzania	28.6	Fish and fish products; wood, pulp, paper and furniture		Textiles and clothing; mineral products, precious metals and stones	
Togo	60.8				Mineral products, precious metals and stones
Tunisia	88.6	Fish and fish products; chemical and photographic supplies; electric machinery		Textiles and clothing; mineral products, precious metals and stones	
Zaïre	87.2			Mineral products, precious metals and stones	Metals
Zambia	97.8				Metals
Zimbabwe	57.8			Mineral products, precious metals and stones	Metals

Source: UNDP/UNCTAD (1994).

African countries have sought measures, including short-term balance of payments assistance in the form of food aid, to compensate the net food-importing countries for higher imported food prices in the Uruguay Round agreement. In order to improve domestic food production and reduce dependency on food imports in the long term, they have also sought commitments – particularly on market access for the region's potential export products and on medium- to long-term technical and financial assistance to accelerate the growth of domestic food production in food-deficit, low-income African countries.

NEW ISSUES

The schedules of specific commitments on trade-related services in the agreement offer some potential benefits for the few African countries where tourism, maritime transport, and cross-border movement of persons are important sources of foreign earnings. The tourism sector and affiliated services – airlines, hotels and restaurants, tourist agencies and tourist guides – have emerged as an important contributor to GDP, employment and foreign exchange in several African countries. But the potential and level of competitiveness of these countries in the sector could be limited by their inadequate infrastructural, technological and managerial capacities to respond to the challenges and opportunities of the rapid changes in the global market for tourism. For African countries to participate more effectively, it will be necessary to place particular emphasis on transfer of technology, training, employment and joint ventures with firms from the developed countries.

The promotion of national shipping and the development of maritime transportation is considered essential for improving the prospects for foreign exchange earnings, and the promotion of economic integration prospects in Africa. But the development of maritime services in African countries also faces obstacles similar to those in the tourism sector. Improvements in maritime services and shipping development could be facilitated through the strengthening of their domestic service capacity and its efficiency and competitiveness; access to technology on a commercial basis; and the improvement of their access to distribution channels and information networks.

The cross-border movement of persons, as a mode of delivery of services, is of particular interest to African countries because remittances of foreign exchange earnings by their nationals abroad constitute a major source of service exports, particularly in the least developed countries. Intra-African and international movement of people has increased significantly in the last two decades, owing to both economic and non-economic factors, and remittances by Africans working abroad have increased correspondingly.

In assessing the overall balance of rights and obligations in the TRIPS agreement from the African countries' viewpoint, it is important to bear in mind that Africa's present world share of registered foreign patents is estimated at about 0.3 per cent. The low level of technological capacity and the current low innovation capacity on the continent does not seem to give much scope for raising this share in the foreseeable future. The benefits from the agreement are limited not only by this factor but also by the increased cost of technology as a result of the longer duration of royalty payments and by the wider choice of countries available for foreign direct investment, the key vehicle for technology transfer. Given these considerations, the obligations in the TRIPS agreement will weigh heavily against African countries in general, and in particular against the least developed among them, which have the weakest technological bases.

Thus it is important for African countries to exploit potential gains from the agreement on intellectual property rights (TRIPS) through better access to advanced technologies. Such access is essential if Africa is to foster new industries able to compete in liberalized international markets. For the most part, these technologies cannot simply be counterfeited; high-tech firms must build local plants or share their know-how with local producers. But such sharing will be a rarity unless firms become convinced that their ideas are safe from copiers. Other potential benefits include a framework more conducive to domestic research efforts, and to technology transfer and foreign direct investment.

Policy Implications and Conclusion

Historically, Africa's external trade has depended on a narrow range of primary products and a narrow market focused on the European Union. Africa's dependence on a few primary commodity exports and on the EU as their traditional market is vulnerable to changes in international market conditions. For some time now, African countries have enjoyed unrestricted and duty-free access in those market. But the Uruguay Round, the global liberalization of world trade and the extension of multilateral trade disciplines into new areas such as services and intellectual property appears to threaten that special relationship. Thus African countries are faced with several challenges with important policy implications in adapting to the post-Uruguay Round trading environment. Paramount are the challenges to diversify their products; to diversify their market and re-examine their relationship with the EU; to exploit regional trade; and to implement legislation consistent with the requirements of the WTO.

As EU trade is liberalized along with the rest of the world's and Africa's privileges are dismantled in that market, Africa will need to explore new markets while simultaneously diversifying its export base. In addition, African countries would have to compete more on the basis of economic factors such as the productivity and quality of products. Although the implementation of national adjustment programmes has improved the macro-economic and trade policy environment in recent years, considerable efforts are required at the micro-economic level to improve production techniques, remove structural bottlenecks and capacity constraints, and enhance both the quantity and productivity of investment. The agreements on new issues such as services and banking imply that African countries will have to diversify their export base into non-traditional areas.

Traditionally the prevailing direction of Africa's trade has been towards the European Union. For example, in the last decade more than 50 per cent of Africa's exports benefited from preferential liberal tariff and non-tariff access to the EU market. The combination of several factors, including the loss of preferential margins under the Uruguay Round agreement, the move towards closer economic integration in the EU, and the loss of global market shares will compel African countries to diversify the market base for both their traditional and non-traditional products. They need to explore trade policies to diversify Africa's exports geographically, to include market destinations in the Asia–Pacific region, Japan and North America; and to open up South–South trade. As the lack of diversification into these markets cannot be attributed mainly to trade restrictions, African countries will need to overcome constraints on both the production and the marketing of their products. A more effective penetration of non-traditional markets will require an assessment of the features of the markets, product specifications, supply and demand conditions, monitoring and processing of market intelligence, product and service adaptation, packaging and quality control.

As part of the evolving relationship between the region and Europe in the context of overall global economic development, African countries will need to explore the potential for intra-African trade beyond the current 5 per cent level. The promotion and expansion of intra-African trade will accelerate the process towards regional economic integration adopted in the Abuja Treaty. The development of intra-African trade will not only help in diversifying the markets for the region's products, but also provide opportunities for African entrepreneurs to broaden their trade marketing skills through sub-regional trade information networks which will be useful in the more competitive global markets.

During the transitional period over the next few years, African countries are required to implement national legislation consistent with the commitments accepted as members of the WTO; and in order to meet transparency obligations for a number of agreements, inconsistent legislation or regulation has to be notified to the WTO (Fortin, 1994: 3). They are required to undertake individual country assessment of the Uruguay Round results in order to determine specific policy responses and strategies to the new trading opportunities and challenges. They will have to improve the trade negotiations skills of their officials so as to enable them to participate effectively in the current and future work programme of the WTO. They will also have to strengthen their institutional and human resource capacities and trade-related information management. Three new issues have been identified as central to the post-Uruguay Round trade agenda. These are the link between trade and environment, labour standards, and trade and competition policies. African countries will need to be prepared for full participation in the negotiations on these issues.

References

Economic Commission for Africa (1994), Draft Report of the Expert Group Meeting on the International Conference on the Uruguay Round of Multilateral Trade Negotiations, Tunis, Tunisia, 24–27 October, 1994.

Carlos A. Primo Braga, Patrick Low, and Piritta Sorsa (1994), 'The Uruguay Round: a "Good Deal" for rich and poor countries,' in Policy Focus No. 7; Overseas Development Council.

Fortin, C., Statement to the International Conference on the Uruguay Round of Multilateral Trade Negotiations, Tunis, Tunisia, 24–27 October, 1994.

GATT Secretariat, 'Note on the outcome of the Uruguay Round and African countries'. Presented to the International Conference on the Uruguay Round of Multilateral Trade Negotiations, Tunis, Tunisia, 24–27 October, 1994.

Ian Goldin, Odin Knusden and Dominique van der Mensbrugghe (1993), Trade Liberalization: Global Economic Implications, OECD Development Center.

Matthew McQueen and Christopher Stevens (1989), 'Trade preferences and Lomé IV: non-traditional ACP exports to the EU', Development Policy Review, 7, 3, London.

Christopher Stevens and Jane Kennan (1994), 'How will the EU's response to the GATT Round affect developing countries,' Institute of Development Studies Working Paper 11.

UNDP/UNCTAD, 'African MTN Project: evaluation of the final results of the Uruguay Round by African countries,' Paper Presented to the International Conference on the Uruguay Round of Multilateral Trade Negotiations, Tunis, Tunisia, 24–27 October, 1994.

7

The Future of African–European Economic Relations: Some Concluding Remarks

• •

OLADEJI O. OJO

In the opening chapter of this book, it was observed that the history of Africa's economic relations with Europe dates back to the middle ages. The relationship has gone through several phases, from colonialism to full cooperation between the two entities. Throughout the several phases of the relationship, trade, capital flows and the movement of people have remained the dominant features. In the wake of political independence in the 1960s, old colonial ties were continued and, in most cases, conscious efforts were made by both parties to strengthen the relationship. The bilateral agreements between the EU and the countries of North Africa, on the one hand, and the various Lomé Conventions between the rest of sub-Saharan Africa (except South Africa) and the other ACP countries on the other, were the results of these conscious efforts. The consequences of these efforts was that, on the eve of '1992', Africa was very dependent on Europe for trade, capital flows and investment. In 1992, for example, about 52 per cent of Africa's exports entered EU markets as against 41 per cent in 1975. In the same year, the EU accounted for 52 per cent of imports as against 50 per cent in 1975 (Table 2.1). Europe's importance in trade is also matched by its role in capital flows and investment. In 1989, for example, EU development flows were equivalent to about 5 per cent of sub-Sahara Africa's GDP.

This book is about African–European economic relations. It is its contention that Africa's special relationship with Europe – a relationship carefully built up and nurtured over the years – could be under threat from the consequences of the Single European Market (SEM), particularly from those aspects of the arrangement relating to trade, capital flows and the imminent establishment of a monetary and economic union in 1997 or in 1999, at the latest. The relationship could be threatened, too, by the latest round of GATT trade negotiations, the Uruguay Round. Similarly, the opening up of the former Soviet bloc to trade as well as to finance could undermine Africa's relationship with Europe, although it must be admitted that the developments in the former Soviet bloc also offer Africa a number of opportunities. There is also the fear that bilateralism may be replacing multilateralism as Europe seeks to channel resources bilaterally rather than multilaterally through the European Development Fund. These developments point to the possibility of a major shift in African–European economic relations. While the magnitude of the shift is unclear, it is certainly the case that the shift is towards reduced interdependence in the years ahead. The rest of this chapter draws together the conclusions of the various chapters. It also attempts to highlight the policy conclusions emanating therefrom.

The Single European Market

With the completion of its internal market, the EU will become the world's second largest market. The European Commission has been quick to emphasize the potential gains from the SEM. In a study carried out on its behalf, (the Cecchini report),[1] it was concluded that the removal of barriers (to trade, persons and capital) will lower the cost of doing business and push down prices as costs go down under the pressure of wider competition across the newly unified market. In turn, the reduction in prices will stimulate demand and, therefore, output; and this increased output will lead to further reductions in costs as economies of scale in production are realized. It is estimated that aggregate GDP will be boosted by 4.5 per cent, with 1.8 million new jobs created, while simultaneously consumer prices will be lowered by 6.1 per cent. The aggregate government budget balance is expected to improve by an amount equal to 2.2 percentage points of GDP. The EU's current account balance with the rest of the world is also projected to improve by the equivalent of 1 percentage point of GDP. Similarly it is expected that an enlarged European market will fuel world economic growth, stimulate world trade and lower interest rates. The world economy, including Africa, is expected to benefit from these gains. The European Commission has also argued that the growth-inducing effects of European integration will enable member states to expand their imports from the rest of the world (including Africa), and enable the EU to expand its aid programme to the developing countries in general and to its Lomé Convention partners in particular.

The completion of the SEM of about 320 million people, with an annual GDP of $2.7 trillion, exports worth $860 billion and imports of $708 billion is indeed a major development in the world economy. The market is bound to attract the attention (and indeed the anxiety) of all those who trade in it, especially Africa. How far, for example, will preferences under the Lomé Convention be affected by the SEM? Will Europe become a

[1] Paolo Cecchini, *The European Challenge: 1992 – The Benefits of a Single Market*, Brookfield, Vermont, Gower Publishing Company, 1988.

fortress? What are the prospects for capital flows and private investment in the new Europe? Will Africa continue to enjoy priority attention now that Eastern Europe is opened up? These are some of the worrying questions facing Africa.

TRADE

Trade creation and trade diversion are likely to accompany the SEM. While the scale of trade creation and trade diversion that will result remains uncertain and the scope for government action to influence the impact may be limited, there are indications that Africa could experience some trade diversion. To the extent that '1992' removes barriers between EU national markets and results in faster economic growth, third parties may benefit. The acceleration of growth should result in increased EU imports, while the removal of internal barriers will make it easier for third-party exporters to exploit the full potential of European demand, but there are several reasons not to expect significant expansion of imports from Africa. For the last few years, the EU has enjoyed the longest post-war economic expansion. But there has been no commensurate feedback effect on Africa. During this period, the share of Africa in the EU's imports has declined progressively in spite of the preferences under the Lomé Convention. Admittedly this is due partly to Africa's poor export performance and partly to the fact that Africa's exports are largely primary products, the demand for which is income inelastic. Furthermore, in spite of the Lomé Convention, African imports still face significant non-tariff barriers in Europe. These barriers could be imposed freely as and when the EU feels threatened by imports from developing countries. Another factor further limiting EU imports from Africa is the current reform programmes which many African countries are implementing. As long as import compression continues under these programmes, EU imports from Africa may not expand significantly. Finally, faster growth in Europe could lead to lower costs of production and thereby render relatively expensive African imports unattractive.

A likely positive impact of the SEM is the possibility of an increase in demand for manufactured imports in the EU. Unlike the demand for primary commodities, that for manufactures is characterized by relatively high income elasticity. The 'income growth' effect of European integration is likely to lead to increased demand for global manufactured imports. The extent to which Africa is able to benefit from this opportunity will depend on Africa's relative competitiveness in the world trade for manufactures and on the extent to which Africa is able to adapt to a harmonized system of standards which will accompany European integration. Although manufactured exports currently constitute a small proportion of Africa's exports, trade in manufactures is one area of immense opportunity which Africa could explore. In order to take advantage of this opportunity, Africa will have to show greater competitiveness in her trade.

Manufactured goods constitute the bulk of African imports from the EU. Increased competitiveness and greater efficiency within the Union could combine to put downward pressure on the prices of manufactures. This in turn could positively affect Africa's terms of trade. It is however possible, under conditions of reduced prices, for Africa to thus become a readily available market for EU manufactures. If this happens, the momentum for Africa's industrialization may stagnate rather than pick up pace.

For the countries of the Maghreb, the SEM could offer other potential problems. Tighter and uniform border controls and more stringent health checks on aliens could slow down the movement of people from these countries to Europe. These could in turn adversely affect the flow of workers' remittances from Europe to these countries.

The North African states are also very vulnerable to the widest range of possible SEM negative effects. Because of their position in the upper echelons of the EU's pyramid of privilege, the internal liberalization aspect of the SEM could increase competition in their traditional markets. As their economies are similar to those of the Southern EU states, the potential for investment diversion is significant.

CAPITAL FLOWS AND INVESTMENT

The importance of Europe to Africa in the area of trade is matched by its importance in the areas of capital flows and direct investment. In 1989, EU development flows are equivalent to about 5 per cent of sub-Saharan GDP. Thus anything that affects total flows of the EU is likely to affect its flow to Africa, and any change in its flows from the EU will have a major effect on Africa. One of the findings of the book is that the prospects for official flows are not very good in the aggregate, partly because of budgetary considerations in EU countries and partly because of the emergence of new EU concerns. Under Lomé V (which is currently being negotiated), there are indications that aid to the ACP countries could be lower still. While the ACP countries are requesting an ECU21 billion aid package, some countries are proposing an increase from the present level of ECU12 billion to ECU14.3 billion to take account of inflation and contributions from the new states of Austria, Finland and Sweden. Some countries favour a reduction, however, perhaps below current levels.[2] What is worrying to the ACP countries is that they have become Europe's third priority, behind Eastern Europe and the Mediterranean countries. Strategic interest, rather than budgetary constraints, may cause the

---

[2] At the recently concluded (June 1995) meeting of the leaders of the EU, it was agreed that aid to the ACP countries should be ECU13.3 billion (or $17.29 billion) for the period 1995–9. Aid allocations to the Mediterranean countries for the same period were set at ECU4.68 billion ($6.1 billion), while allocations to Central and Eastern Europe were put at ECU6.98 ($8.7 billion). The meeting also called for progress to be made in negotiating trade agreements with the Mediterranean countries.

diversion of official development finance from Africa, in particular from sub-Saharan Africa, to Eastern Europe and the Mediterrean countries. Equally worrying is the support in some EU countries for increasing the contributions to the International Development Association (IDA), the soft window of the World Bank, while reducing aid under the Lomé Convention. The rationale behind the thinking is that an enhanced contribution to IDA would trigger more resources from the United States and Japan. A final worrisome concern is the proposal to channel resources bilaterally rather than though the EDF. In addition to the possible reduction in the overall aid package, bilateralism could increase and tighten conditionalities, particularly cross-conditionalities in aid allocations.

Further, there is ground to assume that private capital may now be directed to Eastern Europe. Until now, low labour costs have constituted part of Africa's incentives to foreign investors. But with the entry of Spain and Portugal (countries which also have low labour costs) into the EU, the attraction which Africa holds for European capital may diminish. There is also the fear that EU official and private capital flows to Africa will decline over time as a result of developments in Eastern Europe. Given that Eastern Europe is relatively more developed than Africa, private capital could have a greater incentive to move there in preference to Africa because of a more conducive investment atmosphere, better infrastructure and easy access.

Under 1992 regulations, aid and export credits are expected to be untied. While untying aid could increase its value by 20 per cent, untying export credits could reduce costs to developing countries. One thing which the SEM will achieve is increased coordination of aid policies. The EU decision of 1991 to ensure 'that the policies of the Community and of member states bilaterally are consistent' implies consultation and co-ordination, in such areas as political conditionality. This could reduce variance among aid flows to different donors' 'special clients'. The co-ordination of EU aid to the ACP countries has also been increased.

In the last few years, the flow of EU private investment to Africa has been declining. The constraints on the flow of private investment include the prevalence of relatively small and weak internal markets, inadequacy of infrastructural facilities (which in turn increases the cost of doing business), shortage of skilled manpower, restrictive investment codes and political and economic instability. With the completion of the European integration process, the effects of these constraints will become even more pronounced. With a very large market to exploit, European investors will find it increasingly more attractive to invest at home. The completion of the European market is also likely to affect the flow of private investment from other sources adversely. One of the strategies which EU trading partners have adopted to penetrate what they perceive as Fortress Europe is to increase the volume of their investment in the EU. For example, in 1988 American companies invested over $25 billion in the EU in an apparent effort to secure a strong foothold in the market.

GLOBAL TRADE LIBERALIZATION

The European Commission has argued that Europe will not become a Fortress or more protectionist as a result of the establishment of the SEM. This is because the EU has a fundamental stake in the existence of free trade and open international trade. One of the conclusions of this book is that while the threat of a Fortress Europe is more imagined than real, a real threat to Africa is the loss of preferences in the wake of global trade liberalization. In a study of the impact of the recently concluded Uruguay Round of trade negotiations, it was found that Africa could incur losses of some US$2.6 billion annually as net food importers face increases in world food prices. An additional source of loss will be the erosion of preferences under the Lomé Convention as Europe liberalizes its trade in conformity with the GATT agreement. This is because the liberalization of trade under the Round will mean increased access to Europe of the non-ACP developing countries as Europe liberalizes its trade. This in turn could erode preferences currently enjoyed by Africa and other ACP countries under the Lomé Convention. Thus, trade liberalization under GATT, rather than Europe 1992, could reduce Africa's market share in Europe, and, in the words of Stevens, 'the whole edifice built up over the years by the EU is likely to subside gently as its foundations are weakened by liberalization'.

Indeed, '1992' could make it easier for the more competitive African states to penetrate European national markets in which they have not previously been strongly represented. Much depends, of course, on the supply response of African countries to this changed demand situation. What this implies is that the competitiveness of Africa will determine the extent of its gains/loss under the new arrangement. Of equal importance to Africa's ability to benefit from '1992' is the speed of diversification by Africa of its production base. Thus the pursuit of appropriate macro-economic and trade policies by Africa, and a successful and rapid diversification of the African economy away from the production and exportation of primary products, will remain critical to the continent's efforts to reap the benefits of '1992'. As presently constituted, Africa's exports face bleak prospects in the European market. If Africa remains as heavily dependent on a small group of products in the future as it has in the past, the likelihood is that its share of Europe's imports will continue to fall.

MONETARY COOPERATION

Another development which is likely to alter African–European relations is the move, as part of the process of European integration, towards economic and monetary union in 1997, or in 1999 at the latest. This development, it must be admitted, is more relevant to the French-speaking African countries which are also participants in the CFA franc zone. As Europe moves irrevocably towards a single currency, it is doubtful if France will remain willing to provide the necessary accommodating finance for the CFA franc convertibility. This is partly because the cost of this support will be additional to the adjustment costs (in terms of convergence criteria) which France itself will have to meet in order to enter a single European currency. It is thus likely that we may be witnessing the last days of the currency arrangement which has served the member countries so well.

The possible delinking of the CFA franc from the French franc could provide Africa with a unique opportunity to move more vigorously on the implementation of its own monetary integration. Because monetary integration is one of the principal components of the Abuja Treaty, a successful implementation of that Treaty would *ipso facto* result in the establishment of a single currency in Africa.

Events in the Former Soviet Bloc

The impact of the events in the former Soviet bloc on Africa is no more certain than the impact of the SEM. It will depend on the speed and success of the reform measures taking place in those countries. In a long-term context, growth in Eastern Europe is likely to benefit all regions of the world, but in the short to medium term, there could be negative effects. These will include both trade creation and trade diversion, increased global demand for savings and a potential diversion of OECD resources that may affect developing countries whether or not this is dubbed as 'aid'. The trade creation and trade diversion effects are likely to be most pervasive and complex in the early stages. They may include increased competition in OECD markets from Eastern European exports, increased demand in Eastern Europe for primary products from developing countries, and a shift in demand in Eastern Europe away from imports from developing countries which used to engage in barter trade in favour of other sources, possibly other developing countries. There are two reasons to anticipate some diversion of trade away from developing countries towards Eastern Europe. The first is that economic reform is expected to increase the competitiveness of some of Eastern Europe's exports. The second is that, in responding to the political changes in Eastern Europe, the OECD countries are in the process of elevating some countries in the region in their hierarchy of trade preferences.

The emergence of the countries of the former Soviet Union offers a major challenge to Africa in the area of finance. As these countries grapple with their problems, they will require immense financial resources. Most of these are likely to be direct foreign investment, commercial bank lending and some semi-concessional resources from the World Bank, the new European Bank for Reconstruction and Development, the IMF, and grant aid. To the extent that these resources are non-concessional, there may not be a diversion of resources from Africa. But if larger-scale lending to these countries occurs, it could lead to an increase in world interest rates. And if this is not accompanied by an increase in the supply of funds, it could also affect other borrowers, developed and developing countries alike. For developing Africa, an increase in world interest rates would not augur well for its development prospects, including the external debt problem.

As Central and Eastern Europe grapple with their problems, there could be a decline in their aid to developing countries. Although such aid has been insignificant historically, and was mostly military in nature, its decline could cause developing countries (including Africa) some difficulties.

As the economies of Central and Eastern Europe are restructured, so also will be their competitiveness. Some observers are of the opinion that the areas which look promising in terms of trade are light manufactures, assembly and agricultural products.[3] There is also the possibility of competition with developing countries in the trade for footwear and clothing. On the bright side, however, is the opportunity for increased trade with developing countries. With the removal of the regulations requiring bilateral trade with their (CMEA) partners, countries of Central and Eastern Europe could open their markets to the products of developing countries. Herein lies the opportunity for Africa to expand its trade if it is able to restore its international competitiveness.

In the long run, the whole world will benefit if the reforms in Central and Eastern Europe succeed. Up till now, low *per capita* incomes and government controls have suppressed demand in these countries. As *per capita* incomes grow, and the controls are removed, the consumption of tropical products and imported manufactures may rise.

Conclusion

This book has dealt with recent developments which are likely to alter African–European economic relations in the years ahead. Because the events themselves are still unfolding, many of the conclusions are highly tentative and conjectural. A volume like the present one can do no more than make broad generalizations about the events. The ultimate outcome, positive or negative, will depend on Africa's understanding of the events and how easily it is able to adapt to them. Perhaps the single most important recommendation of the volume, however, is that African countries should understand and take these developments in Europe seriously. Developing such an understanding and studying the consequences of these developments is a task which this book hopes to

---

[3] Christopher Stevens, 'Eastern Europe and developing countries', Overseas Development Institute Briefing Paper, June 1991.

facilitate, but it is also one best undertaken at the national level.

The greatest challenge which faces Africa is the possibility of reduced interdependence between it and Europe in the years ahead. For some time to come, Africa no doubt will continue to derive a significant proportion of its trade, capital flows and investment from Europe. But as the analysis in this book demonstrates, some forces are at work which could reduce that proportion in future. Africa's response to this challenge should be rooted in the search for alternative markets elsewhere, particularly in other less-developed countries of the South and in the expansion of its own internal market through economic integration. This is not to say, however, that it should abandon the single most important market in the world. Rather, it should seek to compete effectively in that market while strategically cultivating other economic relationships.

The challenge of '1992' reaches further. The European integration experience is rooted in the belief that countries can escape size limitations by coming together to form larger economic entities. It is also rooted in the understanding that countries can benefit from economies of scale that result from the formation of larger economic groupings. In the case of Africa, the advantages of economic integration are so overwhelming that the continent may have no choice other than to integrate its various small, pristine economies. Besides, it may be very difficult for Africa to continue to ignore the trend in the world economy towards the formation of regional economic blocs. Because of this trend, it is becoming clear that trade and future trade relations are likely to be conducted along regional lines. Furthermore, and perhaps more importantly, the integration of its most important market – Europe – and the emerging trend of further reduction in Africa's dependence on that market, tend to suggest that Africa should take its own integration process much more seriously.

The inseparable lesson for Africa is that it should pursue vigorously the process of economic integration. Apart from the fact that the advantages are overwhelming, its inability to integrate would run counter to trends in the world economy and it could lose thereby. Thus, the message to Africa of the European integration process and the prospect for reduction in African–European relations is that Africa must develop strong regional markets in order to survive and benefit from the changing international commercial climate. Indeed, without a regional market, Africa will not be organized on a sufficient scale to become an area of economic growth. Without political coordination in other areas – for example, in fiscal, social and legal areas – it will remain weak in the face of the large groupings which are being established everywhere in the world. It was in recognition of the role of larger markets, that OAU members in 1991 committed themselves to the establishment of a Pan-African Economic Community by signing the Abuja Treaty. The lesson of European economic integration is that declarations alone will not be enough. Africa must dedicate itself to the practical implementation of the Abuja Treaty and ensure that there are no slippages in the 34-year time-table for the establishment of an African economic and political union.

Over the years, Africa has lost a substantial portion of its share of world trade. The pursuit of inappropriate trade policies is partly to blame for this loss. Partly to blame, too, is Africa's inability to diversify the range of products it exports and the market to which it exports. As Africa's traditional market (Europe) weakens, partly as a result of technological change which reduces the consumption of raw materials per unit of output, and partly because of the changes in the structure of production in that market, Africa will need to diversify not only the range of products exported but also the market to which it exports. Penetrating the new markets of the former Soviet bloc and other markets of the South is one of the challenges before Africa. If the reform process in the former Soviet bloc succeeds, the resulting increase in *per capita* incomes will lead to increased demand for tropical products and imported light manufactures (textiles, for example) where some African countries (Mauritius, for example) have comparative advantage. But in order to penetrate this market, Africa must be competitive. This requires that Africa's trade policies must be supportive of trade expansion.

As capital flows from Europe dwindle partly as a result of budgetary considerations and partly as a result of new European priorities, Africa will need to enhance domestic resource mobilization efforts. Policies are needed that promote savings (a stable macro-economic environment, financial deregulation and so on), as much as policies that will reverse capital flight. Additional savings could be mobilized by introducing efficiency into the operations of the public sector and through a reform of the tax system.

As the factors which tend to reduce Africa's dependence on Europe come into play, Africa will need to understand the factors more closely in order to develop its internal capacity to respond to them. Either with respect to Europe (where there are signs of decreasing interdependence), or in other markets which Africa may cultivate as alternatives to Europe, the key to success is competitiveness. In the special case of the unfolding events in Europe, the competitiveness of Africa will determine whether it will be able to benefit from an expanding European market, penetrate the emerging markets of Eastern and Central Europe, or compete with the latter in attracting official and private capital flows. Africa's ability in this regard will depend critically on the pursuit of policies which promote macro-economic stability and which, at the same time, foster growth and promote trade.

Index

Africa and Europe was first published in 1996 by
Zed Books Ltd
7 Cynthia Street London N1 9JF, UK and
165 First Avenue, Atlantic Highlands, New Jersey 07716, USA
in association with
The African Development Bank
01 B.P. 1387, Abidjan 01, Côte d'Ivoire.

Cover design by Andrew Corbett
Typeset by Long House Publishing Services, Cumbria, UK
Printed and bound in the United Kingdom
by Redwood Books, Trowbridge, Wiltshire.

A catalogue record for this book is available from the British Library.
US CIP is available from the Library of Congress

ISBN   Cased   1 85649 257 5
        Limp   1 85649 258 3

The views expressed in this book are strictly those of the authors.
They are not to be attributed to the African Development Bank, its Board
of Directors or the governments which they represent.

Africa and Europe
The Changing Economic Relationship

EDITED BY

OLADEJI O. OJO

Zed Books

LONDON AND NEW JERSEY

in association with

The African Development Bank
ABIDJAN